The Teacher's Guide to Open Education

The Teacher's Guide to Open Education

Lillian S. Stephens

State University of New York at Stony Brook

HOLT, RINEHART AND WINSTON, INC.
New York Chicago San Francisco Atlanta
Dallas Montreal Toronto London Sydney

Library of Congress Cataloging in Publication Data

Stephens, Lillian S.
  The teacher's guide to open education

  Bibliography: p. 326
  1. Open plan schools. I. Title.
LB1029.06S72   371.3   73-14754

ISBN: 0-03-007391-X

4 5 6 7 8   038   9 8 7 6 5 4 3 2

Preface

Open education is now recognized as the major educational innovation of this decade. It has survived the attacks of its critics and the over-zealousness of its friends, and emerged as a significant force in schools throughout the United States and many foreign countries as well. For many teachers it is a revitalizing force establishing their profession once again as creative and satisfying.

My interest in open education was sparked in the late 1960s by the early reports of British informal schools, which were enthusiastic, but often ambiguous. They spoke of children's freedom but failed to identify limits, and offered varying definitions of key terms, such as "integrated curriculum" and "free day," and of the role of the teacher. It was evident to me that an understanding of these aspects was crucial.

In 1971, with the cooperation of education authorities in Great Britain, I conducted a study of twenty-four British schools. During the course of the study, I visited more than one hundred classrooms in Oxfordshire, Leicestershire, Bristol, and London.[1] I observed classes that had been practicing open education for twenty-five years and others that were just changing from a traditional approach. I returned from England convinced that the open movement held great promise for American schools, but also aware that the British approach could serve only as a partial guide. No educational movement can be transplanted totally from one society to another.

Since then I have focused on the growing open education movement in the United States, visiting classes throughout the country and exploring its philosophy with my students at the State University of New York at Stony Brook, as well as with teachers, parents, and administrators at workshops and seminars. I have also helped to organize open classrooms and have come to appreciate the practical problems involved in implementing

---

[1] For a summary of this study see Appendix B.

the approach. In my capacity as project director of the New York State University's teacher-training program in Bristol, England, I have returned to England regularly and continued to observe its schools.

Although this book is addressed to teachers, it is also intended for students, administrators, parents, and anyone else interested in the philosophy and practices of open education. The major emphasis of the book is on practice, for in the last analysis an educational theory is best defined in practice, in the realities of the classroom. Many approaches to teaching in open classrooms are presented—methods and ideas that have been tested and proven effective both here and in England. Teachers will select those that best suit their own situations, for what is effective with one class may not work with another. No two combinations of children are alike. Equally important, no two teachers are alike. A noise level that is comfortable for one may drive another to distraction. It is my hope that this book will help all teachers who wish to join the movement toward open education to do so, at a pace and in a manner that is comfortable to them.

A book is rarely the product of one person alone. I wish to acknowledge the contributions of the many teachers both here and in England who invited me into their classrooms and shared their knowledge and experiences, and of the children in their classes whose obvious enthusiasm for learning inspired this book. A few should be singled out: Michelle Grindlinger and Helene Fisher, who related team-teaching experiences; Helen Feder, who contributed suggestions and recipes to the chapter on cooking; Lois Zabriskie, who photographed the parent workshop in Chapter Eighteen; and Linda Stumvoll for her photographs of the Taukomas School. I am particularly grateful to Anne Wild, who was a part of the project from its inception and shared her sensitive insight into classroom practices.

I am most appreciative to Marcia Handler of the Merrick Public Schools for her aid in securing pictures of those schools and her support for the book. The original research in England was conducted primarily under the guidance of Professors Robert Clausen of New York University and Carol Millsom of the University of Michigan. Dr. Millsom also reviewed parts of the manuscript as did Dr. Leonard Gardner and Dr. Sylvia Burns.

I owe a special debt to the members of my family. My husband Bernard was a partner in the work. I relied on his editorial experience, calling on him to react to a passage, edit a section of the manuscript, or advise on the choice of a picture. He and my son Mitchell and my daughter Beth provided the encouragement, support, and counsel that made the book possible.

Albertson, New York   L.S.S.
December 1973

Contents

Preface   v

Introduction   1

Part One   **Understanding Open Education**   9

1   THE PHILOSOPHY OF OPEN EDUCATION   11

  On Defining Open Education   12
  On Children and Childhood   13
  On the Nature of Education   14
    *The Process of Education 14, The Province of
    Education 16*
  On Child Development   16
    *The Views of Jean Piaget 17, Some Implications of
    Piaget's Theories 19*
  On Children and Learning   19
    *Learning Begins at Birth 20, Learning Is Continuous 20,
    Learning Is Personal 20, Learning Is Purposive 21,
    Learning Is Self-Motivated 21, Learning Requires That
    Material Be Appropriate to the Child's Level of
    Development 22, Learning Requires That the Child
    Be the Director, Not the Receiver 22, Learning Requires
    the Active Participation of the Child 24*
  Characteristics of Open Classrooms   25
    The Basic Model 26, Optional Extras 26

                                                           vii

Open Education Defined   27
Other Educational Movements   27
Progressive Education 28, The Free-School Movement 30,
The British Informal Movement 31

2   THE ROLE OF THE TEACHER   33

A Changing Role   34
A Way of Relating   37
The Teacher and Child Responsibility   38
The Notion of Responsibility 39, Freedom in Open
Classrooms 40, Decisions in the Classroom 41,
Sharing Responsibility for Key Decisions 45

Part Two   Organizing the Open Classroom   49

3   CHANGING FROM A TRADITIONAL CLASSROOM   51

Selecting a Starting Point   52
The Teacher 52, The Students 53, Administrators and
Other Faculty Members 53, The Parents 53
Preparing for Change   54
Instituting the Change   55
Starting Slowly 55, Moving Moderately 59,
Changing Completely 60
Arranging the Room   60
The Reading Corner 63, The Writing Corner 65,
The Mathematics Corner 66, The Science Corner 67,
Other Activity Corners 67
A Planned Environment   72
Materials in the Open Classroom 73,
Housekeeping in Open Classrooms 74

4   CLASSROOM MANAGEMENT   76

Organizing the School Day   77
Starting the Day 77, Scheduling the Day 79,
The Class Meeting 82
Organizing and Assigning Work   83
Organizing the Work 83, Signing Up for Activities 84,
Assigning Work 85, Assigning the General Area of
Work 85, Assigning Specific Work 87, Contracts 88,
Activity Cards 96

5   RECORDKEEPING AND EVALUATION   100

Scope and Purpose of Records in Open Classrooms   101
School Records   102
Morning Chores 102, Cumulative Records 105

Internal Class Records   105
    Records of Overall Work of the Class, 106, Records of
    Individual Children's Work 107, Reading Records 116,
    Mathematics Records 117
Summary Comments about Records   119

Part Three   The Curriculum of Open Classrooms   **121**

6   AN INTRODUCTION TO THE CURRICULUM   123

Integrated Curriculum and Integrated Day   124
Children's Play   126
The "Three Rs" and Creative Arts   128

7   TOPICS AND PROJECTS   130

Topics in Open Classrooms   131
    Choosing a Topic 131, Working on a Topic 131,
    The Teacher's Role 132, Summarizing a Topic 133,
    Advantages of Topic Work 133
Projects in Open Classrooms   134
    Choosing a Project 135, Multiple-Class and School
    Projects 138, Planning the Work 138, Groups in Project
    Work 139, Culmination of the Project 139,
    Advantages of Project Work 141

8   SOCIAL STUDIES   143

Transmitting Information about Man   143
    How Objective Are Historical Facts? 144, How Accurate
    Should Reporting Be? 144
Transmitting Values or Citizenship   145
Developing a Critical Attitude   145
Social Studies in the Open Classroom   145

9   SCIENCE   149

What Is Science?   150
Objectives of Science   150
The Scope of Science in Elementary Schools   150
Questioning in Science   151
Science in Open Classrooms   152
    Short-Term Activities 153, Long-Term Activities 154
Living Things   155
    Animals in the Classroom 155, Plants in the
    Classroom 158

10   READING   159

A Critical Look at Some Conventional Approaches   **160**

Reading in Open Classrooms 161
Reading Readiness 162, Beginning Reading 165,
Developmental Reading 168, Fun with Language 178

11 WRITING 181

Stimulating Prose Writing 182
Stimulating Poetry Writing 186
Stimulating Functional Writing 189
Correcting Written Work 191
Dictionaries 191
Bookbinding 192

12 MATHEMATICS 194

The Mathematics Program in Open Classrooms 197
Mathematics Textbooks, Workbooks, or Kits 197,
Activity or Work Cards 198, General Activities 199
The Scope of the Mathematics Curriculum 199
Suggestions for Mathematics Activities 200
Numbers and Numeration 200, Sets: Language and
Symbols 204, Operations on Whole Numbers 204,
Operations on Fractions 205, Problem Solving 207,
Measurement 207, Geometry 210
The Mathematics Corner 212
The Use of Mathematical Activities 214
Recording Findings 215, Maintaining a Class Book
of Facts 216
Computations 216

13 COOKING AND BAKING 218

14 CREATIVE ARTS: ARTS AND CRAFTS, MUSIC, DANCE AND
MOVEMENTS, DRAMA 224

Arts and Crafts 226
Illustrative and Expressive Work 227, Art
Appreciation 228, Art for Art's Sake 229
Music 232
Dance and Movement 233
Drama 236

Part Four   Implementing the Open Approach 239

15 FOCUSING ON THE INDIVIDUAL CHILD 241

Individualization of Instruction 241
Individualization in Traditional Classes 242,
Individualization in Open Classrooms 244,
Individual Interests in the Curriculum 245

Provisions for the Special Child 247
The Special Child in the Traditional Class 248,
The Special Child in the Open Class 249
Assessing the Individual 251
The Assessment of Intelligence 252, The Assessment of
Achievement 254

16 GROUPING FOR INSTRUCTION 257

Horizontal or Single-Age Grouping 258
Ability Grouping: Heterogeneous versus
    Homogeneous Groups 258
Grouping in Open Education Schools 259
Vertical or Interage Grouping 259, The School within
a School 262, Open-Plan Schools 264, Team
Teaching 267
Grouping in Open Education Classes 267
Organization of Groups 268

17 TEAM AND COOPERATIVE TEACHING 271

Cooperative versus Team Teaching 271
Cooperative Teaching in Open Classrooms 272
Team Teaching in Open Classrooms 273
Advantages 273, Disadvantages 274, To Team or
Not To Team 275, Choosing a Team 276,
The Size of the Team 277, Differentiated
Staffing 278, Planning a Team 278,
Organizing the Space 279, Organizing the Students 280,
Organizing the Work 281, Planning the Work 283,
Records of the Team 284, Meeting with Parents 284,
General Comments 285

18 PARENTS, VOLUNTEERS, AND PARAPROFESSIONALS 286

Fostering Parental Understanding 287
Communicating with Parents 287, Parents as
Resources 291
Working with Volunteers 293
Retired People 293, Older Students 293
Working with Paraprofessionals 294
General Comments on the Use of Volunteers and
    Paraprofessionals 296

19 ANTICIPATING SOME PROBLEMS 297

Maintaining a Healthy Working Atmosphere 298
Making Sure That Each Child Spends His Time
    Constructively 300

Learning When (and When Not) To Intercede in a
Child's Activity   301
Sustaining a Child's Interest in an Activity   302
Obtaining Sufficient Materals   303
Handling Negative Reactions from Others   304

20 TEACHER CENTERS   305

Functions of Teacher Centers   305
Clearing Houses for Materials and Equipment 305,
Resource Center 306, Workshop 306, Preservice and
In-Service Education 306, Parental Education 307,
Advisory Service 307, Circulating Equipment 307,
Display Center 307, Meeting Rooms 307,
Social Center 307, Library 308, Miscellaneous 308
Organization of the Centers   308

Appendix A   The British Scene   311

History of Informal Education in Great Britain   311
British Schools Today   314
Organization: Primary Years 315, Organization:
Secondary Schools 315, Faculties of Schools 316, The
Parents 317, Evaluation of Informal Schools 317
Are British Children Different?   319

Appendix B   A Study of British Informal Schools   320

Details of the Study   321
Major Findings   321
The Nature of Classroom Work 321, Organization of
Classes 323, Division of Responsibility 323
Other Findings   324

Annotated Bibliography   326

Index   331

The Teacher's Guide to Open Education

Introduction

Open education did not spring full-grown onto the scene as did Athena
from the forehead of Zeus. Its antecedents lie deep in the history of
Western education. Many of its principles were enunciated centuries ago,
as far back as the days of the early Greek philosophers. Through the ages
there were those who spoke out against the current educational systems,
usually directing their attacks at harsh discipline in the schools, at the
narrowness of the curriculum, or at teaching that stressed unthinking
memorization of facts. As alternatives these critics urged respect for the
child's integrity, a more relevant curriculum, and attention to individual
children's needs and interests. Many also endorsed play as a valid
educational experience. They were advocates of freedom for children and
for childhood itself.

A brief historical survey will demonstrate the continuity with which
these sentiments have been expressed for more than 2,000 years. In the
fifth century B.C., Socrates, for example, used what can be described as
the "inquiry" and "discovery" approaches as he traveled about Athens
instructing the youth. Plato and Aristotle, following Socrates, urged
attention to the whole child, to the training of his body, as well as of
his mind. Plato recognized the value of play; he wrote in *The Republic*:
"Enforced exercise does no harm to the body but enforced learning will not
stay in the mind. So avoid compulsion and let your children's lessons take
the form of play." He also insisted that knowledge cannot be imparted
mechanically, that learning must begin with the student's own desire to
learn.

Much later, in the sixteenth century, François Rabelais satirized the
irrelevant curriculum of those days and endorsed individual freedom for
students. Michele de Montaigne raised another voice against the harsh and

pedantic methods of education in France, endorsing individual teaching, studies with practical application, and play, which he described as children's "most serious actions."

The seventeenth-century Czech philosopher John Comenius had a significant impact on the development of our own ideas. He supported universal education, emphasized the importance of practical experience, integration of subjects, and argued for fitting instruction to the child, rather than the child to instruction. John Locke, an English philosopher of the same century, stressed the need for sensory experience, for taking children out of school buildings into their daily environment to study.

A prominent exponent of the child-centered approach was Jean Jacques Rousseau, who set forth these views in the eighteenth century in the novel *Emile* describing the education of a boy. He urged that children be permitted to develop naturally, free of restraints, and that childhood be valued not merely as a step toward manhood but also as an important stage of life.

J. H. Pestalozzi, a Swiss educator, was a notable contributor in the late eighteenth and early nineteenth centuries to the theories upon which open education are based. He also emphasized the child's sensory experience as the foundation for knowledge and suggested that children must experiment with concrete objects before they can form abstract ideas. He insisted that children must be involved in their education: "To arrive at knowledge slowly, by one's own experience, is better than to learn by rote, in a hurry, facts that other people know and then, glutted with words, to lose one's own free, observant and inquisitive ability to study."[1] Pestalozzi organized schools, directed a teachers' training college, and wrote extensively on education. He had confidence in children's ability to learn from their own experiences; as he expressed it, "Life educates."

In the nineteenth century two Germans, Johann Friedrich Herbart and Friedrich Froebel helped to lay the foundations for educational reform. Herbart was an educational philosopher and practitioner, who in the course of his work devised detailed teaching schemes. Open educators are most attentive to his concern for individual children's needs, his support for activity, as well as for reliance on the child's own interests as motivating factors. He saw interest as an essential prelude to learning.

Froebel was an educator, whose ideas had their greatest impact on the development of the progressive approach to education. He was particularly influential in Great Britain, where there are still Froebel societies and a teacher-training college inspired by his philosophy. He believed that education must start early and founded the first kindergarten (a German word

---

[1] Johann Heinrich Pestalozzi, *The Education of Man,* trans. by Heinz and Ruth Norden (New York: Philosophical Library, 1951), p. 35.

that means "children's garden"). He reaffirmed the value of play and stressed participation by the child in his own learning, the importance of activity, and freedom to make choices. For Froebel there was no distinction between play and work in early education. "Education" meant the unfolding of the child's "inner nature," and it was through the child's contacts with external objects and materials that he would develop and grow. The teacher was to offer guidance and to structure the environment, but he was not to restrict the child's natural development.

The Russian Leo Tolstoy, who also lived in the nineteenth century, based his views on his own experiences in organizing schools for serfs. He urged consideration for individual children's needs and interests and respect for children's ability to exercise responsibility; he insisted that school should be a happy place.

In the early twentieth century many of the views described here found expression in the progressive-education movement, which is closely associated with the name of the American John Dewey. At the heart of Dewey's philosophy was the concept of experience. Education, Dewey believed, begins with a problem or doubt, which the child is motivated to solve. In this sense he and Plato agreed. Both saw the child's own motivation to resolve a problem as the impetus for learning. Through experience, through interaction with the environment the child would resolve his doubt.

Objects, according to Dewey, have meaning only as they are perceived or experienced. A chair, for example, is seen by an adult as an object to be sat upon; for the crawling child a chair may be an object to be climbed upon or a means by which to raise oneself to an upright position. Dewey insisted, "I would have a child say not 'I know' but 'I have experienced.'" From this philosophy flowed his disdain for the more formal methods of traditional education, for teaching children through lectures, for stressing subjects that would prepare the child for a "suppositious" future, rather than those that would interest the child himself.[2]

Beside Dewey there were many other educators associated with the progressive movement. Among them were Francis Parker, who preceded Dewey; Junius Merriam, who organized an influential progressive laboratory school at the University of Missouri; and particularly William Heard Kilpatrick, who devised the project method. (See Chapter One for further discussion of progressive education.)

Other twentieth-century figures also contributed to the development of the philosophy of open education: educators who proposed new curricula or new organizational approaches, psychologists who helped to clarify children's emotional and intellectual development, and sociologists who investigated the school as an institution and its role in society. The con-

[2] John Dewey, *Experience and Education* (London: Collier, 1963).

tributions of some of these people must be acknowledged in a historical survey.

Maria Montessori was an Italian physician whose approach to preschool education represents another important stream in the development of open education. The schools that she established stress individual attention to each child within a prepared environment in which he is free to choose his activities from a number of specified tasks. Although Montessori schools use their equipment in much more structured fashion than do open schools, their provisions for activities, for freedom of choice, and for recognition of individual differences are in keeping with the beliefs of open educators and helped to spur the acceptance of such methods.

Other important figures in Europe were Susan Isaacs and Nathan Isaacs, who were instrumental in clarifying the theory of informal education in Great Britain. Notable also is the work of the Swiss biologist and psychologist Jean Piaget, who has offered insights into children's thinking that have helped to shape the theory of open education. Piaget's views are discussed more fully in Chapter One.

In the United States psychologist Jerome Bruner has directed his attention to education and was active in the curriculum-reform movement of the 1960s. He has emphasized the importance of children's involvement in their own learning, has recognized curiosity as a motivating force, and has argued for the "discovery" approach. Bruner claims that a subject should be taught not to "spectators" but to "participants."[3]

Carl Rogers is another psychologist who is clearly identified with the open-education movement. He insisted that the quality of the relationship between teacher and child and the classroom environment are the decisive ingredients in education. Within an environment of acceptance, he has contended children can be trusted to assume responsibility for their own learning. He deplores the notion of a fixed curriculum, insisting that each child's curriculum must be "self-chosen." According to Rogers, material that can be taught to another is of little consequence. It is knowledge discovered for oneself that is more significant.[4]

Certain currents in American society have also been influential in the development of open education. The past decade in this country has been one of sharp discord. The Vietnam war divided the American people. Racial conflicts have erupted, and crime and drug addiction have reached epidemic proportions. The schools, as always, have mirrored the problems of the larger society. In many areas schools have become stages on which the dramas of poverty, drugs, and racial discrimination are acted out. Guards

[3] Jerome Bruner, "The Skill of Relevance and the Relevance of Skills," *Saturday Review* (April 18, 1970), p. 166.
[4] Carl Rogers, *Freedom To Learn* (Ohio: Merrill, 1969).

in schools, conflicts among parents of different ethnic backgrounds, language difficulties, children who are inadequately fed and clothed, insufficient funds for education have infinitely complicated the problems of teachers.

Teachers themselves have increasingly come under attack for failure to educate the children of the poor and have been accused of ignoring the cultural heritage of children from minority groups. Schools have been called "drab, prison-like environments." Perhaps the most extreme critic of the schools in this period is Ivan Illich, who has called for "deschooling" society, insisting that schools as an institution are no longer defensible.[5]

Less severe critics have also accused the schools of failing students. Charles Silberman has called them "grim, joyless places, governed by oppressive and petty rules."[6] There has been increasing interest in "free schools" and other alternatives to the regimented life in schools indicted by "radical" reformers like John Holt, George Dennison, Jonathan Kozol, Neil Postman.

Criticism of the schools in the last decade, though harsh, has often been perceptive. Although undoubtedly many schools did not deserve these attacks, educators in general could not ignore the charges. Basic school reforms were indicated. The critics of our schools have helped to create a climate for change which has contributed to acceptance of the open-school movement.

It was in this climate that educators in the United States first became aware of the informal classrooms of Great Britain, where children are reputed to work purposively and to learn in a relaxed atmosphere. Discipline problems are said to have been largely overcome. Open education has begun to take root in this country, nurtured at first by a small band of supporters—Charles Silberman, Lillian Weber, Joseph Featherstone, and educators in such disparate states as North Dakota, New York, Massachusetts, Pennsylvania, Arizona, Colorado, California, and Vermont. Although the apparent success of British informal schools has been a significant factor in the birth of the open-school movement here, forces in American society have been primarily responsible for its growth.

Open education is spreading in response to pressures for change in this country. In a few years the children of the "hippie" generation, of the "Consciousness III" generation described by Charles Reich,[7] will be reaching our elementary schools. Among their parents will be those who have rejected much of the materialism of American society, who have rebelled against the computerization of modern life, who cry out against the boredom of jobs in a technological society. The children themselves will need to be

[5] Ivan Illich, *Deschooling Society* (New York: Harper & Row, 1971).
[6] Charles Silberman, *Crisis in the Classroom* (New York: Random House, 1970).
[7] Charles A. Reich, *The Greening of America* (New York: Random House, 1970).

taught to cope with a world that we can no longer anticipate, to adjust to rapid change and to a society becoming ever more mobile. They will need to learn to use leisure, for three-day work weeks may be a reality of their life. Educators are beginning to recognize the inadequacy of teaching yesterday's way to tomorrow's children. In the United States of the 1970s, it can be said that open education is "an idea whose time has come."

This book is divided into four parts. The first is devoted to the historical and philosophical basis of open education and to the teacher's role in the open classroom. Part Two notes methods of organizing and managing open classrooms. In Part Three we discuss the curriculum of open schools. Parts Two and Three also include suggestions for numerous activities for use in open classrooms. Part Four is devoted to various aspects of implementing open education. Finally, in the appendixes, we shall report on the British scene and on British informal schools.

about snakes
Robert: Would like to read cartoon books
Timothy: Would like to read so he can be a policeman

...would like to play with the walkie talkie

Photograph courtesy of New Rochelle Public Schools, New York.

Part
ONE
Understanding
Open
Education

Chapter
ONE
The Philosophy
of
Open Education

"I don't know where this project will lead . . ."

The classroom was a scene of bustling activity. In the back of the room a group of children were constructing a large cage. When asked about its purpose, they giggled and relished the visitor's astonishment at their reply. "For our pet dinosaur," was their answer.

The teacher explained: "I have a series of math activity cards which are intended to offer practice in measurement. One of the cards reads: 'Could you keep a dinosaur in this room? If so, where would you place his cage?' My intention was for the children to measure the room and then conclude that a dinosaur would be too large to fit.

"This particular activity card has been in the room for six months and no one has ever chosen to work on it. Last week a few children who had been reading about dinosaurs noticed the card and became intrigued by it. First, they measured the room and then checked a number of library books about dinosaurs. They found reference to a small dinosaur, *Coelophysis*, which had been only three feet high. They decided they could keep a 'pet' *Coelophysis* and would build a cage for it.

"The whole class is now involved. Some are working with the art teacher, creating a papier-mâché *Coelophysis*. Others are constructing its cage. Children are researching every book in the school and public libraries on dinosaurs, insisting on an accurate replica, investigating *Coelophysis'* habits, and determining what to 'feed' him. I arranged for a trip to the Museum of Natural History next week, where they hope to explore dinosaurs farther. I don't know where this project will lead, but I find myself as excited as the children, learning along with them. . . ."

In this classroom open education was being defined—by the children's enthusiasm for learning, the unpredictable direction that the work had taken, the independence and initiative of the pupils, the provision of materials, integration of the curriculum, the use of outside resources, as well as by the teacher's role in sparking the project, supporting it, and making himself available as a consultant while permitting the children themselves to take the lead.

ON DEFINING OPEN EDUCATION

Definitions of open education have varied widely. Some educators' views have been so rigid that a modern-day Diogenes would have difficulty finding a truly open class in our schools. Some educators have described open education in such mystical terms that it is intelligible only to a few of the "initiated," seeming to others a phenomenon that can only be felt but not really explained. On the other hand, others have interpreted open education so broadly that teachers who merely offer children a choice of the order in which to complete several assigned tasks may believe that they have established open classes.

Part of the problem has been that a number of different terms have been used to designate the open approach. The term "open education" is rarely used in Great Britain. Although British schools are frequently called "informal" by American educators, the British themselves tend to call them "modern," "progressive," "child-centered," "integrated," or schools with a "free day." Here in the United States the term "open corridor" is sometimes used instead of "open," though the former generally connotes a series of open classes located along a common corridor, in which joint activities are conducted.

A further source of confusion is the use of the term "open school," both here and in Great Britain, to define the physical properties of a school, suggesting large, undivided spaces, with only a few individual classrooms, often with removable partitions between them. This type of school is more properly designated "open plan." In such schools open education is not necessarily practiced; nor is an open-plan school required for open education. (For further discussion of open-plan schools, see Chapter Sixteen.)

Another difficulty in defining open education is that it is not at this point a completely evolved theory of education. An educational theory must be forged in practice—tested and refined in different schools and adapted to meet the needs of different constituencies. This requirement applies particularly to open education, which is currently being clarified in practice. The approach as it develops may vary from community to community or even from class to class, each class remaining *open* to the needs of its own students. In a sense, open-education classes may be viewed as part of a continuum; each class progresses slowly and unevenly on many fronts, from traditional to increasingly open. It is not essential to identify a line specifying the point at which a class may be considered truly *open*. It is necessary, however, to recognize that there are certain basic beliefs upon which open education is based and certain common characteristics of the classrooms in which it is practiced. Classes organized in accordance with these tenets can be said to have entered the stream of open education.

In this chapter we shall analyze the philosophy of open education, as it pertains specifically to children and childhood, education, child development and learning, and the organization of classrooms. It should not be surprising that teachers in quite traditional schools may find themselves in agreement with many of the premises of open education. In the "Introduction" we demonstrated that many of the beliefs of open educators are not original but have deep roots in educational history. To a great extent open educators can be distinguished from others who subscribe to the same beliefs by the manner in which they translate their beliefs into classroom practice. For this reason, in reviewing the tenets of open education, frequently we shall refer to contrasting methods employed in traditional and open classes.

ON CHILDREN AND CHILDHOOD

Certain early views of the nature of children, though largely discredited today, nevertheless continue to exert influence on conventional education. One results from the theological doctrine of original sin: that the child is born with evil impulses that must be controlled or stamped out. School officials were expected to enforce harsh discipline, in order to teach the child self-denial and submissiveness so that he would not run wild.

Another notion is that childhood is simply an intermediate stage on the path to adulthood, to be valued not for itself but only as preparation for the future. Children have been viewed as "miniature adults" in training for the important stage of life: adulthood. By extension, childhood has sometimes been viewed almost as a disease, to be quickly cured. The highest compliment that could be paid to a child was to suggest that he was behaving as an adult. Children's concerns have not been considered as having much consequence.

These early perceptions of children continue to affect attitudes toward school today. They lead to notions that children need rigid discipline in school if they are to be capable of self-discipline later, and that the curriculum should emphasize those matters that will be useful to adults, rather than interesting to children themselves. It is feared that play in school will encourage the child to become a frivolous adult.

Open educators reject these views of childhood and their implications. They do not approach the child in moralistic terms, as inherently either bad or good. They recognize that the child reasons differently from the man. Egocentricity, for example, is natural to the young child and not necessarily a portent of narcissism in the adult. Childhood has value not only as a necessary step toward adulthood. Each stage of life is perceived as unique and worthwhile in itself. From an ethical point of view, the child is believed to be as much entitled to a happy life as is the adult; as much of the child's life is spent in school, he is thus entitled to a happy school life. The best preparation for adulthood, according to open educators, is a satisfying childhood in which the child learns to function independently, to define and solve his own problems, and to acquire confidence in his own abilities.

The most significant factor in the open educator's approach to children is his belief that they are *worthy* of respect and trust: the opposite to an approach in which children are viewed as incapable of exercising responsibility or making decisions, their problems or concerns as of little moment. The open educator respects children and their opinions; above all he *trusts* them to assume productive roles in their own education.

ON THE NATURE OF EDUCATION

The Process of Education

There is said to be a dichotomy between the *content* and *process* of education; that is, the value of *what* is learned is contrasted with that of *how* it is learned. Conventional schools are said to concentrate on the former, whereas open schools are said to emphasize the latter.

In a "content approach" subject matter is stressed. Textbooks or curriculum guides break a subject down into parts arranged in a sequence of presumed difficulty, and for each grade a curriculum is constructed from the topics to be "covered" in that grade. Teachers have been known to object when colleagues assign topics to a lower grade which have been scheduled for a higher level or permit children to see a film or read a book that is designated as part of the curriculum for the higher grade. The focus of this approach is on the acquisition of facts, which tends to imply less concern about their use. Application of factual knowledge is often limited to answering questions on unit tests.

The content approach has been criticized on a number of grounds. Subjects do not always lend themselves to the neat compartmentalization designed by textbook publishers and the authors of curriculum guides. In practice topics frequently overlap. Furthermore, the tremendous expansion of knowledge in the past few decades continually threatens to render much of the specific content of many fields obsolete even as it is being taught.

There is still another factor. Although in some schools a specific curriculum may be held sacrosanct, there are in fact virtually infinite possibilities for worthwhile study in elementary schools. The specific choice is to a large extent arbitrary, frequently reflecting the particular interests or biases of textbook publishers or of those who construct achievement tests. For example, the curriculum for eleven- and twelve-year-olds frequently includes Greek and Roman history. Would study of Chinese or African history be less meritorious?

For all these reasons the *process* approach deemphasizes the specific material learned in favor of teaching children *how* to learn. It seeks to aid children to direct their own learning, encourages them to pose their own problems and to solve them by various methods: formulating and testing hypotheses, accumulating and analyzing data, drawing inferences and conclusions. It presupposes a flexible approach to the curriculum, one that avoids raising barriers among subjects. Most important, it poses as a primary goal the training of children in when and how to use their knowledge. There is an additional component in learning how to learn: The child is encouraged to identify the style or process of learning that is most effective for *him* and will best enable him to pursue independent studies.

Although open educators, if compelled to choose between emphasis on content or on process, would prefer the latter, they recognize that this dichotomy is frequently a false one. Process cannot exist in a vacuum. The process approach also leads to increased knowledge—not to collections of isolated facts that can be quickly garnered from a reference book but to knowledge that has meaning for the student and on which he can draw as he seeks to understand his environment.

Open educators do not assume that content is unimportant, that the specific activities which occupy children do not matter. They expect that children may frequently investigate matters not included in their graded textbooks, but that they may nevertheless be devoting their energies to serious intellectual inquiries.

The child whose learning is self-directed but who is satisfied with superficial investigations, flitting from one topic to another, has not adequately learned the process of education. Similarly, the child who has read every assigned book and has achieved high reading-test scores but who never reads a book for enjoyment has been inadequately educated.

The Province of Education

Open educators view the whole child as their province, for they insist that all facets of the child—intellectual, social, emotional, and physical—are interrelated. They demand that education be considered within the context of the child's entire life and dismiss no aspect of his life as irrelevant to his schooling. Although teachers may not be able to prevent children from coming to school angry or hungry, they must be aware that anger or hunger will affect children's ability to function in school. Although they may not be able to resolve their students' emotional problems, they do recognize that unsatisfied emotional needs interfere with students' learning.

This emphasis on the whole child leads open educators to consider that the social and emotional climate of the classroom merits as much attention as does the intellectual climate. The teacher seeks to establish a classroom atmosphere of mutual respect, one in which children listen to one another, respect differences among themselves, and learn to share with one another—to share thoughts as well as materials.

Teachers seek to foster children's sense of self-worth. Studies have revealed a positive correlation between a child's self-concept and his achievement in school. William W. Purkey, who reviewed this correlation, concluded that ". . . there is a persistent and significant relationship between the self-concept and academic achievement at each grade level, and that change in one seems to be associated with change in the other."[1] The teacher in the open classroom strives to create an environment in which each child can experience success, in which each child and his ideas are valued. He builds an atmosphere of acceptance, marked by personal regard for the child, in which the child is free to be honest and open in his relationships, without fear of ridicule or destructive criticism. Such a setting is regarded as essential to open education.

ON CHILD DEVELOPMENT

There are currently three major strands of thought on child development,[2] which may be summarized as follows:

> *Behavioral-environmental.* The child's development is shaped basically by his environment through his learned responses to stimuli.
> *Maturational-nativist.* Development is viewed primarily as the "unfolding" of the child's nature; although it is believed that environ-

---

[1] William W. Purkey, *Self Concept and School Achievement* (Englewood Cliffs, N.J.: Prentice-Hall, 1970), p. 27.

[2] For more complete discussion of these views of child development, see "Educational Product Report No. 42" (New York: Educational Products Information Exchange Institute, 1972); and Lawrence Kohlberg, "Early Education: A Cognitive Developmental View," *Child Development,* 39 (December 1968), pp. 1013–1062.

ment can influence what a child learns, his development is considered to be determined primarily by his genetic patterns.

Interactional. It is assumed that development results from the active interplay between the child and his environment, in which the child's existing mental structures are constantly modified and reorganized as a result of his experiences.

Although open educators have remained alert to the contributions of each of these schools of thought, the interactional view most closely approximates their position. Jean Piaget's work has been particularly identified with this approach, and familiarity with that work is basic to an understanding of the philosophy of open education.

The Views of Jean Piaget

Piaget has been investigating children's intellectual growth since the 1920s, but his research only became widely known in the United States in the 1960s. Recently his studies have stimulated new attention to children's thinking and cognitive development. Piaget was originally interested in discovering how children come to understand their world and how they perceive it at different ages. He observed and interviewed children at all ages, from infancy to adolescence. Much of his early research was based on observation and experimentation with his own three children.

Piaget argues that there are consecutive stages of mental development through which all children pass at approximately similar ages: the sensory-motor (birth to about two years), preoperational (two to seven years), concrete-operations (seven to eleven or twelve years), and the formal-operations (eleven or twelve years on) stages. Although environmental conditions may to some extent influence the pace at which children progress through these stages, the sequence cannot be altered, nor can any stage be skipped. The stages are not discrete, however; each emerges gradually from the earlier stage and merges into the next, more complex one.

The individual develops intellectual structures, or *schemata,* to represent his world. As the result of his interaction with his environment, these mental models are continually modified through two processes: *assimilation* and *accommodation.* As the child is exposed to new experiences, he assimilates these to his existing schemata and then accommodates his schemata to reflect the new elements in the experiences, thus growing more and more able to understand his world. Life, according to Piaget, "is a continuous creation of increasingly complex forms and a progressive adaptation of these forms to the environment."[3]

---

[3] Jean Piaget, *The Origins of Intelligence in Children,* 2d ed. (New York: International Universities Press, 1952b), p. 3.

Basic to an understanding of Piaget's thinking is the idea that each child has his own concepts of reality, which serve as reference points against which he tests and redefines new experiences. In that sense learning is always personal: It is shaped by the child's own existing structures. Piaget believes that young children do not perceive the world in the same way as adults; that human beings reason differently at different ages. The child is at first an egocentric creature, unable to separate himself and his own needs from his environment. Until the age of about six or seven years he has difficulty in distinguishing between appearance and reality. He is unable to accept certain notions that adults take for granted, for example, the principle of *conservation*—that matter can change its shape without changing its volume.

A particular experiment is frequently performed to test the young child's grasp of this principle. Classroom teachers may wish to try this experiment. A child is given two wide glasses of equal size, each half filled with water. He readily agrees that there is the same amount of water in each glass. While he watches, the water from one of these glasses is then poured into a taller, narrower glass; in which it naturally reaches to a higher level. According to Piaget, the child who has not mastered the principle of conservation will insist that the narrow glass holds more water than the wider.

Piaget adds that young children also have difficulty with notions of space, quantity, time, and distinctions among such geographical entities as city, state, and country. A teacher who has struggled to explain. to primary-school children the difference between Paris as a city and France as a country can attest to this difficulty. It is significant that Piaget believes that, when the child finally masters these concepts, he does so through his own reason, after he has had an opportunity to work out the problems for himself.

Another significant aspect of Piaget's theories is his differentiation between language and thought. He suggests that a child's language may not adequately express his thinking, that the development of language is more susceptible to environmental conditions. As a result, a teacher may tend to overrate the thinking capacity of verbally competent, middle-class youngsters and to underrate the ability of children from backgrounds offering little encouragement to development of language.[4]

---

[4] In this brief discussion of Piaget's work we have not included an evaluation or critique of his theories. Readers interested in a summary of pertinent research studies may wish to consult J. M. Hunt, *Intelligence and Experience* (New York: Ronald Press, 1970); and Ellis D. Evans, *Contemporary Influences in Early Childhood Education* (New York: Holt, Rinehart and Winston, 1971).

Some Implications of Piaget's Theories

Piaget's work has several specific implications for elementary school teachers. For example, accepting Piaget's insistence that at any given point a child can learn only what is appropriate to his developmental stage requires an understanding of children's ways of reasoning at different periods before a curriculum can be properly planned. In addition, as not all children reach the same developmental stage at the same chronological age, it seems useless to teach the same curriculum in the same manner to a group of twenty-five or thirty children, as is often attempted in a traditional classroom.

Of particular importance is Piaget's conclusion that it is not until the beginning of the final developmental stage, that of formal operations (usually at age eleven or twelve years), that the child is able to deal with abstract relations. This conclusion means that the child in the concrete-operations stage, though able to draw logical conclusions from concrete objects, has great difficulty in drawing those same conclusions when the problem is presented in verbal or abstract terms.

The child also has difficulty with mathematics before he has grasped the notions of conservation and reversibility. Reversibility implies that certain operations can be reversed; that is that each mathematical operation can be retraced to its starting point: if $6 + 3 = 9$, then $9 - 3 = 6$. To the young child this principle is not clear.

Finally, most significant to educators, is Piaget's reaffirmation of the ineffectiveness of lecturing young children. He emphasizes instead children's needs for concrete experiences, for frequent opportunities to explore their environment and to interact with other students and adults, as well as with materials.

ON CHILDREN AND LEARNING

The ideas about childhood, education, and child development discussed in the preceding pages form the foundation for some of the open educator's beliefs about learning. These beliefs can be summarized as follows:

1. Learning begins at birth.
2. Learning is continuous.
3. Learning is personal.
4. Learning is purposive.
5. Learning is self-motivated.
6. Learning requires that material be appropriate to the child's level of development.

7. Learning requires that the child be the director, not the receiver.
8. Learning requires the active participation of the child.

All these principles are interrelated, as will become apparent in the following discussion.

Learning Begins at Birth

Although it may appear obvious that learning begins at birth, open educators interpret this principle as affirming the individuality of each child. When the child first enters school, he has already learned a vast amount, and in many respects his experiences are unique. Yet some teachers may attempt to treat a class of five- or six-year-olds as if they were all similar, a group of blank slates waiting to be filled. For some children, however, school may violate all their previous patterns of learning. The child who has been taught to be quiet at home may appear to be withdrawn at school, whereas the child who has been encouraged to be active and talkative may appear unmanageable at school. Children do not always easily distinguish between the different values that may be stressed at home and at school. For example, the child who has been cautioned not to sit on the floor or to make a mess may be uncomfortable on the floor or may find it difficult to work with finger paint or with papier-mâché, whereas another may find it a strain to sit straight in a chair while working.

Learning Is Continuous

Acknowledging that the child who enters school has been learning since his birth implies understanding that new learning must be rooted in old learning. The child learns by adding to and reorganizing past knowledge. The teacher must therefore have some familiarity with the young child's home environment, must strive to build a sense of continuity between home and school, and must recognize that new learning should be built upon existing foundations. These foundations may include a different cultural background or a different language or dialect from that of the majority of students. They cannot be ignored, nor can the child be asked to divorce himself sharply from his background at the classroom door.

Learning Is Personal

Piaget believes that each child has his own personal concept of reality largely molded by his unique life history. John Dewey, too, emphasized that each child "knows" a thing only as he experiences it. Although it is true that individuals undoubtedly share many concepts, in another sense no two people understand concepts in exactly the same way. A single word may conjure up different mental images for any two people.

Another aspect of this view of learning is that each child has his own unique *style* of learning. Some learn better aurally, others visually, others through kinesthetic methods. A teacher who recognizes that learning is a personal activity helps each child to identify his own pattern of learning.

Learning Is Purposive

Teachers have long acknowledged that the child who *needs* to learn something will learn it more effectively. They have planned activities with this point in mind: plays to give children a purpose for speaking to an audience and cookie sales to teach him to handle money. This factor, however, requires more than occasional recognition, for it affects the child's attitude toward much of his work. The child who sees no purpose in memorizing the names of the planets or in learning about the American Revolution will probably fail to do so.

A common means of assigning purpose to a lesson is for the teacher to announce that "there will be a test on this material on Friday." But, because this approach provides only a limited purpose for the child, he is frequently able to memorize the material for the test and then to forget it completely by the following week. Nathan Isaacs has offered an effective criticism of learning that is not meaningful to the child, describing it as:

> . . . nothing real at all, only facades, make-believes, and shams. The child can far too readily respond with imitation, verbal reproduction and even with plausible skills of verbal manipulation by which we can let ourselves be deceived if we want to be. Yet we know all too well how easily the verbal facades formed by conventional schools' learning may crumble off as soon as we cease to plaster on new coats; and even those that hold better may be hardly less superficial.[5]

Learning Is Self-Motivated

The principle that learning is self-motivated is closely related to the principles of personal and purposive learning. Learning is viewed as arising from a question, from a problem that the child seeks to resolve. Although certain levels of inquiry are undoubtedly pursued in response to external motivation (in order to pass a test or achieve a grade), learning is most likely to become part of the child's structure of knowledge when it is self-motivated. Implicit in this concept is the view of individuals as inherently

[5] Nathan Isaacs, *Some Aspects of Piaget's Work* (London: National Froebel Foundation, 1955), p. 45.

motivated to resolve problems. It implies that the role of the teacher is not to supply answers but to raise questions, to stimulate doubts that students will be motivated to investigate.

Piaget's view of the organism as constantly seeking equilibrium between his previous understandings and his new experiences—a process called *equilibration*—is relevant here. Piaget sees the child as intellectually restless, striving to explore his environment, and motivated to resolve disparities between his personal model of reality and new ideas to which he is exposed. It is these drives that propel the child toward growth and learning.

Learning Requires That Material Be Appropriate to the Child's Level of Development

Open educators endorse individualization of instruction; they speak of initiating instruction directed at "where the child is," rather than of where the curriculum starts. Piaget's analysis of the different stages of intellectual development suggests the pointlessness of teachers discussing with young children abstract concepts of mathematics, geography, or history. Teachers must provide experiences appropriate to the children's levels of development.

This process has been described as seeking a *match* between the child's existing framework of knowledge and what he is expected to learn. J. M. Hunt has suggested that "this notion of a proper match between circumstances and schema is what every teacher must grasp, perhaps only intuitively, if he is to be effective."[6] For a problem to engage a child, it must lie within his range of challenge: It must not be so easy that it is boring, and it must not be so difficult that it is frustrating.

Learning Requires That the Child Be the Director, Not the Receiver

The Plowden Report contains the statement: "The child is the agent in his own learning."[7] The child as agent or director may be contrasted with the child as the recipient of learning—the person upon whom learning is conferred, to whom it is taught or imparted.

When the child is viewed as mainly a recipient, his mind may be compared to a storage bin that must be filled with information. The teacher presents as many facts as possible to the student. These facts are then "stored," supposedly available for later recall. Some teachers may equate

[6] J. M. Hunt, *Intelligence and Experience* (New York: Ronald Press, 1961), p. 268.
[7] Lady Bridget Plowden, et al. *Children and Their Primary Schools*, I. *Report of the Central Advisory Council for Education* (London: H. M. Stationery Office, 1967), p. 194.

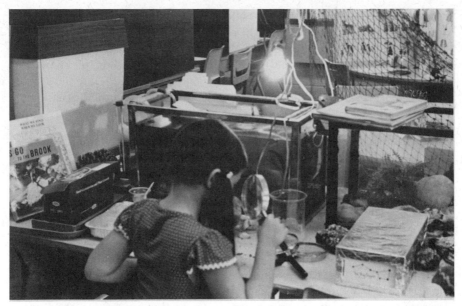

"The child is the agent in his own learning." (Photograph courtesy of Forest Park School, Half Hollow Hills School District, Dix Hills, New York.)

teaching with *telling*. They lecture to students, telling them what they wish them to learn. "Covering" a curriculum may be interpreted as relating bits of knowledge to students: the characteristics of insects, definitions of mathematical terms, dates of historical events, and so on. Tests are then used to determine whether or not the students have "stored" the information and to reward those who can recall the bits of knowledge.

Teaching by telling is reflected in the following complaint by one teacher: "I don't understand what is wrong with my class this year. I have told them how to use quotation marks again and again, and they still don't know how to use them."

Even when a child does "learn" in this manner, much of what he learns is quickly forgotten. Teaching becomes a wasteful and exhausting process for both students and teachers. Tremendous effort is expended to teach and reteach material that may remain with the student only until completion of the unit test. A beginning teacher complained recently about how little she recalled of all that she had "learned" in years and years of school. She particularly remarked on her inadequate knowledge of mathematics: "After twelve years of math in school, I feel unprepared to teach fourth-grade mathematics."

Open educators distinguish between the acquisition and application of knowledge. There are undoubtedly certain facts that the child needs to memorize and "store," just as there are aspects of a cultural heritage that may have to be presented to the child. But open educators argue that, if knowledge is to become useful to a child, he must bring his own thought processes to bear upon it: He must share in the responsibility for his own learning. There is a difference between a superficial facade of knowledge and knowledge that has actually been incorporated into a child's intellectual framework and that he is thus able to apply to other situations.

Learning Requires the Active Participation of the Child

An old Chinese saying holds:

I hear, and I forget;
I see, and I remember;
I do, and I understand.

Open educators believe that there must be ample opportunities in a classroom for children to "do," in the sense of this saying. For it is only by being involved actors, rather than passive listeners, that children learn. The result of this view is a class environment that permits a child scope for activity—freedom to move about, to converse, to explore, and to experiment. All of these activities contribute directly to the child's growth. Freedom to converse, for example, is particularly valuable in language development. Many young children enter school with limited vocabularies, sometimes as a result of the impact of television, which puts a premium on watching and listening, rather than on talking. There is a contradiction between the needs of these children for experience in using language and the "no talking" rules of many conventional classes.

There are additional educational advantages in freedom to converse with other children. Language can be an aid to thinking. Some people think through a problem as they struggle to express it. Social interaction further facilitates learning. Children working together learn to share ideas, to solve problems jointly. Furthermore, encouraging free exchange among students makes it possible for them to seek help from one another. Pupils often make the best teachers.

Freedom to explore and to experiment are other essentials of learning, which permit a child to arrive at understanding based on his own reasoning and through testing his own hypotheses. This process can occur only when there is acceptance of children's errors. It is, of course, possible to prevent children from making mistakes by telling them the one right way to accomplish a task. But effective learning requires that a child be willing to risk error, be free to experiment, seek understanding through trial and error.

Pupils often make the best teachers. (Photograph courtesy of Merrick Public Schools, New York.)

A final point: Active learning does not necessarily imply activity in the physical sense. A child may actively participate in learning while sitting quietly wrestling with a problem that he is attempting to solve. The teacher must recognize this possibility and occasionally ignore the child who appears to be unoccupied.

CHARACTERISTICS OF OPEN CLASSROOMS

Open educators strive to organize classes consistent with their perceptions of childhood, education, development, and learning. Open classes may be conducted in traditional buildings or in large open areas with few defined classrooms. They may be self-contained units of about twenty-five children with one teacher or large numbers of children with teams of teachers. An entire school may be organized in open classes, or there may be just a few.

As is apparent from our discussion so far, there is no single prototype for an open classroom. Acceptance of the philosophy of open education does, however, lead to certain common characteristics of open classrooms. Robert Dearden, a British educator, in discussing the *integrated day,* has suggested an analogy with an automobile: "There is the basic model plus a wide variety of optional extras."[8] This analogy is particularly apt for describing open classrooms.

The Basic Model

The following fifteen characteristics constitute the basic model of an open classroom; every open classroom will reflect them in varying degrees.

1. A minimum of lessons for the whole class; most instruction geared to small groups or individuals.
2. A variety of activities progressing simultaneously.
3. Flexible scheduling, so that children can engage in different activities for varying periods of time.
4. An environment rich in materials, both commercial and homemade.
5. Freedom for children to move about, converse, work together, and seek help from one another.
6. Opportunities for children to make decisions about their work and to develop responsibility for setting and meeting their educational goals.
7. Lack of rigid, prescribed curriculum and provision for children to investigate matters of concern to them.
8. Some integration of the curriculum, eliminating isolated teaching of each subject.
9. Emphasis on experimentation and involvement with materials.
10. Flexible learning groups formed around interests, as well as academic needs, and organized by both pupils and teachers.
11. An atmosphere of trust, acceptance of children, and respect for their diversity.
12. Attention to individual intellectual, emotional, physical, and social needs.
13. Creative activities valued as part of the curriculum.
14. A minimum of grading and marking.
15. Honest and open relationships between teacher and pupil and between pupil and pupil; teacher avoidance of exploiting authority.

Optional Extras

Although the features listed in the preceding section are basic requirements of open classrooms, the actual implementation of each can vary sharply. There will be classes in which there are fairly set periods, others in which there are few or no scheduled periods during the day. For example, in one open school children were permitted to eat their lunches at

[8] Robert Dearden, "What Is the Integrated Day?" in Jack Walton (ed.), *The Integrated Day in Theory and Practice* (London: Ward Lock, 1971), p. 48.

any time during a two-hour period. The day had no set schedule except for approximate arrival and departure times.

There are additional options, practices that are not typical of all open classes but are nevertheless associated with many. Each of these practices will be discussed in greater detail later in this book. These include:

1. *Team teaching.* In many open classrooms two or more teachers are assigned to groups of children.
2. *Interage grouping.* Classes are composed of mixed age groups, rather than of single age levels.
3. *Open plan.* Some new schools are being built on an open plan with open spaces. In some older schools partitions between existing classrooms are being removed to create larger open areas to be shared by two or more teachers.

OPEN EDUCATION DEFINED

The philosophical basis for open education and its characteristics in the classroom have been described. From them a definition of open education can be derived. The emphasis is on the word "open."

Open education is an approach to education that is open to change, to new ideas, to curriculum, to scheduling, to use of space, to honest expressions of feeling between teacher and pupil and between pupil and pupil, and open to children's participation in significant decision-making in the classroom.

Open education is characterized by a classroom environment in which there is a minimum of teaching to the class as a whole, in which provision is made for children to pursue individual interests and to be actively involved with materials, and in which children are trusted to direct many aspects of their own learning.

OTHER EDUCATIONAL MOVEMENTS

Open education has been compared with other movements—notably progressive education, the current "free school" movement, and the British "informal" approach. Although there are undoubtedly similarities among all these movements, equally significant differences do exist. A review of each movement will serve to clarify these differences and to elucidate the philosophy of open education still further.

Progressive Education

A headmaster in one school in Leicestershire, England, recently commented: "If you want to understand our informal schools, look to your progressive schools of the twenties and thirties. In those days we were traveling to America to study your schools. Now you are flocking here to see what we have done with your ideas." There is no doubt that the progressive movement in this country did influence to some extent the development of the very same British schools that are inspiring our open schools today.

The progressive movement in this country started as an elitist movement. It originated in the laboratory schools of several large universities (Chicago, Missouri, and Columbia University), and its acceptance was at first confined to private schools with small enrollments. It had its greatest spurt of growth in the United States during the 1920s and 1930s but died out in this country before many educators believed that it had received a real test. Many factors accounted for its demise. Although it was gradually spreading to public schools, it remained identified with private education. It floundered on widespread misunderstanding of Dewey's principles. Dewey, himself, was critical of the interpretation of his philosophy in the schools. It has been suggested that open classes today reflect this philosophy more closely than did classes in progressive schools.

There is speculation that had it not been for the launching of Sputnik by the Soviet Union, the progressive movement might have overcome some of its "growing pains" and become an important avenue of educational change. When the Soviet Union succeeded in placing the first man-made satellite in space, however, critics began to question the effectiveness of American education; it was said that American schools had failed to produce scientists capable of winning the "space race." These critics sought greater emphasis on didactic teaching and created an atmosphere in which progressive education could not flourish.

Nevertheless, the philosophy of the progressive movement did not completely fade. Throughout the country there were teachers who continued to organize and teach their classes according to progressive principles. Similar concepts also continued to be espoused in the teachers' colleges. In 1962 William Van Til claimed that the ideas of the

> progressive movement in education are not obsolete . . . they will be embodied in the form of new proposals for modern education, new syntheses which build upon our predecessors, as is common in the world of ideas. The over-anxious gravediggers . . . will discover as this twentieth century moves along that what they have mistaken for a corpse is indeed very much alive.[9]

[9] William Van Til, "Is Progressive Education Obsolete?" *Saturday Review* (February 17, 1962), p. 84.

Clearly, progressive education was in many respects the forerunner of open education. Many of its beliefs about children and learning coincide with those of open educators. There is a similarity between the "project method" or "units of work" in progressive schools and the projects that are the base of an integrated curriculum in open classrooms. There are some disparities, however. In progressive schools projects more frequently reflected the domestic and manual activities typical of American society in the early twentieth century. Children in school wove wool, sewed, cooked, worked with wood and tools, raised animals, and so on. Furthermore, projects were frequently the sole means of teaching skills, rather than one method of reinforcing them.

This emphasis led to a failure to teach basic skills, despite Dewey's warning: "The three R's are at all times the tools for introduction into higher studies; they have to be mastered if further initiation is to occur."[10] Other criticisms of progressive schools were aimed at confusion about interpretation of the child's freedom, unplanned and uninspired curricula often marked by a kind of anti-intellectualism, and insufficient provision for reinforcement of learning, all of which contributed to frequent abdication by the teacher of a leading role in the classroom. It is particularly appropriate that we analyze these critiques of progressive education, because many of the errors made in the early stages of the development of open schools in this country resemble those attributed to progressive schools.

Open education is in no sense a carbon copy of progressive education. Its chief points of departure lie in the more active role of the teacher. greater emphasis on planned environments, clarification of the limits of the child's freedom, and greater concern about the curriculum. Open educators view the teacher's role as decisive. They see no conflict between emphasis on the child's responsibility and direction by the teacher. There is not only room for both, but there is also need for both in open classrooms. It would not be possible to caricaturize an open classroom as were progressive classrooms in the cartoon in which a group of children ask, "Do we have to do what we want to do, today?" Open educators define the limits of the child's freedom more clearly.

There is also more emphasis on the role of materials and the classroom environment than was true in progressive schools. Learning is not just accidental; it is aided and structured by activities that are carefully chosen in accordance with the teacher's knowledge of the children. Superficial explorations are rejected in open schools, for only serious investigations are recognized as leading to new and consequential interests. There is a further acceptance of the teacher's responsibility for developing basic

---

[10] John Dewey, *Education and the Social Order* (New York: League for Industrial Democracy, 1934), p. 3.

skills in reading, mathematics, and communication. Open educators use a variety of methods for aiding their students to achieve these skills.

The Free-School Movement

In the United States the 1960s were marked by growing disenchantment with the quality of education in many quarters—parents, students, and educators. A group of "radical reformers," including Holt, Kozol, Postman, Dennison, turned the spotlight on our schools, accusing them of being unresponsive to children's needs, of teaching an outmoded curriculum, and of concentrating too heavily on test scores. Students, especially those in universities, complained about the irrelevance of the curriculum, the growing impersonality of large schools, and unnecessarily restrictive rules. Parents, particularly those from minority groups, expressed dissatisfaction with the education of their children. It was in this climate that the movement for free schools developed. Although in many instances the impetus for this movement arose from the same factors that facilitated the growth of open education, the two movements are decidedly different.

Unlike open education, the free-school movement in this country exists primarily outside the mainstream of public education. Free schools are frequently established for children who cannot adjust to public schools. They have been installed in storefronts, in a few rooms set aside in other buildings, in communes. Some are subsidized for a few students; others charge annual tuitions of thousands of dollars.

Although there is broad variation in the operation of free schools, children are generally permitted to "do their own thing." In reaction to the restraints of public schools, most free schools have removed all restraints. Attendance is generally voluntary, the curriculum completely self-chosen. The relationship between teacher and pupil is decidedly informal, usually on a first-name basis. These schools tend to deemphasize cognitive skills.

Free-school teachers usually reject any role of authority or formal leadership. Kozol has been critical of teachers in free schools for this attitude, claiming that they frequently "build the core of their life style around the simulation of essential impotence with competence admitted only in those areas of basic handiwork and back-to-nature skills where no serious competition from the outside world exists."[11]

The philosophical foundations of open education and free schools differ significantly. Free schools do not merely represent one end of a continuum between traditional and open schools, as has sometimes been implied. Open educators reject many of the approaches of free schools—

[11] Jonathan Kozol, "Free Schools: A Time for Candor," *Saturday Review* (March 4, 1972), p. 52.

the generally laissez-faire attitude toward curriculum, unlimited choices for children, the secondary role of teachers, and absence of attention to cognitive skills. They do find in many of these schools, however, substantiation of the claim that children are capable of making decisions about their own work, sometimes more effectively than adults.

The British Informal Movement

The apparent success of the British "informal" schools has been the single main catalyst in the spread of open education here. As reports of British schools began to reach this country in the late 1960s, many educators found in the British model verification of their belief that schools can be "joyous," "humane" places, where children can assume active roles in their own education.

Of the three movements described here the British informal approach can be said to have the most in common with open education. Schools, however, must be viewed within the context of their own society. There are many differences between American and British societies that result in different emphases in the schools of each. In the appendixes we shall discuss the British scene in greater detail, but we shall mention here a few decisive distinctions between British informal and American open schools. In Great Britain, the following features are more typical:

1. Greater autonomy for teachers and headmasters to set the curricula for their schools and to determine organizational forms.
2. Smaller schools in which headmasters can become acquainted with each child and in which children can move more freely about the building.
3. Frequent instances of headmasters continuing to teach, functioning more as head teachers than administrators.
4. Absence of formal testing procedures and achievement tests.
5. Fewer parents' organizations and lack of parental involvement in curriculum matters.
6. Much less grading of students.
7. Separate schools for younger children.
8. Selective secondary schools in many areas.
9. Local and national systems of advisory and support services for teachers.
10. Schools in which informal education has been developing for more than twenty-five years.

In addition the goals of education differ between the two countries. Only about half the students in Great Britain stay in school past the age of sixteen years, the official age for leaving school. A small minority goes on to receive university education.

Educators in the United States, focusing on British schools, have identified some aspects crucial to the informal approach and have attempted organizational changes patterned on those aspects. For example, Lillian Weber, founder of the Open Corridor program in New York City, has grouped a number of open classes along one corridor, seeking to establish a small-school feeling within a large city school. Teachers come to know all the children along this corridor, and children can move from class to class. There is a deputy in charge who assumes some of the leadership functions of the British headmaster, and Weber has organized advisory services for the teachers. The entire population of the corridor meets together regularly, as do the populations of schools in Great Britain.

Other open-education programs in this country have adopted similar methods, experimenting with organization of "schools within schools" deemphasizing tests and grades, revising report cards, permitting teachers more latitude in determining curricula, and sometimes cooperating in establishment of teacher centers. It must be emphasized, however, that these manifestations do not ensure schools exactly in the British image. Open education is a movement that must always remain somewhat unique to its own society.

Chapter
TWO
The Role
of
the Teacher

"I'm not the only person in this room who knows how to spell!"

The scene was a multi-age grouped class in England. There were children of ages five, six, and seven in the same class. One of the pupils approached the teacher with his personal dictionary. "Please Miss," he said, "could you tell me how to spell 'picture'?" The busy teacher turned to the child. "But why are you asking me? I'm not the only person in this room who knows how to spell!"

This incident illustrates the changing role of the teacher in an open classroom; she no longer considers herself the sole repository of knowledge. This teacher's remarks were in marked contrast to those typical of many teachers in traditional classes, who might have said: "If you have a question, don't ask your neighbor. I'm the teacher in this room. Ask me!"

"I could never go back . . . ."

A year later, in an open classroom of eleven- and twelve-year-olds in the United States, a teacher related the following incident:

A group of children were discussing an article which reported bias against women in children's literature, that women were generally depicted in inferior roles. A debate started. Some of the children cited books they had read which disproved it. Finally, they decided to "find out." They have undertaken a survey of fiction books in the school library to compare the roles of the male and female characters. They are going about it systematically, and with great enthusiasm. Almost every child in the class is screening books and charting his findings. I compare this with the days when my reading program consisted of assigned stories from basal readers. I predigested every story and posed a few superficial questions to test comprehension. I doubt that any of us was ever compelled to think. *I could never go back to that!*

This incident too illustrates a new role for the teacher, one in which she permits children to take the lead in choosing their own topics of study. But it also underscores the personal excitement, the renewed interest in teaching experienced by many teachers who have entered the stream of open education. They speak of growth instead of stagnation, of being in harmony with their students instead of opposing them, of the apparent contradiction between working harder and going home less tired.

Teachers in the past have themselves been victims of "joyless" classes. Creative teachers have frequently been no more welcome in schools than have creative students. The result has been an exodus from the classroom by some of the most capable teachers. Many educators are looking to open education to reverse this trend, as classrooms once more become intellectually stimulating environments.

A CHANGING ROLE

It has been said that the job of the teacher in an open classroom is more to light a fire than to fill a vessel, that teachers are no longer considered primarily as transmitters of knowledge. Several terms suggest this changed role: "diagnosticians," "resource specialists," "learning managers," "consultants," "facilitators," and "interactors."

All these terms undoubtedly do reflect aspects of the teachers' jobs. As they are interested in individual children, they must diagnose each child's needs. Recognizing the importance of materials and a planned environment, they must know about available resources and must manage learning facilities. When teachers encourage children to take an active part in their own learning, they are less likely to lecture than to make themselves available as consultants or facilitators. Finally, teachers believe in dialogues with students, and they thus interact with them.

Even more descriptive of teachers in open classrooms, however, is the term "catalysts." Teachers strive to spark change in their students, to inspire questions, activities, and thought; in the process they themselves change. They are open to new ideas, able to analyze their own work critically, and willing to forgo past methods of teaching and relating to children. These latter facets were stressed by one principal whose teachers had changed from traditional to open classes: "In the past everyone taught behind closed doors. When I entered a room, I always felt somewhat of an intruder. I was hesitant about offering suggestions. Now I find the teachers

There is a new role for the teacher in an open classroom. (Photograph courtesy of New Rochelle Public Schools, New York.)

welcoming visitors, hungry for suggestions, eager for constructive criticism, and willingly sharing ideas among themselves."

Several factors that contribute to tension between teacher and child in traditional classes are absent in the open classroom. Because of seating arrangements, the traditional classroom does tend to make every visitor seem an "intruder." Furthermore, visitors often judge a teacher by whether or not the class is quiet. Efforts to impose outmoded standards of discipline —to keep the class sitting quietly and passively for long periods of time— can be exhausting for a teacher. In all classes there are times when children need to "release some steam." If visitors enter at those moments, they may be critical of the teachers.

In many traditional classes the key word is "control," which is necessary to achieve the required order. Teachers are afraid that they will lose control of their classes. Student teachers are admonished not to attempt activities that will entail movement or laughter because they may not be able to regain control. Much of the day is spent manipulating youngsters in doing what the teacher thinks is best: to answer questions in predetermined ways and to think in terms of the teacher's lesson plans. There is an attempt to regulate every aspect of a child's life—even when he is to use the bathroom. Behavior problems are largely caused by children who chaff at such routines, who feel inadequate or frustrated because they cannot conform to the master plan for their grade.

Because teachers in open classrooms are not expected to maintain complete passivity or to determine what each child must do at every moment, they can relinquish this kind of control, can live with less certainty and also less tension.

It may be said that in the open classroom the key word is "trust." Trust implies confidence that children, given opportunities, will develop self-discipline and will learn—although they may travel unprescribed routes to knowledge. The teacher's awesome responsibility to decide unilaterally what each child will accomplish daily is eliminated.

Another factor with which teachers in traditional classes must contend is competitiveness among children, which leads to undesirable behavior: cheating, immobilization of children by fear of making errors, ridiculing of lower-achieving children by their peers. Although decrying competitiveness, many of our schools simultaneously foster it by constantly grading and testing children, by establishing rigid groupings based on achievement. Ivan Illich has remarked that each child in school is assigned his "level of inferiority."[1] Continual grading of children does indeed remind them of inadequacies and lead them to compare themselves with others. No wonder we hear the constant refrain "What did you get?" when test papers are returned.

In open classrooms there is a different approach to evaluation. Although achievement tests may still be required by the administration, regular classroom tests and grading have largely been eliminated. Papers are not "marked" in the conventional sense. One teacher in an open class who had requested a group of children to complete a page of practice mathematics problems sat down with the group at the end of the morning and commented to each in the following ways: "You did all the examples perfectly, except for three and five. Try them again"; "I don't think you understand this problem. See me later and we'll go over it"; "Ask John to explain this example to you; the others are all correct."

Contrast this approach with one in which every incorrect solution is marked with an X—or even worse, in which a percentage grade is given to the whole paper. In a sense this marking completes the learning transaction. The child frequently does not rework the problems; he may not even learn how to correct his errors. Whereas in the first instance the teacher's evaluation is conducive to further learning, in the second attention to learning is distracted by emphasis on a grade. In the nonevaluative atmosphere of open classrooms competition for grades, cheating to obtain higher scores, and rigid grouping of children are eliminated.

[1] Ivan Illich, *Celebration of Awareness* (New York: Doubleday, 1970).

Other conditions tend to complicate the job of the teacher in traditional classes. Imposing a predetermined curriculum on a class may prevent the necessary "match" between the child and what he is expected to learn. The result is often frustration, boredom, even rebellion. The pressure of a set schedule is another tyranny imposed on teachers and students. In the conventional class there is never enough time. Children are repeatedly told, "We'll be late for lunch" or "Hurry up and finish your reading; it's time for art" or simply "Don't waste time." Both teachers and students have constantly to be aware of the time because a specified number of minutes is allotted to each subject. This need to allocate blocks of time to each activity creates additional problems for the teacher. Children who complete the work quickly pose difficulties because the teacher feels called upon to devise additional work for them to prevent them from disturbing the other pupils or just sitting around doing nothing. Other children cause concern because they do not finish in the allotted time. It is not unusual for some children to be pages and pages behind in their workbooks unable to meet the pace set for them. More flexible approaches to scheduling in the open classroom eliminate much of this tension. Children are permitted to stay with a task as long as they are productively engaged, and they are not expected to follow a common schedule.

It must be emphasized that teachers in open classrooms do not abdicate their responsibilities when they relinquish control or encourage children to share in decision making. An open classroom has been described as both child-centered and teacher-centered. Teachers appreciate that there are many times when children need to receive guidance in their work. Even when a child is pursuing his own investigations, he may want to check his conclusions with the teacher. A child can easily form inaccurate conclusions from his own unassisted observations. A vivid illustration is afforded by a personal anecdote related by Peter Smith, a London educator. Smith had taken his six-year-old daughter to a farm for a week's holiday and was pleased that she had an opportunity to observe the cows being milked by machines daily. Tubes were connected to the cows' teats and to pails, where the milk was collected mechanically. At the end of the week Smith brought his daughter once more to see the cows, confident that she had learned about mechanical methods of milking. To his surprise, he heard her exclaim, "Those cows sure drink a lot of milk, don't they Daddy?"

A WAY OF RELATING

Other facets of the open classroom teachers' relations with children require clarification. Their perceptions of the needs of children mold their behavior as follows:

Because teachers in open classrooms recognize that youngsters are dependent upon their professional knowledge, they remain alert to materials, ideas, and experiences both in the classroom and outside it that can contribute to education of the children. They do not limit the class to investigating only those problems with which they themselves are familiar. They learn to say "I don't know" without feeling inadequate.

The teachers believe that children need to be active participants in their own learning, with freedom to experiment and explore ideas. This belief implies freedom to make mistakes. They therefore refrain from interrupting children who are wrestling with a problem, even when they know a better way to solve it. They are tolerant of errors, calling attention to them without criticizing the child. They appreciate how fragile the egos of many young children are, how easily children may become discouraged.

Teachers in open classrooms assume that children learn best in a humane environment that promotes self-confidence and in which they are treated as responsible people. They therefore encourage children to make significant decisions and to rely on their own strengths to solve problems. They do not, however, confuse freedom with total permissiveness or expect children to make decisions of which they are incapable. $S\top oP$

Teachers in open classrooms are honest with themselves and their students. They recognize that they are not simply one among equals in the classroom: They have authority but avoid exploiting it, avoid using it to manipulate or humiliate children or to escape honest dialogues. They respect children and their varying backgrounds, genuinely accepting differences among them.

Teachers in open classrooms believe that children are entitled to know the difference between sloppy and careful work. They consider it mistaken kindness or lack of appreciation of a child's abilities to accept superficial work that has offered no challenge to the child. They therefore set realistic standards for each child, avoiding uniform standards for all.

Finally, teachers in open classrooms acknowledge that their primary responsibility is to promote children's learning. No matter how humane the environment that they have established, no matter how aesthetically pleasing it is, they recognize that if the students in their classes are not learning they are failing them. They do not simply ignore the slow learner as long as he is happy and the fast learner as long as he is busy. They do not confuse neglect with encouragement for a child to assume an active part in his own education. They meet with each child regularly, assessing his progress, diagnosing his needs, and identifying his strengths, in order to help him to function productively.

THE TEACHER AND CHILD RESPONSIBILITY

One of the most difficult precepts of open education is that of permitting the child responsibility for his own learning. All open educators agree in theory that children should assume such responsibility, but in practice there is confusion about how to accomplish this goal. This question has plagued many teachers in open classrooms.

The Notion of Responsibility

Discussion of responsibility is complicated by the fact that the word itself has various connotations in the classroom. Traditional and open educators interpret it quite differently. The traditional educator's point of view is that the teacher has sole responsibility for the class and for all decisions related to its functioning. In this context, child responsibility is synonymous with obedience; the responsible child is the one who complies with the rules and does the teacher's·assignments promptly, fully, and without talking to his classmates. The responsible child does not skip pages in his workbook—nor does he complete pages that have not yet been assigned. He does not continue to read when the teacher announces that it is time for mathematics or work on mathematics during the reading period. He leaves his seat only with permission and speaks only when called upon.

This kind of obedience to the teacher's authority rules out any independent judgment by students. Children may be afraid to do anything that is not exactly what the teacher prescribes, compulsively checking to be sure that they are·doing things "the right way." This fear may account for a common complaint of teachers in traditional classes: that children are unable to follow directions. "Even after I explain the instructions to the whole class, there are always some students who come to me individually for directions."

In this equation of responsibility with obedience, children are viewed as basically incapable of independent learning. A student teacher who was recently observed during a mathematics lesson expressed this belief when she turned to a child who had completed an extra page in his math workbook and without checking the accuracy of the page, accused him of being "irresponsible" in proceeding on his own, adding, "You can't do that page. You haven't learned it yet because I haven't taught it yet."

Open educators view the child's responsibility quite differently. Their perspective implies the child's participation in classroom decision making. In this sense, responsibility is equated with effective use of freedom. The responsible child is thus the one who is capable of exercising freedom of choice, of making decisions about his work, and of accepting an active role in his own learning.

The responsible child in the open classroom is thus free to organize his day in school, to choose many of his activities, to explore his own interests, and to make other decisions related to his learning. He may spend the morning studying baseball batting averages or preparing a puppet show. He may choose to curl up in a corner of the room to work by himself or go into the corridor with a group to work on a mural. He may decide to use the school library or other facilities. In all these alternative ways he is responsibly directing his own learning.

The day of open-classroom teachers is therefore quite different from that of their more traditional counterparts. They carefully structure environments conducive to independent learning. They are not "on stage" before the class. A casual visitor might have difficulty locating the teacher in an open classroom. She may be exploring science materials with youngsters, teaching mathematics to children at a table in the corner, reading with an individual child, or sitting on the floor with children painting a mural.

The open-classroom teacher's notion of responsibility involves assessment of children as capable human beings, capable of independent judgment and independent learning. She recognizes that many children are entrusted with a great deal of responsibility away from school. Some carry house keys and return home to prepare meals and even to supervise younger siblings. They are ready to assume responsibility in school too. The teacher who views responsibility in this way seeks to organize the classroom so that children have consequential, rather than superficial, choices. Offering a child a choice between two meaningless activities negates the concept of his responsibility for his own learning.

Freedom in Open Classrooms

The equation of responsibility with decision making and freedom of choice requires further clarification of the concept of freedom that prevails in open classrooms. Freedom does *not* imply the choice between functioning or not functioning. Freedom can be equally abused by withholding it or overproviding it. John Dewey complained in 1926 that many progressive teachers misunderstood freedom:

> There is a present tendency in so-called advanced schools of educational thought to say, in effect, let us surround pupils with certain materials, tools, appliances, etc. and then let pupils respond to these things according to their own desires. Above all, let us not suggest . . . to them what they shall do, for that is an unwarranted trespass upon their sacred individuality since the essence of such individuality is to set up ends and means.
>
> Now such a method is really stupid. For it attempts the impossible, which is always stupid; and it misconceives the conditions of independent thinking.[2]

Today there are still reports that some teachers are using the approaches

---

[2] John Dewey, "Individuality and Experience," *Journal of the Barnes Foundation*, 2 (January 1926), p. 4.

that Dewey characterized as "stupid." Bonnie B. Stretch, writing almost fifty years later than Dewey, asked, "Is it enough to simply provide one's children with a school environment more humane than the public schools and then stay out of nature's way?"[3]

Confusion about freedom can also lead to rigidity in the name of "openness." A speech teacher recently reported that she was no longer working with a particular student in an open classroom who needed speech therapy, because she feared that scheduling a regular weekly period for speech constituted a violation of that student's freedom to arrange her own schedule. Thoughtful open educators do not view the child's freedom so narrowly. Both teacher and child have active roles in open classrooms. Respect for the child's freedom does not require teachers to abdicate their own responsibility to assign work, assemble groups, and schedule activities.

One problem has been a tendency to speak of freedom in very general terms. It is more productive to recognize that there can be no freedom without limits, that freedom and structure are not incompatible. The issue is not acceptance or nonacceptance of the child's freedom; it is, rather, to define a structure within which it can be exercised, the specific areas in which children are to be free to make choices.

Decisions in the Classroom

For the teacher in the open classroom the related issue is how and in what areas children are to share in decision making. It is first necessary to delineate the specific kinds of decisions that have to be made in classes. Basically there are two categories of such decisions: those relating to class routines and those relating to initiation and execution of the work of the class.

Decisions about Routines In the traditional classroom there are vast numbers of regulations covering almost every contingency and relating to every aspect of the child's life in school. There are procedures for entering and leaving the room; seating arrangements; conditions under which he may leave his seat, speak to his neighbor, sharpen his pencil, start to work, and so on. A great deal of energy is expended in familiarizing children with these rules and enforcing them. Children sometimes practice walking back and forth in the hall and orderly ways of going to the bathroom. When a child wishes to leave the room, he is often required to raise his hand for permission; sometimes he has to announce to the whole class that he feels unwell or wishes to use the lavatory. Because much of the teaching

---

[3] Bonnie B. Stretch, "The Rise of the Free School," *Saturday Review* (June 20, 1970), pp. 76–79, 90–93.

in traditional schools is directed to the whole class, there are specific rules for discussions. Children must raise their hands to be recognized, and a child who in his enthusiasm speaks out of turn is frequently admonished. Because of the large number of children involved, it is not unusual for several children to vie for the floor during a class discussion; the observer frequently notes obvious frustration and even a sense of rejection among those who are not called upon to participate.

In a traditional class routines are generally imposed by the teacher. The new teacher is reminded to decide on class routines before starting the first day of school. Children are rarely involved in decisions about routines and, even when they are involved, decision making may be only a hollow ritual. Students perceive what is expected of them in school, and when called upon to formulate rules tend to parrot uncritically the traditional regulations.

The open classroom eliminates the need for many rules. Children move freely about the room. They work in different learning areas, frequently conversing about their work. In a typical open classroom a number of activities occur simultaneously, the whole class need not pay attention to any one of them. For example, two children may sit together in one corner, taking turns reading passages aloud from a book. In another corner children may be practicing a play, while elsewhere a group may be trying to lift a heavy pile of books with a pulley. Some children may be writing a story, others binding books, and still others constructing a "wheat farm." The teacher may be working with a group on the use of Cuisenaire rods in addition of fractions. When the children who are reading together finish their story, they may decide to join the group building the farm. They do not require permission to change their seats or to join a new activity.

The open classroom has its rules, but they are kept to a minimum. They are established with the participation of the children and grow out of mutual assessment of the most effective use and maintenance of the environment. Because they are free from preconceived notions of what school is supposed to be like, children in an open classroom can offer valid suggestions for organizing the class, and their contributions are appreciated. They do share responsibility for decisions affecting their daily routines, and they take pride in their class and have a stake in its effective operation.

Decisions about Work   The more significant area of children's responsibility is that involving decisions about the work of the class. Rather than viewing these decisions as a whole, the teacher will find it useful to analyze necessary decisions of this type, as well as the range of choices available in each.

There are actually seven *key decisions* about the initiation and execution of work that must be made by a class.

1. *Initiation of the subject.* Which subject is to be studied: reading, mathematics, science.[4]
2. *Designation of the specific task.* What specific work is to be accomplished in the chosen subject: the particular story to be read, the workbook page to be completed, the experiment to be performed, and so on.
3. *Scheduling of the period.* When the work is to be accomplished: the day or the time of day.
4. *Duration of task.* How long the pupil must devote himself to the task and the points at which he must continue or abandon it.
5. *Determination of procedures and materials to be used.* How the task is to be accomplished.
6. *Choice of participants.* With whom the pupil sits, works, or shares materials in executing a particular task.
7. *Evaluation of work.* Who evaluates the work.

There are three possible ways to reach each of these key decisions: The teacher, the pupil, or both can decide. This will usually be determined by the nature of the task. It may vary for each key decision and from activity to activity. For example, the teacher may make some decisions about a task and pupils may assume responsibility for other aspects. Joint responsibility is exercised either through consultation or through the teacher's designation of alternatives from which the students may choose. Table 2.1 illustrates the different patterns of organizing work in a class depending on where the responsibility for each key decision lies.

An example will help clarify this point. In a classroom the teacher may decide that reading must be included during the day, but pupils may decide which book to read, when and for how long to read it, and whether or not to read it together. The division of responsibility for key decisions in this instance is as follows:

teacher responsibility: initiation of subject
pupil responsibility: all other decisions

The advantage of viewing the work of the class in terms of *key decisions* is that it permits the teacher to define children's responsibility in specific areas, rather than only as a broad generalization.

---

[4] For the purpose of this analysis it has been necessary to view the work of the class to some extent in terms of individual subjects. Actually much of the curriculum of open classes does not readily fall into discrete categories. Children may read, write, and engage in mathematical calculations in connection with a science project, or they may draw and write poetry while composing music. In analyzing the work of the class, however, it is usually possible to identify a primary category. In the first example the category would be science, in the second music. Activities like broad environmental studies, in which no one "subject" can be considered primary, are categorized as "topics" and "projects" (see Chapter Seven).

TABLE 2.1   Examples of Decisions in Each Category of Responsibility

Type of Decision	Teacher Responsibility	Joint Responsibility	Pupil Responsibility
Initiation of subject	subject assigned compulsory for student	pupil's choice of work in a few areas	work on subject voluntary
Designation of specific task	specific task assigned by teacher	pupil's choice of some tasks	pupil's decision about aspect of subject to pursue
Scheduling of period	pupil required to complete task by specified time	pupil's freedom to complete task at any time during specified morning or afternoon	pupil's engagement in activity when he chooses
Duration of task	pupil required to work on subject for specified length of time	pupil's choice of how long he will stay with activity, perhaps with a minimum performance specified	no limits on time spent on particular activity
Determination of procedures and materials to be used	how task is to be accomplished spelled out by teacher	pupil's options to decide how to complete assigned task	determination by pupil of how to proceed and what materials to use, possibly after consultation with teacher
Choice of participants	group assigned by teacher	pupil's choice of established groups	pupil's decision as to whom to sit, work, or share materials with
Evaluation of work	work checked by teacher	joint evaluation by teacher and pupil, perhaps in conference	work checked by pupil himself

Encouraging the child to take responsibility for specific decisions in open classrooms is an approach quite different from that in traditional classrooms, in which teachers make practically all the decisions. In a typical classroom a teacher may organize three reading groups, each may be assigned to read a passage, to complete a few workbook pages, and to "write a summary," "answer these questions," or "define these words." All the tasks and the time in which they are to be performed are carefully spelled out; no key decisions are made by students.

The idea that the teacher makes decisions about work is so ingrained in conventional classes that it remains even when such classes adopt more progressive modes. For example, even in schools that stress "individualization of instruction" a teacher may still consider it as her responsibility to devise a detailed curriculum for each child. Sometimes children may be permitted some responsibility for scheduling their day, but usually all other decisions remain with the teacher.

Sharing Responsibility for Key Decisions

The goal of the teacher in an open classroom is to develop pupils' ability to assume more and more responsibility for decision making. Not that all decisions will eventually be made by pupils. We reiterate that *child responsibility does not mean abdication of teacher responsibility.* Varying patterns of responsibility for different activities will continue to exist.

Within this context the degree to which the teacher shifts responsibility to pupils depends upon the readiness of the class. It may be necessary to start slowly, to permit only choices of scheduling or among a number of activities in a designated period. Happily, responsibility is contagious. As children learn to schedule their work and to choose their own activities, they find it easier to decide how long to spend on a subject, with whom to work, how to use materials. Finally, they can identify how best to learn.

The specifics of sharing responsibility can be better understood if we examine some of the available alternatives in each of the key decisions that we have defined.

Initiation of Subject The teacher has, first, to decide which subjects she deems essential. Must reading, mathematics, and writing be engaged in daily? Some teachers in open classrooms have found it necessary to insist on this, particularly in the early stages of organization. A teacher may also require regular (perhaps weekly) work in other subjects like science, social studies, and spelling. The rest of the class work may then be chosen freely by the students.

Designation of Specific Task Even though the teacher has designated some categories of work as compulsory, there are nevertheless still alternatives for choosing specific tasks. For example, the teacher may assign a particular story to some children, whereas others may be permitted free choice of their reading. Similarly, certain exercises may be specified for a child who needs practice in multiplication, while other children freely choose an activity card, a workbook page, or a survey; still others may be assigned no mathematics activity but may use mathematics in solving a problem in which they are engaged.

Scheduling of Period Most teachers in open classrooms permit each child freedom to schedule his own work. The child is held to be the best judge of when to complete certain tasks. Learning to organize one's day is a skill which open-classroom teachers consciously foster. They recognize that when a child first arrives at school he may want to play before proceeding to mathematics. Another may prefer to finish reading an entire book before tackling a science project. Each is free to follow his inclination as long as he assumes responsibility for performing required tasks. Some children will, of course, need more direct help in organizing their day: some parts of the day will also have to be scheduled by the teacher. Otherwise this category of decision will be primarily the responsibility of pupils.

Duration of Task   Open educators reject the assignment of rigid blocks of time for different subjects. They make it comfortable for a child to continue working on an activity as long as he is motivated to do so and is spending his time profitably. One problem in some open classrooms, particularly those in the early stages of organization, is the tendency of some pupils to flit from activity to activity. The teacher may therefore insist that a pupil complete a task, or a portion of it, once he has begun it or that he engage in a particular activity for a minimum period of time.

Determination of Procedures and Materials   In an open classroom the notion that there is only one "right" way to complete a task or to learn a concept is rejected. Children are encouraged to use materials in their own ways, to develop their own styles of learning. Whenever possible, therefore, they are given responsibility for deciding on procedures. Only when particular procedures are especially inappropriate or necessary does the teacher assume responsibility for this decision.

Choice of Participants   Children in an open classroom are generally permitted to choose with whom they wish to work, sit, and share materials. Children may decide to work together, although their abilities may be quite different. Rigid instructional groups organized according to ability have no place in an open classroom. The teacher chooses the participants in a group only when she has in mind a specific purpose, like introducing a mathematical concept. Even in this situation, however, other members of the class who are interested or wish to review the concept are generally free to join the group.

Evaluation of Work   In an open classroom the notion of evaluation is very different from that in a traditional classroom in which evaluation is often synonymous with grading. In an open class the purpose of evaluation is basically diagnostic. As the goal is to encourage children to accept responsibility for their own learning, it is as important for the child to know his areas of strength and weakness as it is for the teacher to know them. For this reason, children are permitted to correct their own work. Teacher's manuals with answers and other answer keys are made available as children become able to use them. In the absence of grading and competitiveness, children are generally conscientious and accurate in checking themselves. Teachers continue to evaluate some work, but their purpose remains primarily diagnostic or to assess each child's growth.

The teacher in the open classroom will wish to analyze regularly the work of the class, noting which decisions about work are being shared and how effectively, recognizing that responsibility will continue to be distributed between the teacher and pupils. A study of responsibility in British informal schools[5] analyzed 68 classes to determine the distribution of responsibility for key decisions. (Full details of this study are reported in Appendix B.) In a majority of the classrooms a pattern of responsibility was identified. The teacher tended to decide the subjects in which children were to work; then pupils were permitted varying degrees of responsibility for making the other key decisions. This pattern is considered desirable by many British theorists of informal education. Sybil Marshall, for example, has urged teachers to retain responsibility for selecting the subjects to be studied. She has expressed concern about the "extra freedom" of the newer informal classes: "The 'integrated day' appears to have gathered an extra freedom. It does not now merely indicate 'do your work when and how you like' but includes 'do what you like,' i.e. with regard to subject matter to be studied." Marshall concluded that these schools may be "plunging further away from reasonable standards of safety."[6]

The study also noted different distributions of responsibility for the "three Rs" and for other subjects in British schools. Teachers made a much higher percentage of decisions about work in reading, writing, and mathematics.

For the American teacher the finding about the degree to which work is actually structured by the teacher in British informal classes is especially significant. The study concludes that "results . . . should dispel any notion that in British informal classrooms children are 'free to do their own thing,' or make all the decisions pertaining to their work."[7]

---

[5] Lillian S. Stephens, "A Study of Individualization in Informal British Primary Schools." Unpublished doctoral dissertation (New York University School of Education, 1972).
[6] Sybil Marshall, "Back to the Three Rs?" *Times (London) Education Supplement* (July 2, 1971), p. 37.
[7] Stephens, *op. cit.*, p. 129.

Photograph courtesy of Merrick Public Schools, New York.

Part
TWO
Organizing
the
Open Classroom

Chapter
THREE
Changing
from a
Traditional Classroom

Much of human behavior is governed by habit—ways of responding to stimuli that are so well established that they have become automatic and are seldom questioned. These habits serve an important function, enabling people to act without having to stop and think about every move. But they may also act as a barrier to change. Although some individuals welcome breaks in their familiar routines, others become upset when their patterns are disrupted.

Classrooms are also frequently ruled by established traditions and habits that are rarely questioned. Changes in them may also be disturbing. If reading has always been scheduled first in the morning, a suggestion that the day be started with science may either arouse new interest in the science lesson or disturb teacher and pupils alike. Teachers who wish to open their classrooms must confront this factor. They must be prepared to accept change and to help their pupils to do so.

One of the first prerequisites for changing from a traditional to an open classroom is for the teacher to examine critically the current habits of the classroom, almost as an anthropologist surveys another society. She must ask: "What are the mores, the routines, of this class? Which routines support learning? Which tend to inhibit it? Which routines serve a present function? Which have merely been retained from habit or lack of knowledge of alternatives?" She must also examine classroom procedures, asking: "Is it necessary that children refrain from talking or from changing their seats while working? Is it essential that all children work on the same subject at the same time? Are whole-class lessons effective? To what extent are they reaching all the children? Are the children learning? Is there evidence that they can apply their knowledge? Are new interests developing? Are they excited about their work—

intellectually curious? How effective are the procedures for coping with discipline problems? Are the children developing self-discipline? What happens when the teacher steps out of the room? How about groups? Do they tend to remain static? Are children grouped by ability because they really learn better that way? Are the self-concepts of children in the low-ability groups affected by their placement? What is the emotional tone of the class? How much time is spent enforcing rules?"

As teachers analyze their classes along these lines, they identify those areas in which change is most desirable. In the process they also ascertain the extent to which they are committed to the philosophy of open education. Many traditional classrooms provide good education for their students. A teacher should not discard an approach that works without carefully considering what she plans to substitute. For this reason, the pace at which changes are adopted will vary from class to class. Steps toward opening a classroom can be taken at the beginning of the school year or during its course. There can be changes in a few areas at a time or in all areas at once. Several factors will influence the rate of change.

SELECTING A STARTING POINT

Open classrooms in this country are now in various stages of development, ranging from those that have "opened" one subject or one period to those that use the open approach exclusively. It is important that teachers start at points comfortable for them. As an analogy, we may picture a group of people clustered around a swimming pool. Some walk into the water at the lowest level, others enter in the middle of the pool, and a few prefer to dive off the board into deep water.

The point of entry depends upon the current educational program of the class and upon all those affected by the program: the teacher, students, administrators, other faculty members, and parents. It is necessary to assess these groups, to pose some questions about their previous experiences and their abilities to adjust to change.

The Teacher

What are the current teaching methods? Is the teacher accustomed to working with children in small groups? Has instruction been individualized in any subject? Does the teacher become upset if there is a great deal of activity in the room? Can she tolerate ambiguity? Noise? Many teachers enjoy being at the "center of the stage," and find lecturing to the whole class satisfying. Is the teacher prepared to change her teaching style? To relinquish some of her authority? *How does the teacher react to change?*

The Students

Have students had any experience with independent work? With work in groups? What are their academic, emotional, and social needs? Teachers have often worked so hard to establish certain routines that children become dependent upon them and are upset when they are not followed. How many of the children will need individual help in adjusting to the new situation? How many of them will pose special problems in a freer environment? *How do the students react to change?*

Administrators and Other Faculty Members

It must be assumed that teachers who are preparing to establish open classrooms have the permission of their administrators, but will they also have their support? It is almost impossible to organize an open classroom successfully in the face of hostility from the administration. The teacher and students will undoubtedly make some mistakes, and administrators must be prepared to give them some latitude. Furthermore, other members of the faculty may complain because children in the open classrooms may come into their classes early or behave noisily. Although administrators need not be totally convinced of the desirability of open classrooms, they must be willing to support them, to honor the teachers' requests for different kinds of material, and to give these classrooms time to prove themselves. *How does the administration react to change?*

The Parents

Do parents understand the goals of the open classroom? Will they be upset if children do not bring home the same kinds of papers and homework as they have previously done, if they appear to be "playing" more in school, or if they sit on the floor instead of in chairs? Do they generally display confidence in the school and in the teachers? How do they view their own role in shaping educational policy? *How do parents react to change?*

There are alternative routes to establishing an open classroom, differing in the pace at which change is initiated. The preceding questions offer a guide to determining the pace appropriate for a particular classroom and also indicate some of the problems that may arise. Teachers should also be aware that open classrooms reflect totally different approaches to education and require a major commitment of time and effort. They must be prepared to make this commitment.

All these factors should be considered in determining a starting point. Once the decision on how quickly to proceed has been made, several problems can be avoided by paving the way with an orientation period.

PREPARING FOR CHANGE

The duration of the orientation period depends largely upon the pace that has been chosen—slow, moderate, or fast. If the teacher has decided to proceed slowly, only minimum preparation may be required and only the pupils themselves may be involved. If, however, the plan is for complete and immediate change more extensive orientation is essential. Teachers will then have to discuss their plans with each of the concerned groups: students, administrators, other faculty members, and parents. A number of basic points should be considered.

First, in order to secure support, it will be necessary for the teacher to convince others that she knows what she is doing, that she has made a professional evaluation of the learning and developmental needs of the class and is convinced of the advisability of an open classroom. She should also be prepared to justify her plans on theoretical grounds (see Chapter One).

Second, labels should be avoided. It often seems less threatening to speak of a goal, of *working toward* an open classroom, than to announce a *fait accompli*—"We are establishing an open classroom."

Third, the teacher should be sensitive to other people's concerns. The traditional teacher next door may have to be reassured that the open class will not become so noisy that it will disturb her. Parents may have to be reassured that the "three Rs" will continue to be taught. Some of them may confuse open classroom with "free classroom." It may be necessary to define the differences for them.[1]

Fourth, all those who may be involved should be included in the orientation. A custodian can be a valuable resource person in an open classroom; he can also create problems if he is upset by the "mess" in the room.

Fifth, the teacher should not expect complete support. Many people are aware of mistakes that have been made in the name of open education and are legitimately concerned about possible excesses. Others misunderstand open education. Others simply feel threatened by any change. Orientation may have to be a continuing process; it may take a while to convince people.

Sixth, the orientation of the students is of primary importance. It is essential that they be involved in the planning. The teacher should tell them honestly why she is making changes. She should avoid threatening

---

[1] More specific suggestions for parental orientation and involvement are included in Chapter Eighteen.

or appearing as a benevolent dispenser of favors. The teacher who announces in advance, "I will try this but will have to change back to the old ways if you cannot behave" or "If you get too noisy I will have to insist upon absolute quiet" is reminding the class of her authority and challenging it to test her. Misbehavior should not be appraised as "letting me down." Children should not be taught to act responsibly solely to please the teacher. They should be informed that both they and the teacher will probably make mistakes in a new program but that there will be ample opportunity for discussion and joint evaluation of the program.

Seventh, it is unrealistic to expect instant success. Some pupils will need to test limits and will have to be helped to acquire self-discipline, to become more independent. Children from a tightly controlled class often run about wildly when turned loose in the playground, for they are not quite certain how to cope with their freedom. Similarly, some children placed in the freer environment of an open classroom may react with confusion initially.

INSTITUTING THE CHANGE

Having determined the pace at which to accomplish change and prepared the participants, the teacher is ready to initiate the changes themselves. She may proceed slowly, at a moderate rate, or rapidly. Each of these alternatives will be described here, and it will become clear that they are not rigidly separate but usually overlap. The teacher may choose one of the alternatives described or an alternative somewhere between.

Starting Slowly

There are basically two ways of moving slowly toward an open classroom: "opening" one subject at a time and establishing one open activity period per week.

The Subject Approach   A subject in which options can be offered to the students should be selected. Social studies and science lend themselves readily to the subject approach. The teacher, instead of choosing a topic to be studied by the whole class, offers a number of alternative units. For example, she may select three science units like electricity, space, and simple machines. The students may choose to work on any one of them during the coming month. An individual student may also be allowed to substitute a different unit if he chooses.

There should be a number of science books, both textbooks and general publications, available to help children to make their choices. Some newer curriculum units may be used. They have kits on different topics for use by individuals or small groups of children, and encourage children to work independently.[2] Whatever resources are used, it will be necessary for the teacher to discuss some of the different ways of investigating a science topic. For example, students may simply explore materials, or they may do written research, perform a series of experiments and record their observations, or build a model illustrating the scientific principles involved. They may visit related places (like a planetarium), interview people, write for information, or prepare film strips and tapes. They may use several of these methods or choose others.

Students should be permitted to decide whether they wish to work independently or in groups, and in the latter instance to choose group members. At first the teacher will specify a particular time for children to work on their science projects. As they become more interested, the pupils may start reading and writing in conjunction with their topics, and the teacher may permit them to engage in science study in preference to some other work.

The aim of the teacher who "opens" her class for one subject is slowly to encourage the children to assume more and more responsibility for this subject: choosing a topic and determining how to investigate it, when to work on it, with whom to work, and finally how to present it. This process will be gradual. Initially the children may need more specific directions in pursuing their investigations and the teacher may have to make resource information available for each topic. Textbooks and curriculum guides can be used by the children.

When the teacher's written plan is used as a starting point, it should offer a choice of activities and permit each child to complete them in a way that interests him. But plans devised or chosen by the teacher should be viewed as temporary expedients. The goal is for the child to participate in planning his own work and eventually to write some of his own proposals. (Chapter Four suggests one form for students to use in recording their own plans of study.)

There are some techniques for aiding students to plan their own investigations into topics. One rather structured technique was used by a teacher to help children who needed guidance in designing a study. He designed several activities related to science topics and assigned a different

---

[2] Examples of these include: *Elementary Science Study* (ESS), 56 units. Descriptions of units and reports of their use in schools are available from ESS, 55 Chapel Street, Newton, Mass. The kits are marketed commercially by Webster Division, McGraw-Hill Book Co.

Also *Science Curriculum Improvement Study* developed at University of California at Berkeley. Materials from Rand McNally, Chicago, Ill.; and *Science: A Process Approach* developed by the American Association for the Advancement of Science. Materials from Xerox Co., 600 Madison Ave., N.Y.

point value to each. Some activities were worth five points each, others one or two. He suggested that students complete at least ten points of activities for each topic. This system enabled children to decide whether they wished to engage in several easy tasks or a few more difficult ones. Children were also permitted to suggest their own activities and to assign appropriate points to them. The limitations of such approaches must be appreciated. They are reported because they can be very helpful to students who have had no experience in planning their own work, but they do reflect the teacher's conception of an area of study, rather than those of the children. A child working in an open environment could conceivably take a one-point activity and extend it in unforeseen directions. A point system would tend to inhibit this development.

Another technique for assisting students to devise their own investigations of science topics is to maintain a science-resource index file in the classroom. The box can be divided into topics like space, air, and electricity. For each topic, there can be the following subheadings:

Questions about the Topic
Suggested Experiments
Activities
Available Research Material (books, pamphlets, articles, pictures, magazines, film strips, films)
Outside Resources (parents, other members of the faculty, other children, agencies, museums)

The file is available as a ready resource for children who are planning work on particular science topics. They may draw up their plans by choosing from among questions, activities, and other procedures suggested and by adding others of their own. The resource box offers the child who needs it a sense of the scope of the topic and ideas for initial proceedings, while permitting him to choose those investigations that appeal to him. One requirement of such a file is that both teacher and children contribute information for each heading and questions about a topic. The teacher's questions should be open-ended rather than specific: "Which of these will a magnet attract—wood, metal, paper, plastic?" is less useful than "How many objects can you find that a magnet will or will not attract? Can you find anything that these objects have in common?" The children should be urged to file questions for themselves and others to explore.

Some teachers fear that when pupils are permitted to pose their own questions they may pose superficial ones or questions that do not lend themselves to classroom investigation. Teachers will have to address themselves to this, to help children to formulate significant questions that can be investigated at their levels of development. This process is in itself an

important learning experience for youngsters. It should be added, however, that one set of problems related to a particular science topic is not
necessarily superior to others. Textbook questions are frequently chosen
because they have exact answers, like the names of the planets, rather than
because they reflect children's interests in scientific phenomena.

Children should also be encouraged to add to other categories in
the resource box, frequently after completion of their own work on a
topic. They may list additional books that they have found helpful and
experiments or activities that they have devised. In this way the science-
resource file becomes a class endeavor.

Gradually, as children become more responsible in one subject, the
open approach may be extended to other areas of the curriculum, and
similar options may be offered in many areas of work. (Suggestions for
organizing work in open classrooms are presented in detail in Chapters
Four and Five.) It may be necessary to proceed slowly. Months of step-by-
step change may be required before children are ready to accept more
responsibility for their own work.

The Activity Approach   Another method of slowly establishing an
open classroom is to start with one period each week. This period may be
designated for children to choose from a number of alternative activities.
An entire afternoon or morning is advisable, though we caution against
choosing Friday afternoon, rather than "prime" time.

With the children's help a number of activities can be planned for
that period. These activities may be grouped around a common subject like
mathematics, or arts and crafts, or they can be centered around a theme.
For example, if the theme is Latin America, activities may include weaving;
basket making; pottery; modeling "archaeological finds" in clay; cooking;
making felt serapes; constructing musical instruments like tambourines,
maracas, and castanets; learning Spanish dances; Spanish language lessons;
building a store using Spanish currency made by pupils; and making a
piñata. A series of unrelated activities may also be adopted: designing
puppets, film-strip art, painting pictures on light-sensitive paper,[3] bookbinding,[4] rock constructions, and games.

Only a few activities should be initiated at one time. Each should
be conducted in a different corner of the room, and each child should
be permitted to choose one. Activities that are popular and oversubscribed
can be repeated later. Before proceeding, a few simple requirements should
be reviewed with the class:

1. Each group is responsible for its own housekeeping and packing
   away unused material.

---

[3] Work with film strips and light-sensitive paper will be described later in this chapter.
[4] See Chapter Eleven for instructions.

2. No one is to interfere with anyone else's work.
3. Children are expected to stay with the activities that they have chosen for the entire period.

The activity period also affords an opportunity for the teacher to invite a parent or an older child to the class to demonstrate a particular skill: sewing, needlework, tie dying, Morse code, radio building, macramé, or the like. One child in the class may wish to supervise an activity like constructing a wooden cart. He should be encouraged to do so.

During this period the teacher should act as a consultant, prepared to show the students how to use certain materials but not exactly what to construct. Directions should be available for those activities that require them, but strict, preconceived notions about the results should be avoided. The teacher should also observe the entire class, analyzing which activities appear to *fit*: which stimulate children, which engage them, which quickly bore them. Much can be garnered from this observation for planning future work.

At the end of the period the class should evaluate the results of their activities. How were the materials handled? What was produced? Which activities should be repeated? Which discarded? Which extended? What new ones can be suggested? As the weekly activity period is continued, the teacher may find that the children are using some mathematics for measurement, reading and writing on their project topics, and beginning to integrate some of their other school work into the activity periods. This advance may lead to the next step, which is "moving moderately" to institute change.

Moving Moderately

The moderate route toward "opening" begins with an approximately even division between formal and informal work. Often the mornings are scheduled for reading, mathematics, and language arts. The afternoons are reserved for freer work on science, social studies, class projects, and various other activities.

Children should know what is expected of them during the informal periods. For example, they may complete science or social studies projects, work on a play or plan a bulletin board or display, construct special-interest books (see Chapter Seven), or engage in activities like those that we have already described. There should be provision for recording their plans for this work, as well as for the results (see Chapters Four and Five).

As the class becomes more experienced in scheduling its own day, in engaging in diverse activities simultaneously, in employing an "activity approach" in mathematics and language arts, the teacher may find that she can no longer maintain a distinction between formal and informal work. The class may now be ready for a completely open classroom.

Changing Completely

Complete change can be achieved gradually through the steps that we have described or it can be initiated all at once without intermediate steps. Although the latter course may prove more difficult, with careful planning it may nevertheless be the most desirable way to proceed. There will be a uniform approach throughout the day and children will not have to adjust to different rules for formal and informal work. Much, of course, depends upon the participants' ability to adjust to radical change. In this approach, first of all, the room will have to be rearranged for informal work.

ARRANGING THE ROOM

Several considerations should be borne in mind when arranging the room for an open class. First, there must be agreement on a seating plan for the children. In most open classrooms the traditional individual desks have been abandoned in favor of tables that seat six or eight students each. Some teachers continue to use desks, however, either because tables are not available or because the children prefer them.

A London headmaster in whose school individual desks were used explained: "Our children come from areas where they rarely have a desk at home which they can call their own. They enjoy having a desk in school where they can store their belongings and to which they can return for their written work." A New York principal reported, "Our sixth-graders were so adamant at wanting to keep their desks that we decided to retain them." When desks are used, they should be moved together into units of six or eight. There may be an understanding that during the day the tops of the desks may be used by other members of the class.

Those who urge the elimination of desks point to the additional space that they require, the difficulty that children have in moving from one activity to another if they must return to specified seats, and the more rigid seating arrangement that often results. One principal who saw no need for desks insisted that "if children truly feel responsible for a room, they will think of the entire classroom as belonging to them and not need one particular spot." Even when tables are used, however, children may have "home" tables, where they tend to start the day.[5] But some open-class teachers do not encourage the child to identify with a particular desk or table and may not even have a chair for each child: Children sit on the floor during class meetings.

In rooms without desks storage space must be made available for children's belongings: books, workbooks, notebooks, pencils, papers, and

[5] See Chapter Four for further discussion of starting the day.

In rooms without desks, space for children's belongings can be provided in many ways. (Photographs courtesy of Guggenheim School, Port Washington, N.Y.; Teyfant Infants School, Bristol, England; and Taukomas School, Half Hollow Hills School District, Dix Hills, N. Y.)

so on. There are many possible ways in which to achieve this goal. Bookshelves can be built and divided into cubbyholes. In one school in which this method was adopted each child tacked an individual piece of needlework over his cubbyhole to conceal the contents and to create a decorative effect. Plastic trays, shoe boxes, wire files, or cardboard boxes can be used and stored on closet shelves or on open bookshelves. Some plastic trays can be stacked up for easy storage. Carts with trays that can be withdrawn are also popular for this purpose. Whatever the arrangement chosen, it is essential that each child receive an assigned place to store his belongings. It is often advisable to provide a few storage areas around the room so that children do not all crowd into one area. Some teachers color-code different areas so that loose trays can more easily be returned to their proper places. Good housekeeping is an essential ingredient of open classrooms, and it may begin with the teacher's insisting that each child's box be kept reasonably neat.

In addition, each child may also have a file of his work. File folders can be used to hold reports, paintings, graphs, pieces of writing, and the like. These folders are helpful for individual conferences between teacher and pupils, between teacher and parents, and among all three, for they constitute records of what pupils have accomplished and in what areas they need further work.

The next step in arranging the room is to divide it into different learning corners, providing for small areas where groups can work on common activities. This division facilitates the simultaneous occurrence of several different activities. Many materials can be used to partition a room: bookshelves (whose backs can be used for displays), tables placed perpendicular to each other, plywood, poster board, pegboard, portable blackboards. chart racks, screens, heavy corrugated paper, and paneling anchored between desks or tables. Heavy corrugated paper can be used not only for partitioning the room but also for constructing bookshelves and small tables. Raised platforms for stages or additional seating can be constructed by covering lumber with carpet remnants.

Arrangement of activity centers will be determined to a large extent by the basic physical characteristics of the room itself. Painting easels, for example, should probably be placed near the sink. A reading corner is best placed in an area with good lighting and separated from noisy activities. The teacher should also be conscious of the "traffic pattern." Children should be able to obtain materials or go in and out of activity centers without disturbing others. It is important that the pupils be included in planning and arranging the room, that they be responsible for keeping the areas in order, and that learning areas not remain static. Materials in the centers should be changed frequently, and entirely different activities should be substituted as children's interests change.

Initially there will have to be at least three basic areas: for reading, mathematics, and writing. Science and art corners will probably also be included. Other areas will depend upon the grade level of the class, the curriculum, and both the children's and teacher's interests.

The Reading Corner

For a reading corner an area of the room free from interruption, that has good lighting and ample space for bookshelves should be chosen. If bookcases or shelves are not readily available, they can be built by the class. Brightly painted wooden crates or scrap lumber supported on bricks make effective bookshelves. Books should be displayed attractively on the shelves. Book ends can be supplied by the children: Interesting rocks, shells, dolls, wood, pieces of sculpture, and so on are appropriate.

The reading corner should include a variety of books on different topics and at varying levels of difficulty. There should be some basal readers (which make excellent story anthologies), some general books, and many paperbacks. Paperbacks are particularly appropriate, offering inexpensive means of enlarging the classroom library and providing additional copies of books that several children may wish to read simultaneously. Attention should be paid to the length of the books chosen. Some short books that can be read at one sitting are essential for younger children.

"Fort" built by children creates a quiet reading corner. (Photograph courtesy of Bridge Farms Primary School, Bristol, England.)

In addition there should be magazines, pamphlets, advertising catalogues. A mail-order catalogue is interesting reading for children of almost any age. Even outdated catalogues can be used for comparative studies of fashions and prices during different periods. Certain magazines like *Popular Mechanics* are popular in upper grades, as are copies of newspapers. In some classes comic books may be acceptable. A section on poetry is essential. It should include a variety of kinds of poetry: humorous verse, anthologies of miscellaneous poems, and volumes by single authors, limericks, and so on. Books of riddles and puzzles are popular too.

The corner should also provide space for children's original books and poems, individual children's work, and class collections. Some books may be allowed to circulate and a sign-out procedure may then be necessary.

The choice of furniture for the reading corner depends upon the use to which it will be put. There may be a round table where a few children can sit and read, as in a library, or the corner may be arranged for lounging, with a piece of carpeting on the floor, some pillows, and even a comfortable upholstered chair or small couch. An old piece of carpeting and cast-off furniture can generally be obtained without difficulty. The class can help make slipcovers for the furniture. Pieces of carpet can be stitched together to make a rug.

Usually an escape area is required for children, who sometimes need to be alone. If at all possible, there should also be several smaller reading areas in the room, large enough for one or two children. It may be better to place an upholstered chair in a quiet corner where one child can curl up and read by himself. There should also be some small squares of carpet (discontinued carpet samples are available from carpet dealers) and some stuffed pillows that a child can take to a quiet area to read.

Later, as children work on their projects, an Indian tepee, a castle, or a cave large enough for a child to crawl into in order to read quietly can be constructed.

The teacher will want to be aware of which books are being read and which never come off the shelves. It is better to begin with fewer books and to add others gradually than to put everything out at once. It will also be necessary to add books about new interests: baseball in the spring, football in the fall, ecology, mythology, and so on. Children will, of course, use the school library as well.

Particularly in the earlier grades a listening center is an important adjunct to the reading corner. There children may use a tape recorder with individual headsets to hear books read to them. There are many commercial tapes available for this purpose; they are coordinated with books, so that the child can follow the story in a book as he listens to it. The teacher may occasionally tape a "surprise" story for the children, either with or without an accompanying book.

Corner of room divided to provide two writing areas and quiet "escape" spot. (Photograph courtesy of Halford Infants School, London, England.)

The Writing Corner

The writing corner, just as the reading corner, should be placed where there is minimum distraction. It should contain some desks placed side by side or a table. The writing corner should be stocked with papers of various colors and shapes (short pieces for one-paragraph compositions, long and narrow pieces for "tall" tales), pens, pencils, rulers, magic markers, crayons, and felt-tipped pens to illustrate stories. There should also be magazines as a source of cut-out illustrations. An ample assortment of dictionaries, both printed and homemade, is essential.[6] A typewriter, if available, will enhance this corner.

It is important that there be a colorful resource box that includes suggestions for many different kinds of writing:[7]

> Story starters.
> Directions for writing cinquains, haiku, limericks.
> Poetry starters.

[6] Chapter Eleven includes instructions for making dictionaries.
[7] Specific instructions for making each of the items to be included in the writing box are also in Chapter Eleven.

Directions for writing business letters and appropriate stationery with envelopes for mailing.

An address file including addresses of publishers of children's books, elected officials (most of whom will reply to mail received from school children), and of companies that offer free materials to schools.

A file of possible pen pals.

The writing corner should also contain bulletin boards for displaying children's work. Work that is to be exhibited should meet certain standards. Although spelling errors may be overlooked in daily creative writing in choosing pieces for display, the author should usually be asked to rewrite it to correct his errors. The sensitive teacher will, of course, be conscious of what each child is capable of doing and of each child's need to exhibit some work of which he is proud.

The Mathematics Corner

In the open classroom, regardless of the age level of the children, the mathematics corner will stress active involvement in learning mathematics rather than in paper-and-pencil exercises. The mathematics corner for younger children should contain some such structural aids for computations as Cuisenaire rods, Stern blocks, and the Unifix cubes[8] that are so popular in England. There should be materials to provide opportunities for experience in applied mathematics: measurements of surface and weight, money, and time; sorting and classification; counting; graphing; and so on.

These materials should include scales and weights. Postal scales showing ounces, fruit-and-vegetable scales, and scales for weighing people are all excellent investments. Any number of materials can be weighed, classified, and sorted: bottle caps, pegs, sticks, nuts, bolts, buttons, acorns, and so on.

For other measurements rulers (in both centimeters and inches for older children), string, and a trundle wheel (which measures distance) should be included. Also tangrams, attribute blocks, geo boards (preferably made by the children), a cash register for organizing a store, paper money and possibly some pennies, dice, and playing cards (for charting probabilities) are also useful. There may be areas other than the mathematics corner in which children engage in mathematical activities. For example, some may explore liquid measurement at the sink or with a large tub of water outdoors. Others may fill different-sized containers with sand.

---

[8] Unifix cubes are ¾-inch flexible, interlocking plastic cubes in different colors. The cubes are of equal size, regardless of color, and each represents one unit.

Combined mathematics and science corner. (Photograph courtesy of Merrick Public Schools, New York.)

The Science Corner

Organizing a classroom science corner simply as an area in which to display pretty shells or interesting rocks should be avoided. Like the mathematics corner, the science corner should permit children to become actively involved with materials. Depending upon the ages of the children, there should be magnets, bulbs, batteries, wires, test tubes, inexpensive microscopes, lenses, seeds and the like. Some units from the newer science-curriculum kits mentioned earlier in the chapter are helpful. Hamsters, guinea pigs, chameleons, gerbils, rabbits, mice, and other animals are popular and make enlightening studies possible. Their sizes can be measured at regular intervals, they can be weighed before and after feeding, they can be bred, and different aspects of their behavior can be charted. Fish, terrariums, and plants may also be included in the science area. The selection of additional materials will depend upon the particular interests of the class.

Other Activity Corners

In addition to reading, writing, mathematics, and science centers, there will undoubtedly have to be provision for other activities, including art and craftwork—painting, clay, building bricks, needlework, sewing, printing, puppet making, pottery, and infinite kinds of materials for collages (see Chapter Fourteen). Some of the following materials and activities may also be included according to the children's ages:[9]

> Play house
> Puppet theater
> Sand play
> Water play
> Woodworking
> Post office (for issuing stamps and delivering mail)
> Store
> Drama corner with dress-up materials appropriate for all age groups (frequently inspiring creative writing and musical composition)
> Newspaper office
> Junk constructions (see Chapter Fourteen)
> Music center
> Game center (with both commercial and homemade games, as well as materials for constructing games)
> Repair shop
> Weather station
> Cooking and baking
> Foreign-country booths
> Travel center (with books to help children to plan detailed trips that they would like to take)
> Career center (with information on many different careers)
> Television corner, with material for constructing mock television sets (see Chapter Fourteen).
> Puzzles, brain teasers, and codes
> Sports desk
> "Plan a country" area, with materials for constructing communities, maps, and so on, so that students can place their country somewhere on earth, detail its topography, history, customs, and the like
> Research center
> Bank (for printing currency and handling class finances)
> Costume-design center
> Machine shop

Two other activities merit special discussion: bookbinding and photography and film.

A table near the writing corner should provide materials for binding books: fabric, wallpaper samples, contact paper, cardboard, construction paper, masking tape, and glue. (See directions for binding books in Chapter

---

[9] Chapters Seven–Fourteen include numerous suggestions for activities for which additional corners can be provided.

Eleven.) Children should be encouraged to bind stories that they have written, collections of poems, and reports. These bound books may then become part of the class reading corner. They also make excellent gifts for Mother's and Father's Days.

Aside from their intrinsic value as art forms, photography and film offer opportunities for expressive activities related to almost any subject. They serve as means of reporting in language arts, social studies, and science and as a stimulus for writing. Some schools have cameras available for use in classrooms or on trips. It is also possible for a class to construct individual pinhole cameras that will take pictures.[10] Film may be purchased in bulk for classroom use, and a spare closet or unused area can be converted into a dark room for developing pictures.

Film strips can easily be made in a classroom, using old film strips. The procedure is fairly simple. Old 35-millimeter film strips can be obtained from film dealers. The schools too may have film strips that are obsolete. The used film can be soaked in a solution of bleach and water until the old images disappear. When the film has dried, new pictures can be drawn on it with magic markers or grease pencils. The images must fit the size of a frame which is three-quarters of an inch long. One film strip can be cut into smaller pieces to accommodate several children. Sound can be synchronized with the strips by means of a tape recorder.

Film strips can also be made on strips of plain white paper that have been cut to size and lightly coated with cooking oil. Children will enjoy experimenting with this technique. In some classrooms children attempt actual movies. They write scripts, stage and film them, and coordinate the action with dialogue recorded on tape.

Interesting art works can created with wet-media acetate instead of film. Various substances are superimposed on the acetate. One class used glue, jello, nail polish, sand, tea, coffee, and paint. The acetate is then cut to the size of 35-millimeter film slides and inserted in slide holders (which can be obtained from photography supply houses). The projected images can be exciting art forms.

Another activity involves the use of light-sensitive paper available from photography shops. This paper changes color when exposed to light. Placing objects on the paper blocks light from some parts, and the paper in those areas will remain unchanged, thus creating interesting designs. Variation in the opacity of objects, as well as the intensity of light, will also vary the patterns. Children will enjoy experimenting with these possibilities, exposing the paper in sunlight, light from electric bulbs, natural indoor light, and the beam of a flashlight. They can also test the effects of varying

---

[10] See Kodak Pamphlet No. AA-5, "How To Make and Use a Pinhole Camera." (About 15¢ at photo shops or Eastman Kodak Co., Rochester, N.Y. 14650.)

time exposures. When a child is satisfied with his results, the paper can be fixed (placed in a bath of Rapid Fix until it is yellow-brown, then washed in a pan of running water for about five minutes). The dried paper can be mounted on dry mounting paper in various ways. The results serve as unusual illustrations for creative writing.

In addition to activity corners, there are several other aspects of room arrangements that should be considered. Some individual learning carrels can be created by placing heavy cardboard or plywood around three sides of a child's desk for children who prefer to work in seclusion.

An indispensable feature of the open classroom is a class bulletin board, for the use of both teachers and students. It is the place where items that are too time-consuming to be announced to the whole class can be posted: for example, a reminder that there will be an assembly program at 10:00 or that a parent is coming at 1:00 to demonstrate candle making, an announcement by a group of students of a forthcoming presentation, or a request by the teacher to see Beth, Mitch, and Phil at 9:15 for work on multiplying fractions (with an accompanying note that "Anyone who wishes to review this may join the group"). It can also include notices by students who wish to share something that they have learned: "John will explain the use of the microprojector at 1:00"; "Joan is available to help bake 'people cookies.'"

Before proceeding with the actual physical arrangements of the room, the teacher will have to decide which specific learning areas to include. It is desirable at first to keep them at a minimum. It is better to initiate an activity in response to children's developing interests than to impose it. The teacher should strive to keep activities "fresh," to discontinue activities in which children appear to have lost interest, and to add new ones that will extend or spur interests. Sometimes interest in an activity can be reawakened by addition of new pieces of material or by the posing of stimulating questions. For example, the teacher in a Leicestershire classroom had written beside a feather, "How does a baby swan keep its feathers dry?" Encyclopedias and science reference works are good sources of such questions.

In the first few weeks after the room is organized some teachers prefer to supervise the children's schedules closely in order to ensure that each child has a chance to explore each center and remains in it for a period of time. This approach has a number of advantages: Exposing the children to all the centers makes it possible for them to make intelligent choices about where they wish to work when they are later expected to make such decisions for themselves.

It establishes the premise that children are to stay in each center long enough to become involved with the materials, not just to visit and leave. Familiarity with all the materials in the room may enable a child to plan his work more effectively and to coordinate his activities in various centers.

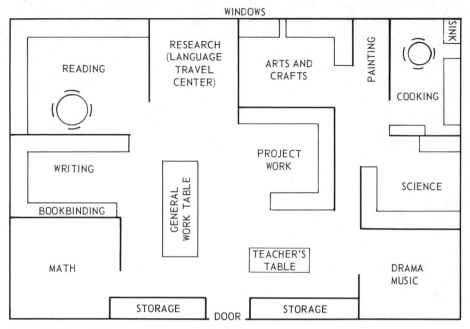

Figure 3.1. Sample Room Arrangement: Large Room

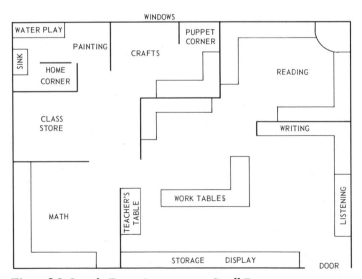

Figure 3.2. Sample Room Arrangement: Small Room

Diagrams of room layouts featuring activity corners are included in Figures 3.1 and 3.2. It should be added that some rooms, because of their sizes or shapes, do not readily lend themselves to individual activity corners in which children can work. Some teachers therefore prefer to distribute materials among different corners of the room, permitting children to work on them wherever convenient. Only a few items remain stationary. Children can thus sit together while working on different activities. A child who is weaving on a small loom may join a child who is weighing objects, for example. Attention to housekeeping becames particularly important in this kind of room, to ensure that supplies are returned to their proper areas.

A PLANNED ENVIRONMENT

The effect of organizing a classroom for open education is a planned environment markedly different in appearance from traditional classrooms. Unlike a traditional room, in which seats are arranged so that the teacher can see all the children at a glance and they in turn can always see her, there is freer use of physical space in an open classroom. Children spill out from the room into the corridor, adjoining classrooms, or small offices to work on projects that require privacy. The classrooms themselves are rich in materials, decorated with children's work—arranged more as workshops, laboratories or research centers than are conventional rooms.

Whatever the physical arrangements are, the environment of the open classroom will reflect the teacher's ideas about how children learn. Materials are chosen to stimulate a child's curiosity, to motivate him to explore, and to provide him with different means of investigating problems. These materials and means should be appropriate to a child's level of maturity. Classrooms are not designed simply to house collections of miscellaneous items but are carefully prepared as laboratories in which children can investigate problems that interest them with the guidance of their teachers.

Attention to the affective domain is a further aspect of the environment that must be taken into account. Opportunities for play, music, art, and other creative activities suggest that these occupations are considered worthwhile in the classroom. Interaction among students can also be stimulated by the physical layout.

An open classroom reflects respect for aesthetics. Sloppy rooms, carelessly maintained with outdated examples of children's work on display, are not only confusing but are also insulting to children, who are expected to spend the greater portion of their days in such environments. In that sense they violate the philosophy of open education. Careful attention to displays, to fine examples of art, to textures, and to colors is appropriate to open classrooms. It is necessary for the teacher occasionally to assess the overall effect of the room, to ensure that it is pleasing and harmonious, a relaxing place to work. Because of the profusion of materials in many different colors, some rooms can become overstimulating and therefore disturbing to some youngsters.

This emphasis on the physical environment of open classrooms may lead to a distorted view of its role. The environment *results* from the philosophy of open education. It is constructed to support that philosophy, but it does not by itself produce it. Room arrangements, no matter how creative, do not alone create an open classroom. It is the *use* of those rooms by teachers and pupils that is decisive.

Materials in the Open Classroom

Within the open classroom materials are recognized as having special significance. They can serve as starting points for stimulating a child's interest in a topic and can lead him to further exploration. But materials are inanimate. Just as with room arrangements, they do not alone create an open classroom. The teacher's knowledge of the potential of materials is frequently required to spark interest. For example, introduction of even a mundane item like a pair of gloves with the question "What other things come in twos?" can lead to explorations on many levels, including use of computers that operate with the numerical base two.

Although the teacher has to be aware of some of the directions in which materials can lead, it is important that she avoid preconceptions about where they will in fact lead. It is the child's freedom to bring his own questions to school, to conceive of the school as a laboratory in which he can investigate problems of moment to him, that is the decisive component of open education. For this reason, the same material can have a variety of functions in an open classroom. A fossil, for example, can be the basis of an art project for some children but may lead to a study of the history and formation of the earth by others. A teacher may bring in some foreign coins to be used for mathematical computations but they may stimulate a number of unexpected projects. Some children may become interested in the country of the coins' origin, others in the history of currency, and still others in how rates of exchange are determined.

It is not essential that large sums of money be spent for equipment in open classrooms. Everyday items are often more useful than commercial equipment, which may be less flexible and limited to specified functions. Many different materials have already been mentioned in connection with activity corners. There are also many others that the teacher may include as she begins to envision their inherent possibilities: old clocks and radios, an egg timer, boxes and plastic bottles of different sizes and shapes, cans, pieces of wood, fabrics of different textures, rubber tubing, wallpaper samples, old magazines, wool, ribbon, plastic-covered wire, vegetable coloring, art prints, small machines, and so on. Some commercial materials can be appropriate—for example, science kits, individualized reading boxes, mathematics activity cards, and games. Ordering fewer textbooks and workbooks (it is no longer necessary to have one for each child) permits savings of money that can be used to purchase stimulating materials.

In equipping the open classroom, it is well to remember the warning of Alice Yardley, an English educator:

> The environment should be well-, but not over-endowed. Some schools, in their anxiety to provide variety, become museums. Every conceivable form of stimulation clutters the child's surroundings. There is nowhere for the eye to rest, nor corner for meditation and no breathing space during which the child can consolidate. Perpetual stimulation allows no time for inner growth. . . . The opportunity to reflect is essential to the development of sound thinking.[11]

A common error of teachers in establishing open classrooms is to put out all the materials at once. When there is much material to choose from, children may explore none of it adequately and may quickly become bored with most of it. It is much more advisable to keep adding new books, rocks to be weighed, colorful pieces of foil to the collage table as the term progresses. It is also important to avoid letting the room became a store-house for junk. It is one thing to include an old pair of curtains in the costume box but quite another to leave old materials around to clutter the room. One English headmaster admonished, "Shoddy materials lead to shoddy work."

Housekeeping in Open Classrooms

Because of the abundance of materials in open classrooms, good housekeeping is particularly imperative. Materials must be accessible, invitingly displayed, and returned to proper places when no longer needed; a missing piece of wire can prevent the use of an entire kit.

Children should be expected to take responsibility for housekeeping. It is frequently helpful to assign primary responsibility for each corner to a different group of children, who are to supervise the housekeeping of that corner and to see that materials in it are properly stored and maintained. Color coding each center also helps. A plastic star or piece of masking tape in one color can be attached to all the material that belongs in a particular corner. A book that belongs in the science corner, rather than in the reading corner is coded accordingly. Some items may also have to be

---

[11] Alice Yardley, *Young Children Learning: Reaching Out* (London: Evans, 1970), p. 54.

number-coded to indicate their places on the shelves. Orderly arrangement of materials will eliminate many problems.

When establishing a new activity corner, the teacher should introduce the class to it in small groups, explaining what materials are included, pertinent facts about their maintenance, and where they are to be stored. Each group should have an opportunity to "walk through" an activity corner and to become familiar with the related materials. The rule that each group using a corner is responsible for its own housekeeping and packing away unused material should be reinforced.

Teachers have responsibility for providing storage space for excess equipment, ensuring that materials are displayed attractively, and replaced when necessary, and guaranteeing that bulletin boards and exhibits are kept up to date. An open classroom should be one in which children take pride for its aesthetic, as well as its intellectual, appeal.

Chapter
FOUR
Classroom
Management

The teacher had just completed her first year of teaching in an open classroom and was discussing her experiences:

> When I started, I was so concerned that someone would miss something that I was constantly checking the schedule of each child. I felt more like a dispatcher than a teacher those first few months. It seems I was always moving people about—excusing some from one center, reminding others to start their reading and worrying about what each was doing at every point. And then I realized that I wasn't really running an open classroom. I was permitting more movement, but I was trying to direct every step. The strange part is that it was still an improvement. Kids enjoyed moving about and having some choice of work within a center.
>
> Gradually I started to relax and trust the kids to schedule their own day. Except for three or four children who needed help it really worked. Some kids would spend an entire day working on a science project, but somehow at the end of the week their other work was completed too. Now I wonder whether we needed that initial period of direction, or whether I could have started out without a strict structure.

The question is one that many teachers have raised and to which there undoubtedly is no one answer. Although there is general agreement on the need for structure in scheduling the work of open classes, the interpretation of structure varies from teacher to teacher and from class to class. Different models for classroom management will be presented in this chapter; some are more structured than are others. Each teacher must decide which model best fits her situation.

Two basic facets of classroom management will be discussed: organizing the school day, and organizing and assigning work.

ORGANIZING THE SCHOOL DAY

Starting the Day

When children arrive at school in the morning, there are a few tasks that must be taken care of. Attendance and in some classes lunch and milk orders must be recorded. Materials may have to be set out. There are often work assignments to be picked up and mailboxes to be checked. Pets may have to be fed, plants watered. Each class will have worked out its routines for such activities. (See Chapter Five for some suggestions for keeping attendance and other morning records.)

Children may or may not have definite areas in which to gather when they first arrive. In some classrooms groups of children start the day in specific activity centers to which they are assigned on a rotating basis. They are responsible for housekeeping and for keeping necessary supplies on hand in those centers. In other rooms there are no predetermined stations.

Whatever the morning chores may be, they will be followed by either a class meeting, an activity period, or a short period of planning by the pupils.

Class Meeting Before general work is begun the entire class may gather with the teacher for a short meeting at which the teacher makes announcements about the day's work, introduces new materials, and ascertains where each child will be working. She may suggest that some children start with mathematics, may simply ask others what their plans are, and may inform a few that she wishes to meet with them in a group. Sometimes this period is used for a short class lesson, discussion of a current event, or aspects of a class project.

Starting the day with a class meeting is the most frequent method during the early stages of organizing an open classroom. It enables the teacher to help the children organize their work and to ensure that they are clear about their plans once work has begun.

Classes that are organized for team teaching, particularly when they are larger than two ordinary classes, tend to begin with meetings in home groups, at which matters similar to those already noted are discussed.

Activity Period After morning chores children may proceed immediately to activity corners to continue previous work or to initiate new projects. This method of starting the day may be most successful when children have had some experience in open classrooms; it has several advantages. Children do not have to wait for everyone to arrive before starting their own activities. In open classrooms some children tend to come in before school has officially opened and are eager to start as soon as they arrive. A class meeting scheduled first in the morning may prove an unnecessary distraction.

DAILY PLAN	
By: _____ Date _____	
My Plans for Today	Completed

DAILY PLAN	
Name _____ Date _____	
Activity	Completed
Reading _____	
Math _____	
Writing _____	
Project _____	
Other _____	

Figure 4.1 Samples of Daily Work Plans

Even when the day starts with an activity period, there may still have to be direction for a few students. Teachers can easily note those children who have difficulty deciding on tasks and can help them to become involved. Sometimes this indecision can be avoided by teachers' checking with students before they leave school each day, to make certain that each child has made plans for the following morning. The duration of the morning activity period varies but generally will average about forty-five minutes.

Planning Period   A short planning period may be scheduled for the start of each day. It differs from a class meeting in that the planning is done by the individual students, rather than in a class group. In this period each child is expected to plan his day's work. He may have to sign up for specific activities or meet with other members of the class to decide when they will work jointly on a common task.

In classes that start in this manner the child must be aware of any specific requirements or plans for the day. He may be expected to check the class bulletin board to see whether or not there are special activities in which he wishes to participate or to which he has been assigned. He will note any special subjects scheduled for the day, any work that is due. He may check his mailbox to see whether or not there are notes from the teacher and previous work to be filed or corrected. His plans for the day are usually recorded in an individual notebook or on a form provided for that purpose (see Figure 4.1). This planning period should be short. Not every facet of a child's activities need be planned in advance.

When pupils have completed their plans they proceed with the day's activities. Beginning the day in this manner is similar to beginning with an activity period, but it requires children to organize their work for an entire day, a valuable skill for them to develop. In classes in which this method is used, there are usually short periods at the end of each day in which children evaluate their plans and indicate which tasks have been completed. Some teachers collect the daily plans and file them in the children's work folders as partial records of their activities and clues to how they organize their days.

In deciding which of these three approaches to adopt, teachers may have to experiment with each and to vary their approaches on different days, depending upon the status of work. On some days children may be involved in projects and wish to continue immediately after arriving at school. On others a meeting or short planning period may be desirable to organize the day.

Scheduling the Day

Several factors influence the class schedule for the day. The schedule will be affected by the children's curriculum needs and by the degree of freedom that the teacher is prepared to permit students in scheduling their own work. It will vary from day to day, depending upon any special activities, class presentations, or assemblies that may be planned. In the early primary grades the mornings may be devoted to language, writing, and mathematics, or the teacher may insist that work in these areas be completed before other work is undertaken. In some instances teachers will permit freer choice of activities in the afternoon or during particular periods; in others there will be free choice throughout the school day.

Where children are required to complete work in the "Three Rs" daily, teachers still must make certain that there is ample time for creative activities: music, art, crafts, drama, and dance. Frequently these activities can be included in project work. They may also, however, have to be organized as separate activities available to children during activity periods.

Three possible programs for a day lasting from 9.00 A.M. to 3:00 P.M. will be suggested here as guides. In each the day starts differently. The times listed are intended to be designated flexible, rather than fixed, periods. Teachers can adapt these schedules to their own requirements.

In devising these programs, grade and age levels have not been taken into account. Actually, the degree of freedom permitted to children in scheduling their own day is less a function of the children's ages than of their experience in working in open classes.

Some first-graders may thus appropriately be permitted as much responsibility in this respect as are fifth-graders. It is probable that schedules that stress long language periods will be more applicable to primary-school classes.

Program A

9:00– 9:45	Free activity period
9:45–10:15	Class meeting (possibly including a short class lesson)
10:15–12:00	Language arts and mathematics
12:00– 1:00	Lunch
1:00– 1:30	Class meeting (with discussion of individual children's work)
1:30– 2:30	Completion of morning work, topics, projects (including social-studies and science projects)
2:30– 3:00	Cleanup Story Planning for the following morning when necessary

Program B

9:00– 9:15	Class meeting
9:15–10:30	Language arts, mathematics, and work on topics
10:30–11:15	Class meeting (including discussion of individual students' work) Class lesson if necessary

11:15–12:00	Directed work or completion of morning work on language arts, mathematics and specific topics
12:00– 1:00	Lunch
1:00– 2:30	Free choice of activities Project work (including social studies and science projects)
2:30– 3:00	Cleanup Evaluation Story

Program C

9:00– 9:20	Period for planning by pupils
9:20–10:30	Free choice of work
10:30–10:45	Class meeting
10:45–12:00	Free choice of work
12:00– 1:00	Lunch
1:00– 1:45	Class meeting Discussion of children's work Class lesson if necessary
1:45– 2:30	Free choice of work
2:30– 3:00	Cleanup Self-evaluation of planning by pupils Story (in some classes)

In adapting these schedules the teacher may wish to include a few breaks in the day for play, snacks, and the like. Some children seem to require breaks during the day; others resent this kind of interruption. To provide for individual differences in this respect, the teacher may permit the students to schedule their own "snack" periods at any time during the day. This approach has additional advantages. The child who has come to school without breakfast may need cookies and milk to start him. Another may prefer a snack later in the morning.

The schedule should be viewed as a framework for the day, not necessarily to be followed rigorously by each individual child. Although programs A and B schedule work in the "three Rs" in the morning, classes using these schedules may nevertheless permit some children to work on their special projects in the morning and on reading and mathematics in the afternoon. It must also be possible occasionally for a child to concentrate on a particular project for the entire day or for the teacher to schedule a task for the entire class. The major consideration in preparing a schedule is to establish a comfortable rhythm for the work of the class. If children are always interrupted in the middle of interesting tasks, if the class never seems to undertake art activities, or if children have difficulty starting, the schedule should be altered. Periods, too, may have to be adjusted. There will be frequent occasions when it is desirable to eliminate class meetings or to increase the time allotted to one. Occasionally experiences may have to be planned for the whole class.

One point must be made in connection with activities of the total group. Although they are kept to a minimum in open classrooms, they need not be entirely eliminated. The class may engage in common movement experiences, view a film, or plan a presentation together. Gathering as a whole class is a valuable social experience. It also teaches children to conduct themselves in large groups and may be a more effective way of presenting or reviewing a general skill when the teacher determines that the entire class requires it. A British government booklet emphasizes: "There is a continuing need for 'class teaching' to start off a major piece of group work, or to round it off, or to convey information quickly and effectively. The newer techniques of class arrangement do not replace the old, they add to them."[1]

The teacher should avoid maintaining a schedule without alteration for the entire school year. Children should be included in periodic reviews and asked to consider these questions: "Is this the best time for our class meeting?" "Do we need more time for the morning activity period?" A final note about scheduling: It may be preferable to move slowly to the freer structure of Program C. In one school that is in its third year of open classrooms the teachers are just beginning to adopt this approach.

The Class Meeting

Teachers may meet daily for brief periods with the whole class to organize work or discuss some aspects of it. In addition to these meetings, there should be one meeting of longer duration each week, a meeting devoted to open discussion of all matters related to the functioning of the classroom. A group of students, frequently the class officers, may be delegated to prepare an agenda for this meeting. Students who have encountered problems during the week should be encouraged to place them on this agenda. Teachers, too, may request that specific concerns be discussed. The primary goals of such a meeting are to aid teachers and pupils to learn to communicate honestly with one another, to establish an atmosphere of mutual respect for one another's opinions.

At these meetings one pupil may act as chairperson. When there

[1] *Open Plan Primary Schools* (Education Survey No. 16; London: H.M. Stationery Office, 1972), p. 4.

are class officers the president generally assumes this role. The agenda should include the problems raised, as well as frank evaluation of all facets of classroom organization, by both teacher and pupils. Students may wish to discuss specific activities, deciding which should be continued, which extended, which abandoned. They should be involved in planning for future centers. It is apparent that a class in which all the activities come out of the "teacher's head," no matter how imaginative they may be, cannot be viewed as truly responsive to students' needs.

Many potential difficulties in a classroom can be eliminated if both teacher and students believe that there are avenues for expressing grievances. The class meeting can provide such a forum. The whole class should be entrusted with decision-making functions and viewed as both a problem-solving and a creative body, established to evaluate existing procedures, to eliminate sources of tension, and to plan future work. Used in this manner, class meetings can be essential tools for establishing a democratic climate that will encourage student participation in organizing a class for learning.[2]

ORGANIZING AND ASSIGNING WORK

Organizing the Work

Organization for learning makes it possible for each child to know what is expected of him; no child has to feel "lost" in the open classroom. As children proceed through the day, they should be able to answer each of the following questions:

> What am I supposed to do now?
> About how long will I do it?
> What do I do when I finish?
> What do I do next?

One administrator has claimed that he can assess the organization of any open classroom by asking a child in the class these four questions. If the child is confused about his answers, the administrator suspects a poorly organized class. The teacher might well review these questions with the students periodically in order to discover whether or not the latter are growing in their ability to function independently.

The second question—how long a child should remain with a particular activity—sometimes poses a problem for teachers in the early stages of organization. They resist setting a timetable for the class in which there are

---

[2] For an excellent description of techniques for conducting class meetings, see William Glasser, *Schools without Failure* (New York: Harper & Row, 1967).

set periods and each child must engage in certain activities for the same lengths of time. They wish, however, to avoid the flitting from activity to activity that sometimes marks a child's initial reaction to a classroom filled with interesting materials. Some teachers have solved this problem by insisting that a child stay with a short activity until it is completed. If he starts an activity card or begins to make a paper-bag puppet, he must finish it before he can go to a different task. Others impose minimum time periods to be devoted to particular activities. Some require a certain number of tasks to be completed daily and are less concerned about the time devoted to the rest. Still others require children to check with them before leaving activities.

No matter what approach is chosen, the teacher will have to be cognizant of the child's ability to continue further with a task and the extent of his interest in it. Children who are truly interested in a piece of work do not have to be reminded to stay with it. On the contrary, they may have to be pulled away from it to eat lunch or to attend a class meeting. If teachers find that children tend to leave activities unfinished, they should assess their classrooms. Are so many materials provided that they are distracting? Are those provided sufficiently interesting? Do they require only superficial involvement, or do they encourage deeper exploration? Are the children sufficiently aware of the possibilities of the materials? Has the teacher introduced the centers carefully enough? Are there children who may be helped by more structure, more detailed suggestions for work? Are others being trained to work independently and to seek avenues of investigation that have not been spelled out by the teacher?

The remaining three questions that we have listed are related to two components of classroom management: scheduling and assignment of work. Both these components must be considered in organizing the class.

Suggestions for daily class schedules have been made. Whatever the plan chosen, the first necessity is that children be familiar with it, so that they will understand what is expected of them at any particular time. As we have shown, each child may have a free choice of activities in one hour but be confined to a more limited choice of whether to work on reading, mathematics, or writing in another. Teachers must be certain that they are not imposing unnecessary limits that inhibit children from taking responsibility for scheduling their own work. They should be concerned about those children who come to them continually to ask, "What do I do now?"

Signing Up for Activities

Related to scheduling the day is the occasional need for children to sign up in advance for certain activities. Perhaps only a limited number of children can engage in one activity simultaneously, or perhaps only limited

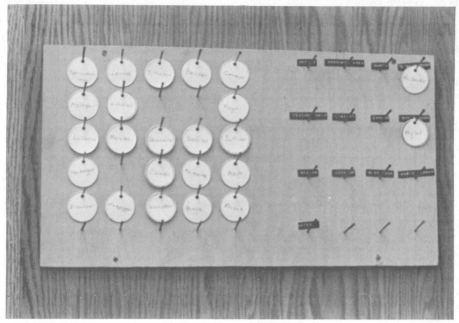

Discs with each child's name facilitate "signing-up" for activities. (Photograph courtesy of Guggenheim School, Port Washington Public Schools, New York.)

materials are available. Sign-up sheets for these activities can be posted in the centers or on the bulletin board, listing specific times and the number of places available. Children may have a supply of discs with their names which they can hang on empty hooks next to an activity removing the discs as they complete their work.

Assigning Work

In Chapter Two we distinguished between two aspects of classroom work: the general subject area in which a child is engaged (for example, reading) and the specific task in that area (for example, the book or pages to be read). We noted that children are usually permitted much more freedom in relation to the latter than to the former. In discussing the assignment of work, we shall suggest possibilities for both of these aspects.

Assigning the General Area of Work

There is great variation in the proportions of work assigned by the teachers. A few methods used in established open classrooms combine teacher's assignments with pupils' options.

First, teachers may ask that each student engage in some reading, writing, and mathematics daily, without spelling out the specific nature of those activities or the time to be allotted to them. This approach is common in British informal schools.

Second, teachers may set daily or weekly general requirements for each area. In one school it was expected that the following assignments would be completed weekly:

> *Readings.*   The reading of a book or three short stories
> Completion of two reading cards
> Work in a skill text
> *Mathematics.*   Completion of two activity cards
> Work in the mathematics workbook
> *Science and Social Studies.*   Completion of one science activity card
> Continuing work on units in science and social studies with specific deadlines
> *Arts and Crafts.*   Completion of two activities
> *Writing.*   Completion of two pieces of writing

Third, teachers may follow a variation on the structure just described. Instead of requesting specific activities one teacher required pupils to engage in twenty-five units of work each week, distributed as follows: reading 5, mathematics 5, language and writing 4, social studies 2, science 2, arts and crafts 2, and freely chosen 5. She defined "unit of work" in each area. For example, an activity card was considered a unit. There were no daily limitations; theoretically the child could fulfill his responsibilities by working in one subject all day or by doing more units on one day than on another.

Fourth, in one school in Leicestershire, England, the number of hours to be spent weekly on each of twelve different areas was specified. They included basic mathematics, discovery mathematics, research reading, basic English, creative English, arts and crafts, science, environmental studies, drama, music, television, and revision (review) sheets. The pupils were free to schedule their time as they wished and even to work at home, but they had to keep daily records of the time spent on each subject.

Fifth, one teacher ensured that each child would participate in certain areas by scheduling each to start in a different area each day and to work at least forty-five minutes in that particular area each day. One group of children started with mathematics on Monday, reading on Tuesday, art on Wednesday, writing on Thursday, and free choice on Friday. These children were expected to complete daily work in other subjects as well. This method of scheduling makes it easier for the teacher to plan work with some students at given times of the week. Some teachers carry this approach further, dividing the class into "clans" and suggesting some daily schedule for each clan, though still permitting "free choice" periods.

Sixth, some teachers permit students to schedule their work freely, but request that they plan each weekly program in advance, outlining the general work that they expect to complete during the week. The teacher reviews each program and may suggest additional emphasis on some subjects or make other pertinent comments.

Finally, the teacher can structure the general work of the class through arrangement of the environment and choice of materials. In primary-school classes, for example, a teacher may emphasize language activities by means of the number of activities provided in this area. The children's choice of activities will thus include a majority related to language. Mathematics, science, and creative work can be emphasized in the same way.

These approaches are useful initially as means of ensuring a diversified program for each student with occasional emphasis on specific facets. But they must all be used carefully to avoid compartmentalization of subjects that would inhibit integrated learning or result in overmanagement of the child's day. Teachers must devise methods that best suit their own classes and must critically review them at regular intervals.

Assigning Specific Work

There are several specific tasks that a teacher will expect children to complete. They may include mathematics examples, certain stories, language activities. The most common method of assigning an individual task in traditional, as well as in open, classrooms is to distribute a dittoed assignment sheet, make an announcement, or write on the blackboard. In open classes the teacher may list the class's weekly assignments on a special blackboard. Recently such a blackboard in a class of eight-year-olds included the following:

> I will need a letter from you to your parents requesting their permission for you to go to the museum on November 30th.

> Practice cursive writing this week by first copying the letters "l," "e," and "t" from handwriting cards, and then writing as many words as you can which include these letters.

> How about two volunteers to take the outdoor temperature this week at 9:00 and 2:30. Sign here

> ———————.   ———————.

> How many words can you think of that mean "happy"? Add them to our class thesaurus.

> Mrs. Romo will be in Tuesday and Thursday at 1:00 P.M. to help with Christmas gifts. Sign up if you wish to work with her.

> Topic books due Friday.

> Everyone is to complete a math activity on measurement.

Another approach is to post a chart with daily notes on an easel or on the bulletin board. It may contain class and individual assignments, as well as notices of special events.

Individual work can be assigned to children in various ways. First, the teacher will frequently note after a conference what work is indicated. She may write the assignment in each child's folder or individual notebook.

Second, in classes in which each child submits his daily work in a notebook, the teacher will often return it with specific assignments. They may include suggestions for a few mathematical computations or for inclusion of some words on a spelling list, reference to some dittos for vocabulary practice, or assignment of a specific skill text.

Third, in a class that has individual mailboxes (see Chapter Five), the teacher may give a child a special piece of work to complete or may simply leave a note saying, "I'd like you to spend more time on your math workbook today"; "I'd like you to complete an SRA card today"; "You haven't done any writing this week. How about a story or poem? You might try a story starter, if you wish." More formal methods of assigning work include contracts or unit plans and activity cards.

Contracts

The use of contracts for assigning work in open classrooms is largely confined to American schools; it is rarely encountered in British informal schools. Such contracts originated in the United States in the days of progressive education during the 1920s and 1930s. Three popular plans of organization in those days—the Morrison, Winnetka and Dalton plans— used work agreements, or contracts. Although these plans were never uniformly adopted in progressive schools, they were widely used, and many of the current contract plans appear to have been influenced by them.

In some respects those early contract plans were compatible with the open approach. They eliminated the conventional time schedule, permitting students to decide when to work on different subjects as long as they fulfilled their contracts. In many instances they emphasized an integrated approach to the curriculum; teachers deliberately designed each contract to cover several subjects. But in one important respect they reflected a different conception of work from that characteristic of open classrooms: It was the teacher who determined in advance exactly what the pupil was to study and then "predigested" the material, breaking it into sequential steps by which the pupil was to master skills. The emphasis was on learning a body of facts, with each pupil proceeding at his own rate. In this sense the contracts resembled later attempts at programmed learning.

Properly used, contracts can have a place in open classrooms, particularly in the transitional stages between the traditional and open approaches.

In open classrooms, however, contracts must be more than a device by which a teacher assigns work ·to the class or prescribes an exact sequence for studying a subject, as is typical of contracts in traditional classes.

These kinds of contracts are *not* consistent with the open approach. By definition, a contract is an agreement between *two* parties. This definition implies that in the open classroom children will be permitted to participate in the formulation of their contracts. Such participation can be stated as a requirement for a contract in an open classroom.

Basically two types of contracts are used in the open classroom: those for specific areas (science and social-studies topics or broad themes like pollution) and those for work on all subjects in a given period of time, usually a week. As in other matters of classroom management, the degree of the child's responsibility for devising his contracts will vary from classroom to classroom. In some the contracts will be completely written by the child; in others they will be written largely by the teacher, with provision for student options. We shall now describe different contract plans, with suggestions for encouraging children's participation in formulating them.

Contracts in Specific Areas   Contracts for specific projects or subjects are sometimes called "units of work" or "unit plans." They constitute agendas for exploring specific topics. For example, the topic may be "the Civil War." In preparing a contract for this topic, there are two alternatives: First, the teacher may assign the topic, list a number of possible avenues of exploration, pose some open-ended questions, and offer various methods of investigating and reporting the information. The child will start with the teacher's contract, but he may select the aspects he wishes to pursue with freedom to add some of his own questions and approaches. Second, the child may decide to investigate a particular topic, to pose his own questions, and to determine his own procedures; the teacher acts mainly as a resource person and consultant.

Each of these alternatives represents one end of a continuum of responsibility, from a major role for the teacher to that of the pupil. In the first the teacher initiates and formulates the broad outlines of the contract, whereas in the second it is basically written by the child, with suggestions from the teacher as necessary. In open classrooms both kinds of contracts are used.

Most children are not accustomed to working freely and to posing their own questions in school. They are usually dependent upon the teacher to tell them what to do. It takes experience in working in an open class before children can effectively decide for themselves what aspects of a particular subject they wish to investigate and how they plan to do so. For this reason, contracts written by pupils are generally typical of a more advanced stage of open-class organization. There are some techniques that may facilitate the child's exercise of responsibility for contracts on specific topics.

The use of a science-resource box was mentioned in Chapter Three as a means of encouraging students to plan their own science projects. This type of resource box can be used in many areas. Instead of writing contracts, teachers can file index cards in a "project" box. For each project, they can supply cards listing possible topics to be explored, some questions to be investigated, available resources, and suggested activities. Both teacher and pupil contribute cards to the box. One primary-school teacher used this box to aid pupils in writing their own contracts. For example, a unit in the box was on transportation. The teacher had listed some suggestions, and pupils had added others. Under topics related to transportation, the teacher had suggested cars, trucks, planes, horses. The students had added camels, magic carpet, walking, crawling. Under questions to be explored, the teacher had asked: "What is the history of this method of transportation?" "Where is it most frequently used?" "Is it used only to transport people? If not, for what other purposes?" Students had added other questions, including "What does it feel like to ride a camel?" "How long does it take a worm to crawl across the room?" The latter question had undoubtedly been inspired by the presence of mealworms in the room.

The teacher, in relating this incident, remarked that she would never have thought of putting the question "How long does it take a worm to crawl across the room?" in a transportation unit. Yet a group of students had incorporated this question into a contract on "insects and transportation," and the solution to this problem had occupied them for days and had involved a number of mathematical computations. In this class students were provided with blank forms to be used in writing their contracts, as illustrated in Figure 4.2.

In one intermediate class children were given the choice of writing a contract on any topic included in the social-studies text for their grade or substituting a teacher-approved contract of their own. The teacher provided a number of different textbooks covering similar topics plus library books. Lists of film strips were available to the students and could be previewed. The library in their school also kept a picture and resource file indexed under different headings. The students were expected not only to choose a topic but also to decide how to explore it. They could use questions posed in the textbooks or in other books. Gradually, as they became accustomed to working in this manner, they were able to define their interests and to formulate more and more of their own problems (see Figure 4.2).

Contracts written by pupils are submitted to the teacher before the work is begun. This procedure permits the teacher to discuss the contract with the students, to determine whether the questions posed are feasible for investigation, and to suggest resources and other areas of exploration. Frequently there are aspects of a subject that have not occurred to a child but that suggest themselves to the teacher when the child indicates his area of interest.

√CONTRACT FOR PROPOSED INVESTIGATION

Name_____ Date_____

Topic_____

I expect to complete work on this topic by_____ .

I will be working by myself/with _____ .

Signed_____

Date_____

Approved by_____

Purpose of investigation (what I expect to learn)

Specific questions

Methods of investigation

Resources (books, magazines, articles, filmstrips, people, or other)

Form of presentation of data

Date completed:

Comments

Figure 4.2   Sample Form for Contracts Written by Pupils

In many classes teachers keep files of contracts in different areas to be used as guides. They can be gradually assembled from contracts devised by both teachers and pupils. In some instances contracts are not written in advance but are kept almost as logs. The child indicates his general plans for investigating a topic, but adds details as he gains knowledge of the subject. This approach permits a child to explore aspects of which he was not initially aware but that present themselves as he continues his research. Although deadlines are always noted and can aid a child to organize his work, the teacher may alter these dates to accommodate the intensity of interest that the child develops as his work progresses.

In this discussion of contracts we do not wish to leave the impression that they are necessary to exploration of a project. Most children, as they learn to work independently, do not need to draw up contracts before proceeding with their work. There are, however, some advantages in using contracts for planning long-term studies of a topic. They enable the teacher to schedule some work in areas that she considers important—for example science or social studies—yet permit children to construct individual curricula. They help the child to formulate questions about a topic so that his research will be focused and not diffuse. They help the child to develop his own methods of research. They help the child to plan and budget his time. They provide the teacher with a means of keeping track of the work in which children are engaged and the goals to which it is directed.

General Work Contracts   In addition to contracts that specify study plans for particular topics, there are contracts that serve to assign general work to children or to record all their activities. These contracts are prepared by both teachers and pupils.

Daily Work Contracts   Teachers may provide printed forms listing specific areas of work—reading, mathematics, writing, topics, crafts, and so on. In some instances specific assignments will be noted on these forms daily: for example, "Choice of topic due today" or "How many math computations can you devise whose solution is twelve?" Sometimes common assignments for groups of children are posted on the class bulletin board, and the children are expected to copy these assignments onto their contracts in the morning. The child generally may complete these tasks at any time during the day.

Daily contracts are also used to help children to plan in advance their major activities for the day. Children add projected activities to the contracts each morning, and at the end of the day the contracts reflect what they have actually accomplished. Each contract is submitted to the teacher, together with any written work, and serves as a log of the day's activities. (The two samples of daily work plans in Figure 4.1 may be used for this purpose.)

Weekly Contracts   Weekly contracts are more frequently used than are daily ones. Sometimes they specify all the work required for the week. Each child may fulfill his contract at any time during the week. This kind of contract can also be used as a record, or log, of a child's total weekly activities. At the beginning of the week, the child or the teacher enters any specific assignments. The child then adds his plans. As a given task is completed, he checks it off. In the course of the week he also records other activities in which he has engaged. Contracts of this type need not list every minor activity. They are not intended as exact diaries but serve primarily to highlight major functions, so that both teacher and child can be aware of the scope of a child's activities during a specified period. It should be borne in mind that writing contracts can become laborious if they are too detailed. Three samples of weekly contracts are illustrated in Figures 4.3–4.5. Again, the form chosen will depend upon a class's need for more or less structure in planning its work.

WORK CONTRACT

The following is the work I plan to complete during the week of_____.

Signed_____

Date_____

Approved_____

Reading

Mathematics

Writing

Science

Topic and project

Arts and crafts

Other

To be entered at end of week:

Unfinished work

Other work accomplished

Figure 4.3   Weekly Work Contract, Sample A

WORK CONTRACT					
Name_____ Week of_____					
			Tasks Completed Each Day		
Plans for Week	Monday	Tuesday	Wednesday	Thursday	Friday
Reading					
Mathematics					
Writing					
Topic and project					
Arts and crafts					
Science					
Social studies					
Other					

Figure 4.4   Weekly Work Contract, Sample B

WORK CONTRACT

Name_____ Week of_____

Reading

   Stories_____

   Dittos_____

   SRA (list cards and colors)_____

   Skill texts_____

   Other_____

Mathematics

   Workbook (pages)_____

   Dittos_____

   Activity cards_____

   Investigations_____

   Other_____

Writing

_____

Spelling

   Unit no._____

   Activities_____

   Mastery test no._____

Topics

   Title_____ Activities_____

   Research_____

   Arts and crafts

_____

Science

   Work on contract_____

   Experiments_____

   Other_____

Other activities

_____

_____

_____

_____

_____

Figure 4.5   Weekly Work Contract, Sample C.

There are difficulties associated with the use of contracts. One problem is that the child with little experience in working with them tends to view the minimum tasks assigned as the only work required of him for the week. Some teachers react by assigning more and more work, so that the areas of the child's choice become limited. In some classrooms a child's weekly contract may consist of an entire folder of assigned work, which negates the concept of open education.

Furthermore, teachers sometimes tend to assign work only in the "three Rs," giving them the aura of "important" school work and thus subtly devaluing other activities. As a result, children shy away from work in the "three Rs" when permitted free choice of activities. Contracts can also serve as a form of pressure on children who find it difficult to anticipate their work for an entire week. They may become almost compulsive about completing their contracts immediately or may neglect them initially and then work feverishly at the end of the week. A further danger is that some contract plans' emphasis on work on individual subjects may perpetuate barriers among subjects, rather than encourage greater integration of the curriculum. Teachers who wish to use contracts in open classrooms will have to be sensitive to the problems associated with their use and must be certain that for their particular classes the advantages outweigh the disadvantages noted.

Activity Cards

A popular means of organizing work in open classrooms is through activity cards, also called "work cards" or "assignment cards." They are cards on which activities are suggested, in self-explanatory terms with a minimum of teacher direction required for their execution. They may be used as a regular part of the instructional program or as a supplement to it.

Activity cards can be prepared for any area of the curriculum. A basic function of such cards is to structure for children experiences that will help them to integrate concepts to which they may have been exposed verbally or through other abstract means. (Chapters Seven to Fourteen offer numerous suggestions for activities that can be adapted to such cards.)

Although some cards may be prepared for practice in limited areas—mathematical computations, phonics, the main idea of a reading passage—usually the problems posed on them are more general and open-ended, designed to stimulate thought and to suggest many possible solutions. When the cards do call for exact answers, like solution to a puzzle or a computation, the answers may be written on the back of the card, so that each card is "self-correcting."

Cards on specific questions may include brain twisters, puzzles, or suggested experiences requiring estimating and researching information. (An example: What do you think the population of the earth is? Of the United

States? Of China? How old is the earth? Estimate; then check your answers.) Children sometimes become intrigued by figures and records, though for young children the concept of large numbers has not yet been established. In one class of older children the *Guinness Book of World Records*[3] was included in the research corner. Children sought unusual information (the smallest fish ever caught, the longest time measure) and put the problems on activity cards; they were expected to estimate the answers and then to check them in the book.

Even activity cards on specific questions can provoke further explorations, by means of follow-up suggestions on the backs of the cards. For example, the back of one card devoted to the age of the earth contained the question "How can this be determined?" More general questions on activity cards could be:

If you had to leave your house and could only take _____ [specify number] of things, which would they be? Why?

If you could choose to be any size, what would it be?

If you could choose to be any person, who would it be?

Set up an experiment to prove or disprove a superstition.

Pretend you are an astronaut exploring a strange planet. You know there were once people living there, but there is no trace of them now. You find one clue—a copper penny. What can you determine about the people from this clue?

At times activity cards can be used as bases for group discussions. Instead of writing their answers, children may prefer to meet and discuss them. Even young children may enjoy a debate on a topic chosen from an activity box, to which children and students have both contributed.

As activity cards for young children should be self-contained, writing may have to be kept to a minimum, and pictures or rebuses can be used to give directions that can be easily understood. In a class in which several age groups are included, older children will frequently read cards to younger ones.

Constructing Activity Cards   Index cards, oak tag, and cardboard all make good activity cards, which can be of various sizes. A card that is comfortable for children to use yet large enough not to be easily misplaced is about 5 by 7 inches or slightly smaller: equivalent to half a sheet of oak tag 8½ by 11 inches.

The activity directions should be written on the cards with felt pens in various colors. They should be as attractive as possible and occasionally

[3] Norris and Ross McWhirter, *Guinness Book of World Records* (New York: Bantam, 1973).

illustrated. When printed matter like clippings from old workbooks or magazines is used, it may be pasted directly on the card.

The cards should have titles, for example; "Creating Puppets," "Using a Scale," "Writing Poetry—A Cinquain." For color coding, the cards themselves can be different colors, or colored squares can be placed in the upper right-hand corners of the cards.

Cards should also be numbered, not necessarily to indicate a sequence of activities but to permit children to record those that have been completed and to facilitate the teacher's reference to particular cards for some children.

Cards may either be sprayed with protective lacquer, laminated in a machine, covered with clear contact paper, or enclosed in acetate folders (folders used for term papers can be cut to size) for protection and durability.

Cards should be filed according to appropriate interest areas. Various devices can be used. A card holder similar to a fabric shoe holder can be made of sturdy fabric on which pockets have been sewn. A commercial index file or a box decorated with contact paper may be used (see picture).

Each storage area should contain some blank cards, so that students or teachers can write additional activity cards.

There are many sources of ideas for activity cards. Teachers' guides, curriculum guides, books on creative activities, puzzle books, art and craft books, magazines, encyclopedias, dictionaries, workbooks, other teachers,

Activity cards can be stored in decorated boxes. Cards and boxes courtesy of Judith Schiffer, S.U.N.Y. at Stony Brook.

parents, and students. Cards offer a ready means of capitalizing on good ideas gleaned from visits to other classes, from books, or from other teachers' suggestions.

Using Activity Cards   Activity cards may be required as part of the work of the class or they may be used by students voluntarily. They are most popular in mathematics study, because they seem an effective means of involving students in concrete mathematical experiences. In many classes students are expected to complete a certain number of mathematical activity cards as part of their assigned work.

It is important that children have choices about the activity cards that they will complete. Children can easily lose interest if the cards become merely substitutes for workbook papers assigned in sequence.

Teachers should attempt to include a variety of cards on similar topics, which permits assignment of a specific area of work while allowing for pupil options. For example, each student may be expected to complete one writing card each week. He chooses a card with suggestions for writing either a story or a poem. Within each category he has further choices. Similarly, teachers may wish to ensure that children engage in an art or craft activity. They may suggest that each child choose from many activity cards in those categories.

In most classrooms cards are chosen freely by students without any restrictions. But sometimes, particularly in an area like mathematics, they may represent a sequence of skills or levels of difficulty. Some teachers color-code cards for difficulty and suggest that students work with cards of a specific color. Others merely color-code cards to indicate the level of difficulty and let students decide whether to tackle "easy," "medium," or "hard" tasks. Occasionally cards may be color-coded simply to facilitate filing: All red cards are filed in one box and all green ones in another, for example.

Students respond to activity cards in various ways. In some classrooms the cards "catch on," and students use them frequently. In others they seem to be used only when assigned. The teacher must assess how the cards are being used. If they are used only when assigned, it may be that the cards do not suggest sufficiently interesting activities to students or that the cards have not been properly introduced to students. From time to time a few cards may be discussed with the class as a means of stimulating interest. Another important consideration regarding their use is that the materials necessary to complete an activity be readily available. Children cannot be expected to complete a science experiment if the necessary chemicals or other materials are not on hand; they cannot do a weight problem if scales are not available.

Another facet of management in a well-organized open classroom is recordkeeping and evaluation. We shall examine these functions in Chapter Five.

Chapter
FIVE
Recordkeeping
and
Evaluation

Glancing about an open classroom in which each child appeared engaged in a different task, a visitor seemed overwhelmed: "But how do you ever know where they are?" she inquired. A school principal echoed the same theme: "My first concern with open classrooms is that there be some method of accounting for each child, that teachers know what each child is doing, that they ensure that none will be overlooked."

When children are working simultaneously on so many diverse activities, recordkeeping may well appear an overwhelming task. Yet it is essential if teachers are to provide a rich educational experience for each youngster and are to be prepared to communicate his progress to other adults. To achieve these objectives, teachers must maintain records of a decidedly different scope from that of records kept in traditional classes.

In traditional classes records are primarily related to gradings. The teacher prepares a curriculum for the class in advance and then records how well the children have mastered that curriculum as measured by their grades on classroom tests. The teacher's grade book is thus the basic class record. Grades can be misleading, however. One teacher's grade of 65 percent may mean something different from another teacher's 65 percent. Two children in the same class, both receiving grades of 70 percent on a given test, may have very dissimilar needs. The use of numerical figures, however, has a flavor of objectivity and provides a convenient tool for communicating information to parents and others. By denying themselves this tool open educators have assumed more complex recordkeeping and evaluation tasks. Treating children as many-faceted individuals who cannot be neatly summed up by single grades requires more diversified records on students.

SCOPE AND PURPOSE OF RECORDS
IN OPEN CLASSROOMS

Teachers in open classrooms need the following information about their students: work engaged in, choices made, interests, needs, strengths, talents, and progress. For this purpose, they seek details of how a child schedules his time, to what he devotes his energies, what he can accomplish, and the quality of his work. They determine whether or not the child's work is consistent with his abilities. In reviewing the child's choices, they note the activities that the child engages in when he is permitted free choice and whether or not the tasks that the child sets for himself tend to be too easy or too difficult, with the result that he is either unchallenged or frustrated. The teachers question whether or not the child's choices contribute to a diversified educational experience for him.

In observing a child's interests, teachers seek to extend existing interests and to encourage formation of new ones. They also look at the child's needs, in order to determine which specific assignments or lessons should be scheduled and how the child's developing skills can be reinforced. Information about a child's strengths helps the teacher to decide what learning style seems most effective for the child, what resources he can offer other children, and how his talents can best be used in the class.

Finally, teachers record the child's academic, emotional, and social progress, to reflect whether or not he is developing competence in areas like oral and written communications, reading, and mathematics. Is the child growing into a self-disciplined individual, motivated to learn and inquisitive, sufficiently confident to explore unfamiliar paths, able to organize his work, to make effective choices, and to enjoy his creative abilities? The teacher's evaluations in these respects, are guided by many considerations. Evaluation that implies comparison of one child with others is to be avoided. A child is not graded according to a single standard for the whole class, but his performance is assessed in the context of his own pattern of growth. Evaluation is not simply a search for errors in a child's work. Children in open classrooms have the freedom to make mistakes and are encouraged to attempt tasks that may appear difficult. Evaluation in open classrooms is primarily for the purpose of diagnosis.

Such diagnosis is not limited to the teachers themselves. The child, too, must learn to evaluate his work diagnostically and to keep appropriate records, so that he can plan experiences for himself. Marion Jenkinson commented at an international curriculum conference: "Teachers need to teach children how to learn diagnostically. . . . The learner needs to realize what he does not know and correct his errors as soon as possible so that wrong learning is not reinforced."[1] It is for this reason that children in open class-rooms are frequently encouraged to mark their own work.

In devising a recordkeeping system that will embody the types of information outlined, teachers must consider a number of guidelines:

1. Children should participate in recordkeeping.
2. Records should be visually uncomplicated, so that information is readily revealed.
3. They should be easy to understand (not written in unintelligible code), so that others can interpret the information recorded.
4. Duplication should be avoided; for example, a single copy of a diagnostic test may be an adequate record of a child's phonic skills, a folder of his work a sufficient record of his progress.
5. Work that is part of a record should be dated, to facilitate evaluation of a child's growth over a period of time.
6. Each record should have a clear and specific purpose; it may be unnecessary to record every task in which a child engages each day.
7. Extraneous information should be avoided; if a child misses a few words while reading a page, they may be noted, but if a child chooses a book that is obviously too difficult and then misses many words, recording his choice of the difficult book is more significant than entering every word that he has misread.
8. Records should not be so time consuming that they divert the teacher from working with children or involve disproportionate shares of the children's efforts.

There are two kinds of records that teachers are expected to maintain. One kind includes records for the school, like attendance sheets and cumulative folders of data on a child's entire career in school; the second includes records of the child's daily experiences in a single class. Suggestions for each of these types of records are offered here. Teachers will undoubtedly wish to adapt ideas to their own purposes and preferences. To a large extent, recordkeeping may be viewed as a personal endeavor.

SCHOOL RECORDS

Morning Chores

There are classrooms in which the required morning records, particularly when combined with other morning chores like making announce-

---

[1] Quoted in J. Stuart Maclure, *Curriculum Innovation in Practice: Report of the Third International Curriculum Conference, Oxford* (London: H.M. Stationery Office, 1967), p. 41.

ments and distributing papers, may occupy a good portion of the first hour. Many open classrooms have organized more efficient ways of handling these administrative matters.

Attendance Records   In classrooms where there are no assigned seats, attendance taking can be troublesome. Many teachers have therefore delegated to the children the responsibility for recording their own presence. There are many possible procedures.

One teacher of a five- and six-year-old group mounted a photograph of each child, which she had taken at the beginning of the school year, on a piece of cardboard and wrote his name on the back. A hole was punched in the top, a string attached, and the picture hung on the wall with the name showing. Each morning as a child arrived, he turned his picture around so that his face showed. The names of those who were absent could then be easily listed. In this instance the teacher wrote down the names of absentees. In a group of older youngsters a child can be assigned this responsibility. At the end of the day one child reversed all the pictures in readiness for the next day.

Attendance is taken by each child turning his picture around as he enters the class. (Photograph courtesy of Merrick Public Schools, New York.)

This method of taking attendance has many virtues. Beside placing the responsibility for indicating his presence on the child, the use of his own picture "personalizes" his participation. It emphasizes those who are in school, rather than those who are absent.

This approach has been adopted and is used in many other classes. One teacher asked each child to draw a picture of himself on a name tag (similar to a luggage tag) and to print his name on the reverse side. Another teacher used blocks of wood, another tongue depressors that the children decorated. In each instance holes were drilled in the markers so that they could be hung on hooks and easily reversed each morning to indicate children's presence in school.

In another class children are responsible for moving index cards with their names from an "absent" box to a "present" box as they arrive. At the end of the day all the cards are returned to the "absent" box. Some teachers use a "sign in" procedure. Class lists are posted each morning, and children sign their names or initials to indicate their arrival. Check marks next to the names are not recommended, as they involve greater possibility of error.

Lunch and Milk Counts   In many classes teachers are expected to count the number of children who will be buying lunch from the school cafeteria or ordering milk. This procedure can be coordinated with that for keeping attendance. In a class that uses one of the name-tag approaches described, a child may also be expected to hang a colored disk on his hook together with his name tag to signify that he wishes to order lunch or milk. It is then easy for one class member to total the number of orders.

In classes in which sign-up procedures are used, children may also be asked to sign their names on a sheet of paper or an appropriate place on the board to order a hot lunch or milk.

Two teachers working as a team with fifty fourth-year students have devised an effective method of recording administrative details. They have divided their class into six administrative units, each led by a unit chairman (a rotating post). Each unit is assigned for one month to one of the six permanent interest centers in the room—reading, mathematics, science, social studies, writing, or arts and crafts. The unit is responsible for taking its own attendance, the lunch and milk count, returning papers, reading announcements, and keeping its particular interest center in order. Each unit chairman lists the absentees from his group on the board and gives the lunch order to a class secretary, who is elected monthly by the whole class and is responsible for clerical procedures.

In all these schemes responsibility for indicating his presence in class or for ordering lunch is shifted to the child, fostering his growth as a self-directed individual. These methods subtly represent the classroom. A list of absentees that is available to all indicates the cooperative nature of the class and general concern about who is absent on a particular day. This attitude is appropriate for several reasons. Children may be working together on a project; others may wish to take the time to send notes or cards to a child who is ill.

Cumulative Records

The school maintains cumulative records of basic information on each child: his birth date, number of siblings, information on his parents and home, previous schools attended and teachers, attendance record, pertinent comments about physical development, and results of achievement and intelligence tests. There is no doubt that such records can help a teacher in working with a child. For example, information that a child was absent for a long period during his first year in school or is currently living in a foster home has obvious meaning to a teacher.

Many cumulative records also contain anecdotal reports by previous teachers and their value varies considerably. Teachers have occasionally remarked, "I never read the anecdotal records until I get to know the child, because I don't want to be prejudiced." This attitude is unfortunate and probably a reflection on many such records, which tend to be judgmental, critical of a child's personality, or written in jargon that makes it difficult to distinguish one child from another.

Cumulative records can be particularly helpful to teachers in open classrooms. In writing them, teachers should be guided by the question, "What is important for the pupil's succeeding teachers to know?" It is of little consequence that he committed a minor infraction and of doubtful value that one teacher found him difficult or a pleasure to live with. Children change and relate differently to different adults. Nor is a general statement that he showed growth useful; presumably most children will grow in the course of a year. Certain specific details are important, however. What a child's interests were, what areas he chose to work in, how much initiative he showed, what his strengths were, where he seemed to need help are what teachers want to know. Some children may fall into a pattern of repeating work in some areas in succeeding years; if teachers are aware of such tendencies they can encourage children to try new paths of exploration.

If a particular test score does not seem valid, it may be mentioned in the anecdotal reports: for example, "John's I.Q. of 90 seems low from my knowledge of him." Reports of conferences with parents are also helpful— as long as information divulged by parents in confidence and not for the general use of the school is not included.

INTERNAL CLASS RECORDS

Aside from the records mandated by the school, each teacher will want to maintain at least records of the overall work of the class and records of individual children's work. Examples of each of these kinds of records will be presented here.

Records of Overall Work of the Class

In traditional classrooms teachers are generally expected to maintain a plan book, detailing the work that they expect to complete in every subject each week. These plan books do not lend themselves to recording the work of open classes. As alternatives, teachers can use notebooks, frequently in conjunction with photographs.

Teachers' Notebooks   A loose-leaf notebook may be used to summarize the overall work of the class. There are separate pages for subjects, projects, and various activities, as well as weekly summary sheets. On the subject pages the teacher lists highlights of the week's work, group assignments, and general plans. For example, the new book that was introduced in the reading corner, the need for more practice in punctuation, and the observation that "John, Bill, and Joan are writing stories for the five-year-olds" are all recorded. The pages on activities may report excitement about weaving resulting from the gift of a loom or may describe briefly how a center was used during the week. General comments may describe some children's growing interest in communication and sound after the visit of a telephone-company representative; they also include some overall goals for each week.

The notebook is used both for planning work and for chronicling events. It is not intended as a complete review of the work of the class or of each child. Rather, its purpose is to help the teacher to focus on each subject, project, and activity weekly; to evaluate each in relation to the overall work of the class; and to assess whether or not certain experiences should be planned, additional materials provided for a center, some activities abandoned, or others introduced.

Photographs   Another method of recording class work is to photograph the class in action. If a teacher has a camera available, 35-millimeter color slides make excellent permanent records. They can be taken at any time during the school day: while the children are engaged in activities, during a speaker's presentation, or during a group lesson. Displays or centers can be also photographed. The slides should be dated and filed. Such a slide file is extremely valuable. It may be used to explain class work to parents, visitors, and school officials. Color slides can be viewed by the children, and sometimes they inspire further activities. They also serve as a resource file for the teacher when she may wish to remember later how a certain corner had been arranged. When several teachers in a school photograph their classes' activities, slides may provide a ready means by which they can exchange ideas.

Records of Individual Children's Work

Teachers will want to be aware of the tasks that engage individual children, both the general nature of those tasks and their specific details. Some teachers require that certain general areas of work (like reading or mathematics) be included daily and wish to ensure that each child has complied with this requirement. There are various methods of providing the teacher with a visual means of quickly noting the work a child has engaged in during a given period.

Pegboards A pegboard is a simple but effective device that has been used in a number of open classrooms. The teacher puts the names of the students on a piece of pegboard, plywood, or bulletin board. Each curriculum area is color-coded perhaps red for reading, blue for mathematics, yellow for writing, and green for project work. Other colors may be added to correspond with work required of students on a given day. As a child completes work in one of these areas, he places an appropriately colored peg or tack next to his name. The teacher can see at a glance who still has work to accomplish in one of these areas. One teacher using this system said:

> I prefer to permit students freedom to schedule their own work each day, but the pegs are my security. In the afternoon, I generally check to see which students haven't done any reading or math. I can find out with what they have been occupied and whether they are getting experiences in these subjects through other areas of the curriculum. If not, I may suggest to a child that he work on his math at this point, or that he start with it the following day.

Graphs Alternatively, the names of all the students in the class can be listed on a large sheet of graph paper. Each subject or project is designated by a different color; as with the pegboards, students fill in squares on the graph paper with the appropriate colored pencil when they have completed work in certain areas. The advantage of using graph paper is that the record can be continued for a week or even longer, enabling a teacher to note quickly whether or not a child has varied his activities within that period.

Another teacher used graph records quite differently, and, though his method was valuable for his group of ten-year-olds, it might be difficult for younger children to use. In his class each child kept a weekly bar graph of his work. Each day of the week was coded in a different color—red for Monday, blue for Tuesday, and so on. Different areas of work were listed along the horizontal axis and fifteen-minute intervals along the vertical axis. The time spent on each area was graphed daily. In this manner each pupil had a visual record of the time he had devoted to different activities each week.

Sign-Up Sheets Another teacher, who wished to ensure that her students completed certain activities daily, posted a sheet for them to sign as they completed these activities. In a school in Leicestershire, England, the sign-up sheet in Figure 5.1 was posted daily.

●	Have you worked on these today?		
Reading	Writing	Number	Craft

Figure 5.1   A Sample Daily Sign-Up Sheet

Frequently some written work carries a specific due date. Teachers will wish to provide some organizational devices which facilitate the flow of written work within the classroom. The most common method of achieving this is by providing adequate deposit places for work as it is completed.

Baskets In some classes there are baskets in each activity center in which pupils place written work that they have completed in that center. In others, a common "in" basket is provided. One teacher used a large dishwashing basin for this purpose.

Folders Some teachers prefer to use an individual folder for each child. One used a dish drainer that had sufficient slots for her twenty-five students. A folder was placed in each slot, and children deposited work in the folders as they finished it. The teacher checked the folders regularly and also utilized them for written comments to the students. A master sheet listing all the centers may also be included in each folder. Children can be expected to check off the centers in which they have worked in order to provide a more complete record of their daily experiences.

Mailboxes A popular method of facilitating the flow of written communications between teacher and student is the use of individual "mailboxes." These boxes can be made from quart milk containers or large cans with the tops removed. They are then placed side by side and taped together. Corrugated cartons with individual dividers like those used for shipping liquor can also be used. There can be some boxes for incoming mail and some for outgoing mail. As a child finishes some paper work, he files it in the "outgoing" box for the teacher. At any time during the day the teacher can note at a glance whether or not a particular student has completed any written work. After the teacher reviews the work, she places it with the student's incoming mail, together with any comments about future work. Children can "post" mail in the classroom, eliminating the time-consuming

Mailboxes aid the flow of written work. (Photograph courtesy of Taukomas School, Half Hollow Hills School District, Dix Hills, New York.)

task of distributing individual papers or giving verbal instructions to individual children.

Some types of records lend themselves to more specific detail on what individual children have accomplished. They may be maintained by the children, the teacher, or both together.

The Notebook Children may complete all their written work in one notebook, which they may also use each morning to plan their day and later to record the activities in which they have engaged. Sometimes children also enter brief summaries of work that may not be reflected in the written assignments in the notebook. In some classes children keep individual notebooks for mathematics, writing, research, and so on. Notebooks are reviewed regularly by the teacher and returned with appropriate comments or suggestions for specific tasks.

When team teaching is adopted, children may carry their notebooks with them. As they meet with different teachers, each enters assignments or recommendations in the notebooks. This procedure permits all the teachers to be aware of each child's progress in difference areas, as well as of the work that has been assigned to him by other teachers.

Notebooks can also be used in an entirely different way. One notebook, similar to a guest book, may be kept in each activity center. When children work there, they sign the book, indicating the date and possibly the time spent. Teachers can glance at these notebooks to find out who has worked in each center and to learn which children tend to work together. It is significant that some children tend to sign in and out of a center at the same time.

Index Cards   When the class is organized as a large unit headed by a team of teachers, recording individual children's work may be a more complex task. In one Hartford, Connecticut, school a number of ways to ease this recording have been devised. Each child is assigned a minimum number of tasks by his "home teacher" each morning. Then he is permitted "free flow" time during which he is expected to complete those tasks and to choose others from among a number of possible activities. In this program a child must complete any activity that he has started. As he finishes each task, he must secure permission from some adult in the room—a teacher, an intern, a paraprofessional—to go on to another. Each adult carries a pack of index cards. As she excuses the child, she enters the particular task he completed—for example, "math bingo game." Comments can be added when appropriate. At the end of the day these cards are collected and filed for each child. A complete record of a child's activities thus emerges. In some units in this school, the child wears about his neck a card on which his daily assignments, as well as the activities in which he is involved, are noted. As the child meets with his "home teacher" at regular intervals during the day, the teacher can observe how he has been occupying himself and make any necessary recommendations.

A teacher in a self-contained classroom also uses index cards, which he files on a rotary wheel. There is a group of cards for each child, separated by colored tabs. The cards contain information about each area of a child's work and constitute his basic record. They include comments on the child's performance in reading, mathematics, specific topics, science contract, and so on. They provide a comprehensive picture for the teacher of each child's work.

The Log   Some teachers ask children to keep daily or weekly logs, similar to the contracts that pupils write for overall work, which we described in Chapter 4. But the logs are not completed in advance of the work. The child logs the work that he has completed daily or weekly and, in some instances, the amount of time that he has spent on each task. Again the purpose of the log is to indicate to both teacher and child whether the child is engaging in a balanced program or whether any area is receiving insufficient or disproportionate attention. It should be emphasized, however, that the goal of the teacher in an open classroom is not necessarily to balance a child's program within a stated period of time. It is perfectly acceptable for some children to remain with a single project or field of study for long periods of time. The teacher may ensure that he will not indefinitely neglect some basic areas of work but does not necessarily require that any one area of work be included each day. (A sample pupil log is included in Figure 5.2, on which children list each activity engaged in daily.) Some teachers may not require the exact times devoted to each.

A danger to be avoided in using these methods of recording work is that they may become too cumbersome and time-consuming for the children or too difficult to keep accurately. The same criteria should be applied to records kept by pupils as to all others. They should provide only essential

WEEKLY LOG				
Name_____ Date_____				
MONDAY	TUESDAY	WEDNESDAY	THURSDAY	FRIDAY
S F	S F	S F	S F	S F
S F	S F	S F	S F	S F
S F	S F	S F	S F	S F
S F	S F	S F	S F	S F
S F	S F	S F	S F	S F
S F	S F	S F	S F	S F
S F	S F	S F	S F	S F

Note Lunch 12:00–1:00
          Special subjects: 1:15–2:00 daily
Key S: Time started
          F: Time finished

Figure 5.2 Sample Form for Individual Pupil Log

material that is not readily available elsewhere and should be reviewed regularly to ensure that their use is necessary. Most teachers find more detailed records important in the early stages of organization, as an aid to children in budgeting their time and planning their work. But they often find that they can eliminate much record keeping as children become more accustomed to working in open classrooms.

Check Lists   One of the most popular and probably the easiest means of recording work in open classrooms is the check list. Some teachers build their entire record-keeping system on check lists. Such lists fall into two categories: general check lists to ensure that certain assignments have been completed and specific check lists of skills that children are expected to acquire.

The general check list is an alphabetical list of the pupils in the class. A number of such lists are prepared for use of both pupils and teachers. Pupils may be asked to sign them when they have completed specific tasks, and teachers may make notations on them about any phase of a child's work.

Teachers may wish to have lists of the pupils who work in each interest center. We have already observed that notebooks that children sign as they work in a center are a means of accomplishing this goal. But check lists have an additional advantage, in that they reveal at a glance which children have participated and which have not. All the children's names are posted. When a child works in an interest corner, he signs the list, sometimes specifying "time in" and "time out."

Sometimes specific assignments may be posted in an interest center. For example, the mathematics corner may contain a list of children who are to work on fractions during the week. As the children complete each posted assignment, they initial the list and, where pertinent, also indicate the date they have completed it. Various items can be recorded on class lists; in one class students were asked to note the dates of the following:

> When you have completed a writing assignment
> When you have finished your science contract
> When you have started a new spelling unit
> When you have taken a math mastery test
> When you have chosen a new topic

Check lists can serve as a record of which activity cards a child has completed; a class list or notebook can be posted near the cards, and the number of each activity card can be entered, as shown in Figure 5.3. As the child finishes a card, he brings his work to the teacher if it requires review. If it is satisfactory, either the teacher or the child enters the date on which the activity was completed.

Because of the variety of work in which children are involved in open classrooms, teachers sometimes express concern that individual chil-

RECORD OF EXPERIENCES WITH FRACTIONS								
	Date Completed							
	Activity Card Numbers							
Students	1	2	3	4	5	6	7	8
J. Athens		2/28		2/25	3/2			
A. Barrow							2/27	
C. Charles					3/2			
D. Christie	3/1			2/25				
L. Daniels								

Figure 5.3   Sample Record of Mathematics Activity Cards Completed

dren may neglect certain skills. For example, a teacher may wish to ensure that a particular child has studied fractions or has learned particular punctuation skills or the meaning of some suffixes and prefixes. In many schools lists of specific skills associated with subjects like reading and mathematics have been developed. They can be used as guides in diagnosing a child's work and as aids to the teacher when he prescribes subsequent work or forms a group for instruction.

The check list illustrated in Figure 5.4 was developed for use with a group of eight- and nine-year-olds who were exploring fractions. As they acquired each concept, it was checked off the list.

Although check lists do offer the advantages noted, some cautions should be borne in mind when they are used. Check lists often subdivide subjects into so many parts that they become unwieldy. They can also be misleading, for it is difficult to determine the point at which a child can be said to have mastered certain skills. Must he have passed a test, and if so what level of achievement indicates mastery? Even if he has acquired the skills by a certain date, there is no guarantee that he has really mastered them, for another factor enters in. Check lists tend to represent learning as sequential, with certain skills following others in tidy progressions. In fact, children may not learn them in these sequences at all. Lists of skills can be useful in open classrooms, but they should be used with these warnings in mind.

Grade Books for Recordkeeping   In most traditional classes the basic records are the grade books. Each subject and test is listed, and grades and scores are recorded. The limitations of this information for teachers in open classrooms have been noted. The format of grade books does, however, lend itself to recording the work of individual children. Teachers in open class-

| CHECK LIST FOR THE STUDY OF FRACTIONS
Skills | | | | | | | | | | |
NAME	Concept of a Whole	Equal Parts of a Whole	Equal Parts of a Group	Numerator	Denominator	Equivalent Fractions	Addition of Like Parts	Subtraction of Like Parts	Mixed and Improper Fractions	Application to Problem Solving
F. Johnson										
L. Jones										
B. Holmes										
D. Swanson										

Figure 5.4   Sample Check List for Acquisition of Concepts Related to Fractions

rooms may use grade books to record a variety of information about a child's work other than grades. For example, one section may be used to list the topics that a child has chosen and the dates of initiation and completion of each. A few comments may be included on the outcome of the work. Another section may include information about projects or mathematics, reading, and the like. When test scores are recorded the teacher may include a comment about the kinds of errors made. The other children with whom a specific child chooses to work are noted. A grade book used in this manner, together with a child's work folder, may constitute adequate recording of the work of individual children.

Anecdotal Records   Some teachers choose to keep anecdotal records on each child, considering them more descriptive of the kind of work done in open classrooms. Teachers may keep these records on index cards or individual pages of a loose-leaf notebook. An entry is made as a child completes a significant piece of work and also at stated intervals, usually once each month.

These records are not limited to comments on academic work but also include notes on each child's social and emotional development—his ability to accept responsibility and to make significant choices, his interests, his relations with other children, his initiative, his powers of concentration, his use of materials.

One problem with anecdotal records is that, when teachers have to enter comments about twenty-five children, they may tend to make only general statements. It may therefore be desirable not to work on anecdotal records all on one day but to space this work out throughout the month or to do it after conferences with individual children. Even in discussing generalized areas of growth, the teacher should attempt to be specific in anecdotal records. "John is showing more initiative" is a less valuable comment than is "John showed initiative in developing the pollution project. He took the lead in producing the group skit"; just as "Jim needs to show more initiative" is less valuable than "Jim seems to be losing interest in animal project but doesn't move to other work. Suggested he join group building a bird feeder."

The Child's General Work Folder   In most open classes folders are compiled for all the children's work. The folders may be complete enough to serve as basic records of the children's overall work. Each folder may contain most of the work that the child has completed in a certain period of time, or it may contain only selected pieces. All entries should be dated. Procedures for deciding what is to be included vary. Children may determine what work they wish to file, whereas the teacher merely ensures that the folders adequately represent their activities. Or children may prepare work each month especially for their folders: pieces of writing, paintings, summaries of activities. These efforts are sometimes supplementary to other material that has been filed. A child's progress can frequently be assessed by these folder pieces, which are accumulated over an entire term or even longer.

In addition to samples of a child's work, the folder may contain details of a child's activities. His weekly logs or a list of activity cards completed or of activities explored in various areas can be included.

The general work folder is an important component of the records of open classrooms. It is most useful in conferences between teachers and parents. One teacher has stressed the value of such a folder in reassuring an apprehensive parent about work in open classrooms. A common reaction of parents reviewing their children's folder was "I didn't realize my child did all that work!" Not only is the folder helpful as a record of the actual work in which a child has engaged, but it also provides a means of assessing his progress in specific areas. A headmistress in London has emphasized the value of art work included in the folder over a period of time as an indicator of a child's growth. She has insisted that she can judge a child's development by reviewing samples of his paintings.

Conferring with Individual Children   Other primary means of ascertaining the progress of each child are daily and weekly conferences. The daily conference with a child may last only a few minutes. The teacher checks briefly with all the children, at the end of the morning and the remainder in the afternoon. Although each meeting may be brief, the teacher does use it to record significant details. She may use check lists for this purpose, commenting on a few items that had previously been listed, entering brief statements next to the children's names, or recording assignments suggested during the meeting. If a child requires more time or help, the teacher schedules an appointment with him for later in the day.

In addition, a longer conference is held with each child at least once a week (aside from the individualized reading meeting to be described in Chapter Ten). At this conference the teacher and child review the child's work folder. This session does not necessarily involve teaching, though some teaching may occur. The teacher may point out to a child errors in a mathematical problem, may show him how to punctuate a sentence, or may correct his spelling of a word. But if more prolonged teaching is necessary it will generally be scheduled for a different period—as part of group instruction whenever possible. The weekly conference is primarily diagnostic and evaluative. Together with the child the teacher evaluates what has been accomplished and discusses future plans. It is at this point that the teacher sets individual standards for the child:

I think you could do more work.

I suggest you concentrate on learning to spell these words.

How about collecting your poems and preparing a bound volume for our reading center?

That is a lovely poem. How about trying to set it to music? If you need help, ask Laura; she composed a lovely piece to go with her poem.

You might try a potato print for the outside of that booklet. There are directions in the art activity box.

That was an outstanding bit of research; let's schedule a time when you can discuss the results with the class.

Reading Records

Reading records are maintained by both teachers and children, separately or jointly. Generally they take the form of reading folders, reading cards, or notebooks.

Reading Folder   There may be a reading folder for each child which includes copies of his written work, information about the books that he has read and other reading activities in which he has engaged, plus appropriate comments: lists of words with which he has had difficulty or notations on passages that he wishes to discuss. Most reading folders also provide spaces for the teacher or children to enter specific reading assignments.

In some classes reading folders are the sole reading records. In these instances, they must also provide for entries by teachers and children and contain such diagnostic information about children's reading as copies of informal reading inventories or skill tests. Regular file folders can be used. Forms for records to be maintained by students are stapled into the front of each folder, and those for records to be maintained by the teacher are stapled into the back. Student records include the information described in the preceding paragraph. The teacher's records include notes made during reading conferences (for example, the book or pages discussed, the pages read orally, the child's response to reading, diagnostic information, and words misread or misinterpreted), other comments and assignments. Examples of forms used for student and teacher records are included in Figure 5.5.

At the end of each reading conference the child's written work is transferred to his general work folder, so that the reading folder contains only current reading work. The reading folders are stored in a file or central box. The child removes his folder when he is working in it or when he meets with the teacher, and he is then responsible for returning it to the central storage area. Teachers may occasionally screen the folders between conferences to assess the work that is being done, or may add personal comments for the children.

Reading Card   Some teachers prefer to keep their records of each child's reading separately, which permits more private comments about a child's work. Individual cards approximately 4 by 6 inches are used for each child. They may be filed in a card file or in one folder. Letter-size commercial folders in which cards for an entire class can be placed are available in stationery stores. Information is generally recorded at each reading conference, together with other necessary data and diagnostic notes. Each card is a running record of the child's reading in the conference, including the date of the conference, the pages read, comments, and further assignments.

Reading Notebook   Other methods of recording information about a child's reading include a loose-leaf notebook, in which a page is kept for each child and in which pertinent information is noted by the teacher. In some schools small notebooks are kept jointly by the teachers and children. The child enters information on his reading activities, and the teacher comments on his work and the reading conference.

Mathematics Records

In many classrooms each child also records the kinds of mathematics activities in which he has engaged, thus providing an overall record of his work in this subject. This record may include copies of his written work in mathematics for a specified period of time. The record is generally main-

STUDENT'S READING RECORD

Date	Name of Book and Pages Read	Other Reading Activities	Comments	Reading Conferences	
				Date	Assignments

TEACHER'S RECORD OF CONFERENCES

Date	Book or Pages Discussed	Oral Reading	Comprehension	Vocabulary	Observations and Follow-Up

Figure 5.5 Sample Forms for Reading Records To Be Maintained by Student and Teacher

tained by the child, with provisions for the teacher's comments and assignments. Its appearance may be similar to that of the reading folder, with pages stapled to the front for the pupil's own records and others stapled to the back for the teacher's comments. The pupil's record indicates the work that has been done in a given period of time.

In one school in England in which no mathematics workbook or common mathematics curriculum is used, assignment cards are filed as records of work. A week's basic mathematics assignment for each child is entered on a 3 by 5-inch index card, which is placed in a card file. The child works on his assignment at any time during the week, initialing each item as he completes it. After all the work assigned on the card is completed, the child enters any additional mathematical work that he has accomplished on the back, removes the card from the original file, and places it in a "completed" box. The teacher reviews the child's work and finally files the completed card as a record of the basic mathematics curriculum followed by each child.

SUMMARY COMMENTS ABOUT RECORDS

Several kinds of records have been described in this chapter. Those that the teacher chooses to maintain will have value only to the extent that they are consistently kept. For this reason, it is essential that teachers decide what records are necessary for the efficient functioning of their classes, keep them in the simplest and clearest fashion possible, and do not impose unnecessary recording on either themselves or their students. The teacher must be satisfied that students are capable of keeping the records requested of them. Just as records should not be so complex as to divert the teacher from the more important work of the class, they should also not divert the students from more important activities. If students frequently fail to keep their records up to date or resist turning in some records, the teacher must determine whether or not recording responsibilities are unnecessarily burdensome, whether or not the children have had sufficient practice in recording, and, most important, whether or not certain kinds of recording are really necessary. Teachers will undoubtedly have to experiment with many different types of records before deciding finally on those most applicable to their own classes.

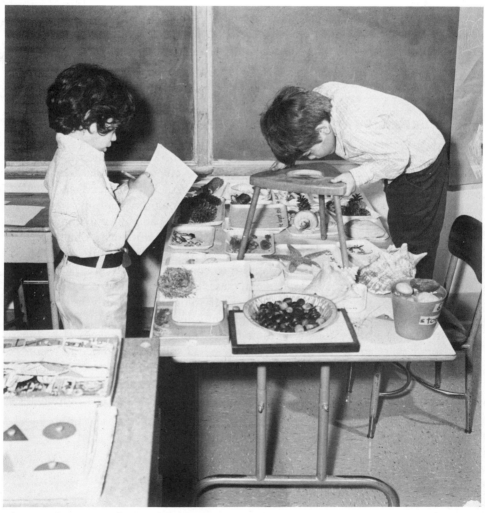

Photograph courtesy of Merrick Public Schools, New York.

Part
THREE
The Curriculum
of
Open Classrooms

Chapter
SIX
An Introduction to the Curriculum

There is an oft-repeated story about the child who returns home from a busy day at school and is asked by his parents, "What did you do at school today?" The child replies, "Nothing!"—even though the teacher may have packed numerous activities into the day. There are many possible interpretations of this story. One is that some children are simply unable or unwilling to communicate about their school day. Unfortunately, there is another possibility: that much of what occurs at school leaves children relatively unaffected. They often function as onlookers, disengaged and present only in body.

The curriculum of the open classroom is designed to involve the child, to touch him, to encourage him to become responsible for his learning. It is a flexible, dynamic curriculum forged in interaction between teachers and children. Teachers bring to curriculum development a general knowledge of areas to be included and skills appropriate for certain age groups, plus their own previous experiences and interests. From this background they design the outlines of their curricula. Children in turn help to shape their curricula by their reactions to materials, their changing needs, their blossoming interests. The open curriculum is thus both planned and unplanned. It is planned in the sense that teachers do not simply drift from day to day, waiting for things to happen. The environment is carefully constructed, materials are chosen to provide particular experiences, lessons are planned in response to individual and group needs. Yet the curriculum can also be unplanned in the sense that directions are not always prescribed: There is room for unforeseen explorations. A teacher may provide the spark, but, once the fire of learning has been lit in a child, it may burn in many directions.

Back in 1931 a British report described the curriculum of informal schools in terms that apply equally to those of open classrooms today: "The curriculum is to be thought of in terms of activity and experience rather than of knowledge to be acquired and facts to be stored."[1] More recently the Plowden report has reaffirmed this statement but cautioned that clarification is necessary. The statement is not to be interpreted as suggesting that "activity and experience did not lead to the acquisition of knowledge." On the contrary: "The context makes it plain that the actual implication is almost the opposite of this. It is that activity and experience, both physical and mental, are often the best means of gaining knowledge and acquiring facts. . . . Facts are best retained when they are used and understood." The Plowden report has also noted that teaching must be appropriate to the child's previous experience: "Instruction in many primary schools continues to bewilder children because it outruns their experience."[2]

The curriculum of the open classroom in the United States can be "thought of in terms of activity and experience," within the limits proposed by the Plowden Council. Activity is defined as both physical and intellectual, and its goal is indeed knowledge—knowledge that has meaning to the child, that can be applied, and that will contribute to his growth as a responsible and fulfilled individual able to enjoy his own unique talents. Experiences are structured to match each child's level of maturity.

Some general facets of the curricula of open classrooms require further elaboration: the notions of integrated curriculum and integrated day, as well as the roles of play, creative arts, and the "three Rs."

INTEGRATED CURRICULUM AND INTEGRATED DAY

Open educators object to the sharp division among subjects common in traditional classrooms. They argue that learning cannot always be neatly wrapped in separate packages marked "mathematics," "reading," "science," and the like. Many activities involve a variety of subjects. Mathematics can sometimes be more easily learned while designing a toy building, and reading while in pursuit of scientific information. Open educators therefore propose an *integrated curriculum*, in which subject boundaries are less distinct. The work of the class is organized around broad, unified themes, which encompass many subjects. Skills are studied as they are required by the activity and are practiced in the course of significant tasks, rather than simply in isolation.

[1] *Report of the Consultative Committee on the Primary School* (1931), see *Primary Education,* British Ministry of Education (London: H.M. Stationery Office, 1959), p. 7.
[2] Lady Bridget Plowden, et al. *Children and Their Primary Schools,* I (London: Her Majesty's Stationery Office, 1967), p. 195.

The child works through an *integrated day*, that is, a day in which there are minimum fixed periods and no barriers between subjects; he is free to follow any activity as long as his interest in it continues. This approach contrasts with arrangement of the day in specified periods for various subjects and reflects recognition that the duration of children's interests in subjects varies, that "it is folly either to interrupt it [the interest] when it is intense, or to flog it when it has declined."[3] Other boundaries are also blurred during an integrated day: those between play and work, between cognitive and affective domains, among different ages in the same class. Much of the children's work is chosen by themselves.

Although both the integrated curriculum and the integrated day are important components of open education, they can easily be misunderstood. Neither is to be interpreted rigidly or construed as eliminating the need for occasional separate teaching of individual subjects or the scheduling of some class work by the teacher. For example, it is probably impossible to introduce all the necessary mathematics skills as part of an integrated curriculum. At a conference on the integrated day in England Jack Walton reported that "Many people were concerned about the acquisition of basic skills," particularly of mathematics skills, in an integrated curriculum. Some expressed the opinion that relying on the teaching of mathematics through a wholly integrated curriculum was "hardly likely to lead to a logical development of understanding of this subject by the child." Walton also noted, "Whilst maths appeared to be particularly intransigent as far as integration was concerned other subjects appeared to present difficulties."[4]

In practice the degree of integration in the curricula of open classrooms varies. Some subjects, like spelling, grammar, and social studies, lend themselves more readily to this approach. Teachers recognize that all subjects can be learned more easily when they are approached through stimulating activities, but they remain conscious of certain skills appropriate to the age levels of the youngsters and include training in them. Similarly, teachers encourage each child to plan his day and to choose his activities responsibly; they hesitate to interrupt a child who is profitably engaged in a task, yet they strive to ensure a variety of work within a period of time. If a child constantly shies away from an art activity or never does mathematics, it may be because he is intensely interested in a particular science project or because he lacks confidence in his ability in the neglected area and requires further instruction in it. The sensitive teacher will find means of exposing children to many activities, in order to help them to become more competent to choose for themselves.

[3] *Ibid.*, p. 197.
[4] Jack Walton, *The Integrated Day in Theory and Practice* (London: Ward Lock, 1971), p. 11.

CHILDREN'S PLAY

The role of play in children's learning is central to an understanding of open education. The Plowden report has referred to play as "the principal means of learning in early childhood."[5] It is an integral part of the curriculum of an open classroom and is considered a valid educational experience in itself. Through the years theories of the necessity for play have been expounded. In the nineteenth century F. S. C. Schiller and Herbert Spencer considered play a release for surplus energy. Later Karl Groos described it as an exercise that prepares a child for adult life. Stanley Hall viewed it as a means of recapitulating the history of the species. To Friedrich Froebel play was the unfolding of the "divine essence" of the child.

More recent theories credit play with satisfying important psychological needs of the child. Through play a child may compensate for frustrations or dissatisfactions in his life. He can structure situations as he wishes and bring them to successful conclusions. It has also been considered cathartic, releasing stress or aggression. In addition, play has been envisioned as a means by which children can reenact experiences that have significance for them. Repetition of an unpleasant event may help the child to understand and accept it.

Jean Piaget considers play indispensable in a child's development. He has identified various stages of play, which coincide with the child's intellectual growth. Other psychologists have also noted that there are stages of play.

There is not, however, universal agreement on what constitutes play. R. F. Dearden has insisted that it is "fundamental": that play is "non-serious in the sense that it has no ethical value. . . . What we play at is intrinsically unimportant."[6] On the other hand, both Michel de Montaigne and Froebel had earlier referred to play as "serious business." In schools play has sometimes been defined as a relatively limited range of activities like games or unsupervised experiences with toys, water, sand, and the like. Conversely, it has also been viewed quite broadly as including diverse activities in art, music, and drama. It is probable that the authors of the Plowden report had a broad definition of play in mind when they argued that "a distinction between work and play is false" and "lies in past notions that what is done during school hours is work and what is done outside of school is play."[7]

Contributing to the difficulty of defining play in open schools is the fact that much of the *work* may fit the category of *play*. Children play

[5] Plowden, *op. cit.*, p. 193.
[6] R. F. Dearden, *The Philosophy of Primary Education* (London: Routledge & Kegan Paul, 1968), p. 97.
[7] Plowden, *op. cit.*, p. 193.

store and learn mathematics. They bake and learn to measure, play a reading game and learn phonics, play a social-studies game and learn geography.

Two definitions do offer some basis for distinguishing work and play. Michael J. Ellis has argued that "play is commonly considered to be the behavior emitted by an individual not motivated by the end product of the behavior."[8] A somewhat similar definition was offered in an exchange of correspondence between Susan Isaacs and the headmistress of a British school. The headmistress had written briefly: "I want a psychological definition of play. Would you give me one? I am giving a lecture on the Play Way with Infants and find my own definition too limited." Isaacs replied: "I would suggest that play is any activity of a child which is freely chosen and entered into spontaneously for its own sake, without reference to any end beyond itself. It makes no difference what the material of play is, it is the attitude of mind that defines it."[9]

From these definitions, work appears to be a more purposeful activity than does play, one with a goal, an "end beyond itself." Even following this distinction, however, the line of demarcation between work and play in open classrooms often seems blurred. A reading or mathematics game might be considered work in this context, whereas a game of checkers might be considered play. Or a child might enter an activity like dressing up in play clothes in an attitude of play, with no particular "end" in mind, but might be led to create a dramatic skit, a piece of work. It is thus easy to understand why open educators frequently conclude that there is no real difference between work and play in the open classroom.

Particular values have been attributed to play in school. Beatrice Mann[10] has stressed release of tension, development of self-discipline through perseverance in a task, social development, and growth of creative skills. Gertrude E. Cooper has emphasized social gains, noting, "There is an adhesive quality about play that unites the groups."[11]

The Bristol Education Authority in England in a release to its infant schools (for children approximately between five and seven years old) urged them to furnish ample opportunities for play, noting seven positive effects: language development, growth in self-confidence, development of concentration, greater facility in solving problems, cooperation among children, growth in independence, and broadening interest in the world. The sensi-

---

[8] Michael J. Ellis, *Why People Play* (Englewood Cliffs, N.J.: Prentice-Hall, 1973), p. 2.
[9] Reported in D. E. M. Gardner, *Susan Isaacs—The First Biography* (London: Methuen, 1969), pp. 100–101.
[10] Beatrice Mann, *Learning through Creative Work* (London: National Froebel Foundation, 1971).
[11] Gertrude E. Cooper, *The Place of Play in an Infant and Junior School* (London: National Froebel Foundation, 1968), p. 6.

tive teacher can learn more about a child by observing his play than in almost any other way, for children reveal their concerns as they act them out in play.

Teachers in open classrooms provide opportunities for many kinds of play: exploratory, imaginative, dramatic, constructive, destructive (for example, knocking down a pile of blocks that the child has himself built up), social, muscular, indoor, outdoor. The child comes in contact with many kinds of raw materials in his play: water, sand, clay, wood, paint, paper, textiles, and so on. Play is viewed as a facet of the curriculum, one that satisfies a child's need to explore his world and to understand it. It is thus directly related to how a child learns: "A child learns by wiggling skills through his fingers and toes into himself; by soaking up habits and attitudes of those around him; by pushing and pulling his own world. Thus a child learns. . . ."[12]

THE "THREE Rs" AND CREATIVE ARTS

Two final observations about the curricula of open classes are pertinent. One is directed at the role of the "three Rs" and the other at the role of creative arts. First, it must be emphasized that open educators do stress reading, writing, and mathematics in the curricula and that experiences in these subjects, in one form or another, occupy the major portion of the day in most open elementary school classrooms. A study conducted in British primary schools by the author (see Appendix B for details of this study) revealed that 66 percent of more than 2,000 children observed were also primarily engaged in activities classified as reading, writing, or mathematics, in addition to work in those subjects included in other areas of the curriculum.

Realistically, no system of education can expect to be accepted in the United States if it neglects these subjects. But, even more decisive, failure to achieve competency in the "three Rs" can result in a child's perceiving himself, or being perceived by others, as inadequate, which may seriously affect his future. As elementary schools are charged with basic responsibility for providing instruction in these areas, teachers in open classrooms devote much of their energy to finding effective means of helping their students to acquire competence in the "three Rs."

Creative arts are also valued and stressed in open classrooms. There is no conflict between these two emphases on the "three Rs" and on the creative arts—just as open educators see no inherent dichotomy between the cognitive and affective aspects of the curriculum, between the intel-

12 *"Thus a child learns . . ."* (Bristol: Bristol Education Authority).

lectual and the emotional and social aspects. They are interrelated ingredients of the education of the whole child. A final point bears emphasis. In some instances, as a reaction to the virtual exclusion of the arts in conventional classrooms, teachers in open classrooms have made these the major emphases of their program. This is a distortion of the role of creative arts in the curriculum.

In the eight chapters that follow the curriculum of the open classroom is presented in detail. It should be understood that the arrangement of material according to distinct subjects is dictated by organizational needs, rather than by any fundamental independence of one subject from another.

Chapter
SEVEN
Topics
and
Projects

A unique characteristic of the curriculum of open classrooms is its emphasis on topics and projects, which may supplant many of the traditional subjects or serve as means of integrating them. Topics and projects also provide a primary medium for permitting children to explore their own interests.

Historically, there have been several attempts to integrate the curriculum around broad areas of work. The "activity" program basic to progressive education in the United States was largely based on units of work, which encompassed many subjects. Earlier in this century a Belgian educator, Ovide Decroly, endorsed a project approach in which the focus was on children's centers of interest: food, housing, animals, and the like. Currently in England projects are widely used as the basis of an integrated approach to the curriculum. They are frequently generated by aspects of the environment.

Several terms are used for projects in elementary schools: "themes," "units," "centers of interest," "environmental studies," "topics," "projects." Although distinctions have at times been made among these terms, these distinctions tend to become blurred in practice. For this reason, we shall use only the terms "topics" and "projects" for the kinds of activities generally included under all these headings in open classrooms. Topics and projects will be distinguished from each other here: A topic is a unit of work pursued by an individual child or small group; it is usually more limited in scope than is a project, which encompasses a longer unit of work for a larger group, the entire class, or in some instances the entire school.

Most teachers have at times included topics and projects in the conventional curriculum. Children have done research on topics or constructed objects in conjunction with science or social studies units. These projects have frequently been supplementary features of the curriculum, for "extra credit." In open classrooms projects are viewed somewhat differently. Together with topics they constitute an essential part of the work of the class, and their execution may involve work in every elementary school subject.

TOPICS IN OPEN CLASSROOMS

In addition to his other work, each child in an open classroom is expected to investigate at least one topic of his own. The time devoted to such a topic will vary. In the course of a year, some children will explore two topics, others more.

Choosing a Topic

Topics should be freely chosen by the children to reflect their own interests. At first children may require suggestions for topics. The teacher may help to compile a list of possibilities, but the students should always be permitted to make the final choices.

One teacher used a novel method of helping a child to choose a topic. She suggested that he empty his pockets. A toy car or figure, baseball cards, coins, rubber bands, a wrapper, a pencil: any item in a child's pockets can suggest a topic. Constructing a flow chart with the aid of other children can help a child to recognize further ramifications of his topic. (The flow-chart technique is described later in this chapter.)

Working on a Topic

Topic work is generally performed individually, but there are times when small groups may wish to work together. The methods of exploring a topic vary with its nature and the maturity of the children. Most children keep topic notebooks in which they record research about their topics and include pictures or original illustrations. Others make constructions or displays, either in addition to their notebooks or as primary means of presenting their findings. Some may choose to paint murals, prepare sculptures, produce film strips, write skits, or combine several of these activities.

The emphasis placed on topic work in a particular class varies. In some classes teachers will insist that the children work on their topics regularly and may even set aside periods for such work. In others topics are pursued more sporadically. The degree of involvement depends upon the individual child. Some children may wish to work on their topics to the eventual exclusion of many other subjects, whereas others work only for minimal periods.

Peter Rance claims that the chief function of topics is to teach the

Boys construct fort to illustrate their topic. (Photograph courtesy of New Rochelle Public Schools, New York.)

student "how to learn." From experience gained while pursuing an area of interest, Rance suggests, the child will "develop a simple but logical method of systematically seeking, absorbing, organizing and recording knowledge."[1]

The Teacher's Role

Teachers must be available as consultants and resource persons for work on topics, ready to help children as they proceed. They should be careful not to direct the actual course of the investigations. To the greatest extent possible, children should determine how they wish to pursue their studies, deciding for themselves "how to learn." Teachers will have several other responsibilities connected with topics. They should be aware of the choice of topics made by each child, in order to ensure that his choice is consistent with his level of maturity. Some children tend to narrow their choices to areas with which they are familiar. In such instances teachers must determine whether the child's failure to diversify his choices results from insecurity or from absorbing interest in the chosen field. Their reactions will depend upon this assessment.

[1] Peter Rance, *Teaching by Topics* (London: Ward Lock, 1968), p. 13.

It is also sometimes necessary for teachers to stimulate and even to suggest new avenues of exploration to children as they work on their topics. They will wish to make certain that each child's interest in a topic is maintained. When interest wanes, the child may be ready to complete his study, or he may be stymied in his investigation. In the latter instance, the teacher may have to suggest new directions for study or additional resources. The decision to consider a topic completed should be made jointly by teacher and child. It is unwise to suggest that a child stay with a topic in which he has lost interest, but it is important that he be encouraged to explore his topic in a depth commensurate with his ability, rather than superficially. Frequently a child is not aware of the ramifications of his topic.

Summarizing a Topic

When work on a topic has been completed, the child should have an opportunity to share some of his new information with the class. This presentation serves the dual purpose of enabling him to display his own work and of stimulating new interests in other members of the class. Such sharing need not take the form of reports to the entire class. Children may list their topics on the bulletin board and invite interested members to participate in discussions about them or to view displays at particular hours. In some instances, the work will deserve a larger audience. Work on topics can be shared through school assemblies, class meetings, or school exhibits. Not every child will, however, wish to report to others on his topic. Some children will prefer not to share a particular piece of work; once they have satisfied their own interest in certain subjects, they may not want to discuss them further.

Displays should always be appropriately labeled with the name of the "authors." It is also advisable to maintain a class index file, including the title of each topic and the child who investigated it. This file serves as a "resource list" of children who are "authorities" in different fields. If a child wishes to study a particular subject, he may find that another child has already done so and can be used as a source of advice.

Advantages of Topic Work

There are many advantages to work on topics.

1. It permits each child to pursue an individual interest within the curriculum.
2. It enhances the acquisition of research skills, teaching a child how to investigate a subject.
3. It encourages initiative, enabling a child to plan an important part of his own work.

4. It eliminates artificial barriers among subjects and provides a means by which a child can integrate and use what he has learned.
5. It leads to greater knowledge of many areas.
6. It stimulates new interests.

Possible topics are literally unlimited. Here are some examples:

Famous people, chosen by profession or race	Women's Liberation movement	Movies
Fictional characters	Civil rights	Medicine
Sports (statistics, origins of games, athletes)	Presidents of the United States	Pets
Authors	State capitals	Flowers
Holidays	Radio	Elections
Musical instruments	Television	Birds
Witches	Codes	Insects
Astrology	Puzzles	Holidays
Printing	Toys or games	Stamps
The school	States	Coins
The community	Foreign countries	Unusual customs
Cooking	Dress	Myths
		Superstitions

(See also titles listed under *Projects* later in this chapter)

PROJECTS IN OPEN CLASSROOMS

There is often no clear-cut distinction between topics and projects. A subject that begins as an individual topic may come to interest a larger group and may develop into a class project. The suggested topics listed may well be the themes of projects also.

Each class generally has a project on which it is working as a group. This project may supplement work on individual topics. In open classrooms social studies and science are frequently taught through class projects. For example, in one open classroom in New York City the children became intrigued by Ancient Greece and a project developed. They set up an Athenian senate, which they used as an actual governing body. They studied Greek history, staged several skits and an "olympics," constructed a model of the Greek marketplace and a section of the Parthenon. Another group became interested in Greek art, visited the Metropolitan Museum, and made pottery modeled after Ancient Greek vases. The project continued for months.

The length of time spent on a project will vary with its nature and the interest that it engenders. One class spent an entire semester on a project on vocations. The children surveyed and graphed the vocations of their parents, did research on different careers, invited speakers, and visited factories and businesses; then each member of the class chose to study a specific vocation in depth. The information became part of a really worthwhile book of careers, which contained valuable data used later for a unit on vocational education in other classes in the school.

Choosing a Project

Interest in a project can be sparked in many ways: It can begin with a topic that one child has been exploring: a television broadcast, a newspaper item, a book read to the class, a discussion, school visitors, a collection lent to the school by a museum or parent, current events, and field trips. For example, a visit by one child's father, who was a stockbroker, led one class to engage in an extensive project on the stock market; it included "purchasing" a group of stocks, following their daily ups and downs, studying the operation of the market, and exploring the responsibilities of stockholders in a corporation. In another class a parent who was a lawyer inspired interest in law and the American system of justice. The parent arranged a class visit to a local court and the participation of the class in preparing a bill for introduction to the state legislature.

During the world chess-championship matches one class undertoook to study the history of the game and the biographies of world champions. Some members of the class built chess sets and organized a tournament. The Olympics intrigued another class and led to many related projects. Sometimes a project can be stimulated by a piece of material. The teacher or a child may bring in an old clock, a rock, a shell, a bird's nest, a bottle, or an old pair of shoes. A project can develop through the preparation of a *flow chart* based on such an object. The title is written on the blackboard or a large sheet of paper. The children discuss all the various possibilities for exploration that come to mind, each suggestion leading to others in a process called *brainstorming*. The children then decide which areas they wish to pursue.

We have mentioned that the contents of a child's pockets can stimulate a topic. A few grains of sand in one pocket led to an extensive project on sand. The teacher posed three questions: "Where is it found?" "What is it used for?" "What can we do with it?" The class constructed a flow chart on sand in response to these questions. (See Figure 7.1.) They then divided into groups, and each group undertook a major area of investigation from those suggested on the chart; the children also used sand in creative projects. The results were impressive.

An old pair of shoes led to some particularly imaginative studies. Stories were written about the people who had worn the shoes, materials

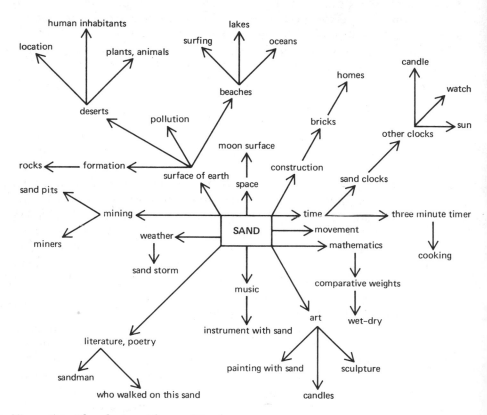

Figure 7.1 Flowchart on Theme of Sand

for making shoes were investigated, research was conducted on kinds of shoes and where they are worn, other shoes were sprayed to create pop art, and one group examined things that come in pairs.

A class of six- and seven-year-olds decided to study the color blue. They explored why the sky is blue, the primary colors, paintings from Pablo Picasso's Blue Period; they noted the number of children in the class with blue eyes, made Venn diagrams showing the ratio of blue eyes to the total number of boys and girls in the class, wrote mood poems entitled "When I Feel Blue," and worked on a variety of blue artistic creations: mosaics made of bits of blue paper, eggshells dyed blue, paintings, sculpture of blue clay, and collages. They also made a display of different blue objects. Colors make convenient themes for class projects.

This same class was so intrigued by the idea of developing a project around a single common dimension that it then decided to collect objects that are round. This project also led to a number of studies, from the discoveries of Copernicus to an imaginative examination of the environment based on the proposition "What if everything in the world were round?"

Environmental studies are the impetus for many class projects. Children may visit the seashore and decide to investigate the sea; a nature preserve may interest them in facets of plant and animal life; they can look into the background of a historical landmark; or they may undertake study of a particular neighborhood. The last approach is popular in England. A group studies the history of the neighborhood, its residents, the architecture of its buildings, its shops, its trees, and so on. Usually this type of study is limited to a small area of a few blocks. The group often constructs a model of the area.

One class became interested in early man and investigated some significant archaeological finds. They decided to organize a "dig." They contacted the mayor and the local historical society and finally secured permission to work at a nearby site. They invited an archaeologist from the local university to discuss procedures with them and ran a white-elephant sale to raise funds for equipment. Finally they began work. First they surveyed the land and planted markers. Then they began to dig. Photographs were taken as the work progressed, the area was mapped, and notes were taken of all artifacts discovered. The group has a collection of bricks, a piece of bottle, bits of pottery, a door hinge, and a tool. There was one other offshoot of this project: The discovery of the bottle fragment aroused interest in bottle collecting, decorating bottles, and classifying them.

Environmental studies are frequently linked with ecological investigations—for example, study of pollution in the environment. As a result, many classes have become interested in recycling waste products, and many projects have developed around the use of "junk." (See the discussion of junk art in Chapter Fourteen.)

Although initially some projects may be inspired by the teacher, it is essential that pupils participate in choosing class projects, which are important avenues for expanding children's interests. Frequently class meetings provide a forum for deciding on a new project. Jack Walton has warned of one potential pitfall to be avoided at such meetings: Sometimes one child who is more verbal than the rest may quickly offer a suggestion for a project and then the rest of the class may simply go along, so that the teacher mistakes one child's choice for that of the whole class. He cautions: "We must not be misled by moving from 'this topic was suggested by a member of the class' to 'this suggestion came from the class.' If one does, then it makes us think that we are running our class in a democratic way, whereas in fact the suggestion has come from one child."[2]

---

[2] Jack Walton, *The Integrated Day in Theory and Practice* (London: Ward Lock, 1971), pp. 25–26.

Multiple-Class and School Projects

Projects can involve more than one class or even a whole school. Four open classes grouped in the same wing of a building decided to collaborate on a project on black history. Each room became the center for a different theme. In one children cooked "soul food" and wrote recipes. In another poetry, literature, and music by black artists were stressed. Another concentrated on art and sculpture, the fourth on politics, government, and the professions. Each room wrote material for the project and made displays. Children chose the areas in which they wished to work for the duration of the project, which lasted two weeks. Every afternoon they went to the rooms where their chosen activities were centered. The project culminated in a joint exhibition and fair open to the entire school.

A school in England devotes one month at the end of each school year to a school project. One year interest in medieval history was sparked by a Breughel print, a scene of games and jousting in the Middle Ages. The entire school undertook to recreate the scene depicted. Each class chose a different aspect. Medieval history was studied; games, food, scenery, and costumes were duplicated; and the project culminated in a grand pageant. Another year the school chose "story-book characters." Younger children drew nursery-rhyme figures or composed nursery rhymes. Older classes wrote new stories, placing characters in original situations. Costumes were made and skits based on familiar books presented. Classes voted for favorite books. Individual children presented their choices in a variety of ways. A book fair capped the project.

Planning the Work

Once the theme of the project has been chosen, the class will still need help in determining which aspects to explore. Constructing a flow chart has been mentioned as one approach. The teacher may make additional suggestions for research or provide some materials on the subject. Sometimes a group of children may agree to share responsibility for developing ideas for the project. They may screen the literature and then meet with the teacher to draw up a list of possible avenues of exploration. Lists of resources may have to be compiled. They may include books, reference works, films, displays, people who can be invited to the class, field trips. Some of them may be attended to before work actually commences; that is, a speaker can be invited or a field trip scheduled. This prior planning serves both as a means of stimulating further interest in the project and of indicating its dimensions.

In some instances, a work plan is prepared before the project is begun. (In Chapter Four we discussed techniques for writing contracts, which can be applied to project work.) Even when a project is carefully planned in advance, however, there must be provision for exploration of facets not originally included. For example, one class studying Japan became aware that the Japanese are baseball fans. A group of ten-year-old boys then extended their original plans to include research on baseball in Japan. The result was a productive investigation in which the Japanese consulate and American athletes who had played in Japan were consulted for information.

Groups in Project Work

Although groups are not essential, children generally do work on projects in groups. These groups are usually based on the interests of class members. There will be times when a teacher may wish to balance the composition of a group in terms of the members' talents or to place a particular child with one group for social or other reasons. Nevertheless, groups established by the teacher should be the exception. Children tend to show good judgment in organizing groups and may work more effectively when they are responsible for deciding with whom they will work.

A group member should be designated as the leader by the students, and there should be some provision for rotating leadership responsibilities in the course of the school year. Each group should be expected to plan its work and to make a tentative schedule for completing it. The leader will be expected to keep an up-to-date record of the plans and the work that is being done. This record enables the teacher to check with the leader regularly to ensure that the project is not bogging down. Space may have to be allotted to each group for work in progress; provision should also be made for storage of materials used by the group.

Culmination of the Project

A project should not be allowed simply to fade away. The entire class should be able to survey the work that has been accomplished, so that each group sees more than only the aspects on which it has concentrated. There are many methods for accomplishing this goal. There may be individual group presentations, or the whole class may cooperate on a presentation summarizing all the different facets. Reading of long written group reports to the class should be avoided. A group may make a film or tape material, so that individual children can look or listen. Children may perform an experiment, prepare a bulletin board, work on a mural, duplicate their results for distribution to the class, or write and bind a book. Sometimes an entire class will cooperate on a book summarizing all the findings; photographs of displays or models and other illustrations will enhance such a book.

A group of children making clowns as part of a class project on "The Circus." (Photograph courtesy of Merrick Public Schools, New York.)

Advantages of Project Work

Many of the values attributed to projects are similar to those associated with work on topics. Projects serve important functions in open classrooms:

1. They help to integrate the curriculum around unifying themes.
2. They permit study of subjects in a manner that has meaning for children, stimulating varied avenues of exploration.
3. They allow pursuit of individual interests.
4. They enhance ability to use varied means of investigating a subject.
5. They help to develop social skills connected with working in a group.
6. They encourage student leadership.
7. They foster student initiative.
8. They lead to increased knowledge about many subjects that are not usually part of the curriculum.
9. They stimulate new interests.

Because of the advantages of topic and project approaches in the classroom, many teachers have attempted to organize their entire curricula in this manner. Although there are undoubtedly projects that can become all-encompassing and there may be periods of time when they will replace individual subjects, the teacher must still make provision for teaching certain skills not included in work on the project. It is possible, for example, to exaggerate the mathematical skills developed in connection with a project. Measurement may be required for a construction, for example, but measurement is only one aspect of mathematics. It is unlikely that work on the "three Rs" can be completely replaced by project work. Other subjects, however, do lend themselves to teaching through projects. Social studies and science have been mentioned in this connection. Spelling, grammar, art, and music are others.

In discussing projects we have emphasized an integrated approach. A further note of caution is in order: It may not always be desirable to try to integrate all areas of the curriculum around a project or theme. If attempts to include many different subjects in the development of a project become labored, the project may seem contrived. There is an additional factor: Concentration on one project as the central work of the class may be valuable for a certain period of time while the class is really interested, but if it continues too long it may offer too narrow a focus. A class deserves a rich curriculum, and the teacher who concentrates on one project should be certain that it meets this criterion.

Many of the subjects mentioned as possible individual topics may also be appropriate for class projects. Here are suggestions for other possible projects:

Animals	Time	Seasons
Reptiles	Careers	Communities
Fish	Transportation	Sound
Flight	Space	Minorities
Colors	Films	Environmental studies
Historical events	Art and artists	Pollution
Periods of history	Boats	Government
Farms	Automobiles	Law
Architecture	Food	Senior citizens
Archaeology	United Nations	Public health
Scientists	Foreign countries	Communication
The human body	Post office	Homes
Symbols	Light	The sea
Times of day (morning,	Pantomime	Trees
afternoon, evening)	Cybernetics	Beaches

Considerations of age or grade level have purposely been excluded from this list. The same theme can be used for projects on many different levels. For example, a first-year class and a sixth-year class can each investigate boats. In the first year children may cut out pictures of different boats and ships, make models, and write short pieces. Older children may pursue this subject by studying the history of commerce, different kinds of ships, products shipped from a particular harbor and their dollar value, maritime laws, the shipping industry, unions, fishing laws, territorial limits, and waterways.

We have noted that in open classrooms social studies and science are frequently taught by means of projects. The next two chapters are devoted to further exploration of these subject areas.

Chapter
EIGHT
Social
Studies

The label "social studies" encompasses many academic disciplines: history, geography, economics, sociology, anthropology, and political science. Its potential scope is considerable, embracing the entire history of civilization, the physical environment of man, and the social institutions that he has created for living in that environment. Because of these broad dimensions, the social studies curriculum must be highly selective. Most elementary school textbooks stress history and geography, adding some elements of sociology through study of communities.

Three purposes of teaching social studies in elementary schools have been put forth: to transmit information about man, his heritage, environment, and institutions; to transmit values associated with society and citizenship; and to encourage a critical attitude toward contemporary events. Although these objectives may seem easily acceptable, achieving them is more complex. Several issues have been raised in connection with each.

TRANSMITTING INFORMATION ABOUT MAN

Much of the social studies curriculum in conventional schools is focused on transmission of information about man. Students are supposedly presented impartially with facts about human history. In the past some educators have debated what facts are to be presented and to what extent they must be committed to memory by children—but not the facts themselves. Yet the notion that a body of historical facts exists and can be presented wholly impartially may itself be challenged. We may ask "How objective are historical facts?" and "How accurate should their presentation to young children be?"

How Objective Are Historical Facts?

Textbook authors have often been accused of distorting aspects of history through their selection of material and particularly by their failure to take adequate account of the contributions of minority groups in American history.[1] Textbooks are said to reflect consistently the point of view of the dominant group in society. "Facts" reported about a particular event may actually represent a very narrow interpretation of that incident. Textbooks also tend to reflect national biases. We wonder how differently the *facts* about the Bay of Pigs incident are reported in the textbooks of the three countries involved: the Soviet Union, Cuba, and the United States.

Carl Becker has discussed objectivity of historical facts: "We talk much about the 'hard facts.' . . . By virtue of talking in this way, the facts of history . . . seem something solid, something substantial. . . ." He has demonstrated how each fact presented reflects selection of a single incident from a conglomerate of events, concluding: "The simple fact turns out to be not a simple fact at all. It is the statement that is simple—a simple generalization of a thousand and one facts. . . ."[2]

How Accurate Should Reporting Be?

Teachers have wondered to what extent controversial issues should be raised in school. Should young children, for example, be exposed to discussion of atrocities committed in Vietnam? Or to some of the facts about the Spanish-American war of 1898?

There is a related consideration. Should social studies teaching glorify American heroes and treat myths as history? From the perspective of the white man Daniel Boone was a hero, from that of the Indians an intruder in their lands. George Washington is remembered by most school children for having confessed to chopping down a mythical cherry tree, but they might be shocked to learn that he was actually also a slaveholder. Some teachers have argued that children need myths and heroes, even presented in the guise of history, and that schools should encourage the attitude that our country is always "right." Others suggest that this kind of teaching only leads children ultimately to distrust what they have been taught and those who have taught them.

---

[1] For example, few children are aware that about one third of all cowboys in the West have been black or Indian.

[2] Carl Becker, "What are Historical Facts?" in *Detachment and the Writing of History* (Ithaca: Cornell University Press, 1958), pp. 43–61.

TRANSMITTING VALUES OR CITIZENSHIP

It has often been argued that schools should teach values, or "good citizenship." This demand also poses problems for the teacher, who has to deal with the question "Which values?" We suspect that some of those who insist on the teaching of values may view schools not as social melting pots of society but as paint pots from which each child emerges, purged of his ethnic origins and clothed in the manners and values of the majority groups. The values to be taught are frequently interpreted as those held by majority groups in American society, with which children from minority groups cannot always identify. Nor are all groups' conceptions of good citizenship similar. Where these factors are considered, bland generalizations are frequently taught as values in school. Furthermore, social values change from generation to generation. Youngsters may distrust teachers who fail to recognize that many values of the "good old days" are no longer relevant in our rapidly changing society.

DEVELOPING A CRITICAL ATTITUDE

It has been stated that one purpose of teaching social studies is to help children to examine current events critically. Yet traditional schools are not always prepared to cope with students who do adopt truly critical attitudes that may lead them to challenge established practices. In fact, it is the conforming student, who accepts what he is told unquestioningly, who may be most comfortable in a conventional school. Teachers who encourage students to view society critically may be unwelcome, too.

It is clear that the professed objectives of teaching social studies are not always attainable or even considered desirable in elementary schools.

SOCIAL STUDIES IN THE OPEN CLASSROOM

Although the issues described are also relevant to teaching in open classrooms, the atmosphere of the open class does lend itself to easier resolution of some problems. In a relationship between teacher and pupils characterized by openness and honesty, American heroes, for example, can be presented as men and women who suffered from human frailties without detracting from their accomplishments. As there is less emphasis on facts, dates, and places, a more rounded picture of an event can be offered. When questioning is emphasized in all areas of the curriculum, a more critical attitude toward events is also acceptable.

The teacher's main goal in teaching social studies is to ensure that students acquire certain broad outlooks: a sense of history as a continuous process with multiple causes, appreciation of past civilizations, a sense of man as a social animal who has established many different forms of institutions and cultures deserving consideration and respect, and recognition of change as a constant factor in life. Geography is studied as it affects mankind and as it is affected by mankind. Economics and politics are examined within a social context.

Most social studies in open classrooms are pursued through individual topics or class projects. Children choose aspects of social studies that interest them and are encouraged to explore these aspects individually or in small groups. In addition, a class project in social studies may be centered on themes like Colonial America or the role of women in American society at different periods. Work on individual topics and class projects proceeds as we have described in Chapter Seven. It will obviously take quite different forms from that of the social studies curriculum in traditional schools.

First, the areas of study are not limited to units included in the textbook for that grade level. The open-classroom teacher respects children's interests in many subjects: African and Latin American history are considered just as valid as are Western and Middle Eastern history, for example.

Furthermore, the methods of study differ from the traditional garnering of information from textbooks. In one class children studied periods of American life through the folk songs of each era. They found that, by collecting and analyzing the songs actually sung at different times, they were able to gain insight into the philosophy and history of those periods, as well as into the contributions of various ethnic groups.[3]

In another class a group of children was determined to study history through postage stamps. Recognizing that postage stamps are issued to commemorate key historical events, they collected United States stamps, organized them chronologically, and then investigated the people and events pictured. This approach has further possibilities. The history of foreign countries can also be investigated through postage stamps and other items like coins and paper currency.

It is often desirable for students to maintain a time line, a chronology, if they are to appreciate the sequence and interrelations of apparently discrete historical events. It can be constructed by means of stamps, coins, or currency—or simply by listing events discovered in research. Students can also construct chronologies of current events, charting daily occurrences that they deem significant.

Children need ample opportunities for concrete experiences if they

[3] As a reference for such an approach, see John Anthony Scott, *The Ballad of America* (New York: Bantam, 1966).

are to absorb social studies concepts. Young children cannot readily understand many concepts like time and space. Geographical notions may be quite confusing if presented abstractly. Children can best comprehend maps, not through coloring or tracing them, but through actually mapping a locality —perhaps one block near the school. This approach led to an interesting project in one class of ten- and eleven-year-olds.

The children undertook to study a local shopping center. Initially they made a map showing the location of each store in the center. Various investigations followed. Some children concentrated on the commodities sold in the stores and their origins. Others were interested in the quantities of certain items sold over a period of time. By interviewing the manager of the supermarket, they discovered how many quarts of milk, loaves of bread, and dozens of eggs were sold weekly. Another group focused on the people who worked in the stores, still another on the number of people who shopped in the area, undertaking detailed counts to determine this figure.

Child decides where to locate mythical country developed in social studies project. (Photograph courtesy of Merrick Public Schools, New York.)

An attempt to integrate more abstract social studies concepts also led to an extensive class project. The children decided to "make up" a country. First, they placed it on the globe, named it, described its weather and topography, and made a series of maps and constructions illustrating it. Then they drew its flag and gave it a government and a history. They described the people who lived in it; what they wore; how they traveled, worked, and played; the foods that they ate; and the plant and animal life. The children recognized the relation between the physical environment that they had created and the life of the people and were required to justify their placement of different communities; they had to do a great deal of research into the geography and history of the hemisphere in which they had located their country before the project was completed.

It should be apparent that social studies are indeed broad subjects in open classrooms, that actually combine many fields of study. In teaching social studies the open-classroom teacher who follows consistently his philosophy of how children learn will encourage them to pursue investigations that interest them and to participate in experiences related to their studies, rather than simply to read about social studies. In this connection we should add that the democratic environment of the open classroom is in itself a significant statement of social values: By living in this atmosphere children are in effect learning a great deal about "social studies."

Chapter
NINE
Science

The headmaster of a British informal school reported rather apologetically: "I'm afraid we don't teach science. I suppose we just don't seem to find the time." An elementary school principal in a quite traditional American school announced proudly, "We teach a great deal of science in our school."

After visits to classrooms in their respective schools, it appeared that both were incorrect. In the informal school children were incubating chickens, inspecting embryos, and keeping detailed records of the incubation periods, and the weights of the chickens both at birth and before and after each feeding. They explained how eggs were fertilized and the difference between fertilized and unfertilized eggs. They were experimenting with pendulums, growing plants, and baking. They were speculating on the relation between the size of an object and its shadow and gathering other kinds of data about their immediate environment.

In the traditional school most of the classes relied on a science textbook. The children read the textbooks (often together in class) and then answered questions that followed each chapter. A written test followed treatment of each topic. There was little opportunity for any member of the class to form hypotheses, to observe, to test his hypotheses, or to draw conclusions. Problems were presented and answered in the book. For example, one class was reading about gravity. The page in the textbook began: "Did you ever wonder why it is easier to carry something down hill than up?" The answer was immediately given: "Gravity helps you." Two pages later the children were asked, "Why is it easier to skate down hill than up?" Learning science in this class appeared to consist of memorizing words.

WHAT IS SCIENCE?

XThere are two aspects to the study of science: content and process. The content of science is a vast body of knowledge about man and his environment. The process of science is a method of discovering that knowledge. The content of science is all about us; its domain is infinite. It encompasses the nature of moon rocks brought back by astronauts and of pebbles on the school playground, the principles behind the flight of a jumbo jet plane and the operation of a toy airplane. This vast scope offers unlimited possibilities for worthwhile investigation. It is necessary, however, that children understand how to conduct such investigations. For this reason the process of science receives most emphasis in open classrooms.

The process of science involves formulating a problem, stating a hypothesis, investigating, drawing conclusions, and verifying results. This method of problem solving can be applied to many areas of the curriculum other than science. In open classrooms children are expected to use it in much of their work.

OBJECTIVES OF SCIENCE

Five objectives of science teaching in open classrooms may be stated:

1. To develop interest in and sensitivity to the environment.
2. To develop ability to pose questions about the environment.
3. To develop ability to observe, to experiment, and to formulate and test hypotheses.
4. To develop the ability to interpret findings.
5. To engender new insights into the physical world.

THE SCOPE OF SCIENCE IN ELEMENTARY SCHOOLS

Science in the elementary school encompasses several branches: physics (light, sound, energy, matter), biology (living things), geology (composition of the earth), astronomy (stars and space), and chemistry (atoms, molecules, chemical changes). Any serious study of these fields requires understanding of sophisticated concepts and mathematics that is way beyond the grasp of young children. It therefore becomes necessary to select for study aspects that interest the child yet are possible for him to explore. The scope of science is defined as the child's own environment. The word "environment" is used broadly: The stars at night are part of the child's

The open classroom is a laboratory where children observe, experiment, and test hypotheses. (Photograph courtesy of Merrick Public Schools, New York.)

environment, as are materials provided in the classroom. The study of science in the open classroom begins with the child's own questions, arising from his need to come to terms with his environment, to comprehend it.

QUESTIONING IN SCIENCE

Children are naturally curious. Preschool children want to know the "why" of everything. If they are not discouraged, they will continue to be inquisitive about their environment as they grow older, asking questions like "Why is the sky blue?" "How does water get into a faucet?" "How does a light bulb work?" "Why does the moon change shape?" "How does a television set work?" Children's questions tend to fall into four categories:

1. Questions that can be answered precisely and require little explanation: "How far is the moon?"
2. Questions that can be answered through simple investigations: "Will a magnet attract a metal object through paper?"
3. Questions that can be answered through more complex investigations that are still within the child's grasp: "How does an airplane fly?"
4. Questions that involve concepts too sophisticated for the child to grasp at his current level of development: "How does the sun stay in the sky?"

Teachers' replies to each of these kinds of questions will be different. In the first instance, a teacher may help a child to find the appropriate reference material, in the second to find the materials necessary to solve the problem. In the third instance, depending upon the child's maturity, the teacher may direct him to perform experiments or to study written material and devise his own experiments. In the last instance, a few general comments may suffice for the young child.

In every instance the teacher seeks to help the child to distinguish between different categories of questions and to strive as much as possible for his own solutions. Teachers encourage the view of the classroom as a laboratory in which the child can wrestle with scientific problems. They do not consider themselves experts; their objective is to foster children's ability to pose scientific questions without expecting immediate answers from the teachers. In effect, they suggest that the child ask not "How far is the moon?" but "How can I find out how far the moon is?"

Although science teaching often begins with a child's own questions, as in other areas of the curriculum, teachers have also to stimulate questions, to provide materials and experiences, and to be aware of what they expect children to learn—which is not necessarily the same for each child. Albert James has expressed this notion: "It is now well-established that science . . . should come from the child's own interest and questions. . . . But one should not assume that this means setting out like Abraham . . . [who] 'went out not knowing whither he went'. . . ."[1]

SCIENCE IN OPEN CLASSROOMS

Teachers who encourage a questioning attitude will find that science programs often develop naturally from daily experiences. Children will "discover" and investigate water. They will observe what floats in it, what sinks, what displaces it. They will feel it, pour it, blow bubbles in it, boil it, freeze it, melt it, and determine how long it takes to do each under varying conditions. They will study its temperature at different points and check its effects on fabrics. They may proceed from such studies to investigation of boats and how they stay afloat.

Other children may be interested in light. They will plot shadows and the sun's path at different times of day. They will investigate reflections in mirrors, water, kaleidoscopes, and prisms. They will construct periscopes and will also try to comprehend the speed of light and related measurements.

Science programs may also be more organized. They will generally

[1] Albert James, *et al.*, *Structures and Forces*, trial ed., Science 5/13 (London: Macdonald, 1970), p. 11.

consist of two kinds of science activities. First are those of relatively short duration undertaken in response to specific problems: "What materials make good conductors of electricity?" "Which foods contain starch?" "Do all plants require the same amount of water?" Second are those of broader scope and requiring longer periods of study. They may be approached as individual topics or as class projects.

Short-Term Activities

There are many opportunities for short-term science activities in open classrooms. They can be generated by problems posed by either pupils or teacher. Science activities frequently result from contact with materials. An interesting science corner can stimulate experiments in any number of areas: electricity, chemistry, weights, machines, air, geology, fossils, and so on. A stethoscope, for example, may lead to an interest in respiration and its relation to circulation. There are many general books that suggest science experiments which can be part of the science corner.

An interest in crystals can result from "growing" crystals on charcoal. Four pieces of charcoal are placed in a bowl; six tablespoons each of water, salt, and bluing are combined with two tablespoons of ammonia and a few drops of food coloring, and this mixture is poured over the charcoal. After several hours crystals will grow, much as coral grows.

A science-activity box can help to stimulate short-term activities. It should contain a file of activity cards. Each card should contain a problem that can be solved by reference to or experimentation with materials at hand. It is important that children help to write the activity cards, both to ensure that the problems interest them and to teach them how to formulate questions that can be answered through relatively short investigations.

Some teachers suggest that the child complete a certain number of short-term activities in a period of time, perhaps one a week. Others permit children to decide whether or not to engage in such activities. In either instance the teacher must be aware of the child's interest in order to help him choose an appropriate card—and also to recognize the broader implications of his activity. A successful activity should engage a child in thought, should lead him to pose further questions and additional experiments. The teacher may have to help an interested child to appreciate the directions in which a short-term activity can lead him. Here are some examples of short-term problems that can be posed on activity cards:

Do all liquids have the same weight?
Does dye evaporate when water turns to steam?
What is a beam of light composed of?
How can you measure the height of a tree without climbing to the top?

How can the distance to the moon be calculated?
How can you float a wooden block in a pail of water?
Do any fabrics shrink when washed? Using as many different fabrics as
you can, determine under what conditions and how much each will (or
will not) shrink.

Some activities may require longer periods for investigation:

What is mold? Does mold grow on all foods? Set up some experiments
to determine what conditions are necessary to grow mold. Summarize
your conclusions.
What is iron rust? Does it add weight to a piece of iron? Prove and
explain your hypothesis. Set up some experiments to show which materials rust and the necessary conditions. Can you prevent iron from rusting
under these conditions?

An excellent source of science activities is the series of books for
teachers resulting from the *Science 5/13* project in Britain.[2]

Long-Term Activities

Long-term activities take the shape of individual topics or class
projects.

The Science Topic   In Chapter Seven we discussed individual topics
that children may choose to investigate. Frequently they are in science and
represent particular interests of the students. The manner and depth of exploration depend upon the individual child, his maturity, and the extent of interest in the topic.

There may also be more formal attention to science in the open classroom. Some teachers may expect each student to study a certain number of
science topics in the course of the school year. The number should always
be flexible, permitting more extensive work in some areas than in others.
Topics are chosen by the student from among a number suggested by the
teacher or by the student himself or from commercial kits offering materials
and suggestions for investigating science topics. In some classes teachers
expect the student to submit a "contract" before beginning work on a unit.
(See Chapter Three for information on science kits, suggestions for using a
science-resource box, and other methods of helping students to plan work

---

[2] Science 5/13 was sponsored by the Schools Council, Nuffield Foundation, and Scottish
Education Department and based at the University of Bristol. The books are on general
topics, such as *Working with Wood, Time, Structures and Forces, Science from Toys,*
and one particularly recommended for early primary teachers, *Early Experiences.* These
are published by Macdonald Educational, 49–50 Poland Street, London, W1.

on science topics; see Chapter Four for discussion of contracts.) Students may choose to work on science topics individually or in groups.

The Science Project Another method of introducing science activities is through class projects. The class agrees on a broad science theme, like the human body, to be studied. Work is then organized as in other class projects. Children choose the aspects that they wish to pursue and form appropriate groups. The science project differs from the science topic in that in the former, the entire class is engaged in work on a common theme. There is room for both kinds of science activity in open classes.

LIVING THINGS

An important facet of science in open classrooms is the care and study of living things. Animals, fish, insects, and plants are part of the environment of the class.

Animals in the Classroom

As so many open classes keep animals, a few basic points should be reviewed, especially the many advantages of housing animals:

Training children to accept responsibility for the care of animals.
Engendering respect for other forms of life and understanding of the needs of living things.
Opportunities for first-hand observation of biological processes and animal behavior.
Observing the processes of birth and animals' care of their young, which leads children to broader understanding of these natural processes.
Inspiring work in many subjects—reading, mathematics, writing, art.

Many small mammals make good pets: For example, mice, guinea pigs, rabbits, hamsters, and gerbils. They adapt easily to the classroom environment but must be kept in an area that is not directly in the sunlight, too close to a radiator, or subject to drafts.

It is important that children be instructed in the proper handling of animals. Cages should be cleaned regularly. It is axiomatic that no animal should be kept unless there are proper arrangements for its care and feeding and the teacher can guarantee that it will not be mistreated. When animals are mistreated, they may become frightened and may bite. Local pet shops will generally advise on proper methods of handling each species.

If animals are to be mated, it will be necessary to find out whether they should be placed in the same cage for prolonged periods or only at certain times, how to care for the pregnant female, and finally how to handle the young. Some species may eat their young if the latter are not removed soon after birth.

Activities with Animals   Many activities, spanning various parts of the curriculum, can develop from housing animals: reading to gather information about a species, mathematical calculations, behavioral studies, writing and art. Here are some specific examples:

Measuring and weighing food.

Weighing animals regularly, especially before and after each feeding.

Making charts of the overall dimensions of the animal and of its different parts, comparing growth, calculating proportions between certain parts and total size, and observing placement of eyes and ears.

Observations of animal behavior including "Pavlovian" experiments.

   a. Training an animal to respond to outside stimuli

   b. Observing treatment of young

   c. Observing responses to fear

   d. Observing patterns of sleep, exercise, and feeding

   e. Observing reactions to color

Research on species, encompassing history, characteristics, gestation period, size of litter, and life span.

Animals are weighed regularly and the results carefully recorded. (Photograph courtesy of Merrick Public Schools, New York.)

Other species also offer good opportunities for observations in the classroom: earthworms and insects like praying mantises, ants, moths, and butterflies.

Incubating Chickens   Incubating chickens requires fertilized eggs, an incubator, and a brooder. Local 4-H clubs can supply information on sources of fertilized eggs and incubators, as well as directions for making incubators and brooders. Agricultural colleges are another source of such information.

Fertilized eggs require twenty-one days to hatch. During that period some eggs can be broken open to reveal the different stages in the development of the embryo, so that children can see how the chick evolves from a single cell: formation of different organs, changes in weight and shape, and the eventual hatching of the live chick.

Watching chickens hatch is an absorbing experience for children and can stimulate many specific interests. One class in a suburban school was motivated to build a pen and to keep chickens. The children became interested in chickens as a species: life cycle, habits, method of fertilization, and behavior in hatching eggs. The class sold eggs, raised and sold chicks, recorded weight and other measurements, and used eggs shells to make mosaics. By using bits of shell painted different colors they were able to create striking designs.

Aquariums in the Classroom   Classroom aquariums can vary in size from small ones, each housing a few guppies, to large commercial tanks for tropical fish. The small ones offer a good beginning and have the added advantage of making it possible for individual children, or a few together, to keep their own. They also permit comparisons among the various aquariums.

Almost any size jar will do, preferably one larger than a half-gallon in capacity. The jar should be washed and rinsed carefully and a layer of clean sand added; if the sand is taken from a beach or sandpile it should be washed thoroughly. The jar should be filled about half or two-thirds full of water and allowed to stand for about forty-eight hours so that the chlorine will evaporate. A few water plants can then be set into the sand, with pebbles to help hold them in place. Finally, the fish may be added; a pair of guppies, male and female, is inexpensive and multiplies rapidly. A few snails may be added to help keep the water clean. It is important not to feed the fish too much; a pinch of food every few days is sufficient.

Children should be encouraged to compare what happens in the various jars. Those placed in the sun may develop a green color caused by the growth of algae. The water in some may develop an odor, probably as a result of feeding the fish too much. Guppies produce about fifty young every four to six weeks, but they will eat their young. Children should observe their behavior; they may then decide to separate the adult fish from the young. Children will also want to chart other aspects of the guppies' behavior and may devise comparative studies of their own.

Plants in the Classroom

A popular means of observing plants in the classroom is by growing them in a terrarium—a miniature garden in a container. Almost any glass container will do. A layer of crushed charcoal should be placed on the bottom of the container. If a jar is used, it should be placed on its side to provide a larger planting area; a wooden base may have to be constructed to prevent the jar from rolling. Potting soil should be added to a depth of about two inches. Then small plants like ivy, philodendron, mosses, and ferns can be planted. They should be watered immediately.

If the terrarium is sealed it should not be necessary to add water again, as water will evaporate and then condense, "raining" on the plants. Some worms or small animals can be included in the terrarium. Several small terrariums can be prepared so that children can chart their own observations and plan comparative investigations.

A number of other activities can be planned around growing plants in the classroom. Children may sprout seeds or beans on moist blotting paper and examine their structures. They may plant seeds and compare different factors in their growth. They may note the effects of different conditions—light, darkness, moisture, heat, cold—and calculate the rates of growth of various plants. They may observe parts of a plant, noting the functions of each, and may discover that some plants reproduce without forming seeds. They can also learn to distinguish among different plants.

Not the least of what children learn from living plants is an appreciation of their role in the cycle of life. In some schools small plots of ground can be used for gardening. Planning and tending a garden will prove a valuable learning experience for many children.

Studying living things is particularly relevant in open classrooms because such study can be dynamic and exciting. Open classrooms illustrate Jerome Bruner's notion that children should be taught not "about" a subject but the subject itself. Science in open classrooms is taught as Bruner would have subjects taught—not to "spectators but to participants."[3]

[3] Jerome Bruner, "The Skill of Relevance and the Relevance of Skills," *Saturday Review* (April 18, 1970), p. 66.

Chapter
TEN
Reading

"Reading is said to be a thorn in the flesh of practically every primary head," concluded a *London Times* survey of London primary schools, indicating that concern about reading is not confined to the United States or to traditional schools. In fact, educators throughout the world have had to cope with reading problems. In the United States school officials are well aware that schools are frequently evaluated solely by their pupils' reading scores.

The impact of reading achievement on an individual student is formidable. His reading score may determine his class placement, his success or failure in school, and his status with teachers, peers, or sometimes even parents. Difficulty in learning to read may lead to serious emotional problems that can affect the child's entire life. No area of school work is so directly related to a child's self-concept.

Because of the damage inflicted on children who are deficient in reading skills, some educators question whether or not such great emphasis on reading in schools is justified. They even challenge the assumption that reading is a necessary skill in our society. Neil Postman has suggested that the development of electronic media has made it possible to evolve a definition of "literacy" different from one based on the printed page alone. He has argued that television cameras, films, computers, audio and video tape, radio, and still cameras might be substituted for textbooks to aid students in achieving "multimedia literacy." To the claim that a high level of reading ability is a precondition for success in adult vocational life, Postman replies, "The number of jobs that require reading skill much beyond what teachers call a 'fifth-grade level' is probably small and scarcely justifies the massive compulsory, unrelenting reading programs that characterize most schools."[1]

[1] Neil Postman, "The Politics of Reading," *Harvard Educational Review*, 40, No. 2 (May 1970), p. 246.

Another group of educators believes that reading literacy is important but suggests that *instruction* in reading should be delayed and is for the most part unnecessary. It is this group's claim that "reading is caught not taught" and that teaching it has been disproportionately stressed in schools. It believes that learning to read is "natural," that many reading problems arise not from lack of emphasis on teaching reading but from overemphasis. These educators suggest that, if children are exposed to a rich environment, including attractive books, opportunities to express their ideas, freedom to read when they wish, and some instruction when they request it, they will naturally want to read and will therefore learn to read.

Despite arguments like the preceding ones, most open educators do believe that reading instruction in our schools is essential and that in our society those who fail to achieve reading proficiency are severely handicapped. They may suspect the reliability of measures of proficiency and may argue that the price exacted for low achievement according to those measures is indefensible or that some teaching methods are inadequate. But open educators do insist on careful attention to the teaching of reading in their schools. They too are concerned about the massive failure in reading characteristic of many children in our schools; they seek means to eliminate it. Although no one can promise that every child in an open classroom will learn to read at a prescribed level, teachers can create an atmosphere that precludes the sense of personal failure surrounding many children in conventional schools who have reading difficulties and that becomes increasingly self-defeating for those children.

A CRITICAL LOOK AT SOME CONVENTIONAL APPROACHES

The most common method of teaching reading in elementary schools is to assign a basal reader and to require the class to read it, story by story, while keeping up with corresponding workbook pages. The whole class may read the same book or be grouped by ability and assigned two or three different books. The children read both orally and silently, often in groups. Oral reading frequently takes the form of a "round robin," each child reading a few sentences or a page in turn while the rest of the group follows along. Instruction in silent reading may consist of the teacher requesting children to read a designated portion of the story. That is then dissected, frequently paragraph by paragraph, as the teacher checks "comprehension." Some children have learned to read with an eye to anticipating the questions that they will be asked. The entire process has a mechanical aspect that is not conducive to pleasure in reading.

For teachers who wish to supplant or supplement the basal readers, there is an ever-growing profusion of available materials, supposedly designed to teach different skills. It is difficult for a teacher to decide which of them to use. One problem is that the merit of a reading program is generally determined by how well children score on achievement tests after using its materials. It is therefore advantageous for publishers to pattern reading materials after the skills measured on reading-achievement tests. These tests are unrelated to the world of books; they usually consist of lists of words to be defined and short, discrete selections followed by questions to test comprehension. The questions are focused on narrow details of the selection, for the answers must be stated in single words or short phrases. Many reading materials follow this format too. Children work on isolated vocabulary exercises or short paragraphs for practice in comprehension.

The point is that all these conventional reading materials, though not by themselves either good or bad, frequently constitute the entire reading program of the class. Reading *literature,* that is, complete books, may be relegated to a library period once a week. Open educators would agree with Charles F. Reasoner, who has remarked that it is "discomforting to hear teachers refer to literature for children as *supplementary* reading, something which children can enjoy not for its own sake, but for the sake of a unit."[2]

A result of this approach is that children often view reading as a displeasurable school task, and do not indulge in it after school hours unless required to do so; they turn to other media for relaxation. It is possible that, if popular music were taught in school in the same manner that reading is —short selections analyzed and used as the basis for tests—the billion-dollar record industry might quickly collapse.

READING IN OPEN CLASSROOMS

Reading instruction in open classes may superficially resemble that in many traditional classes. Some of the same materials may be used: basal texts, library books, skill books, reading cards, and the like. The children may read individually or in groups, but there are some important differences in the reading programs of open classes:

Reading is more closely integrated with other means of communication: listening, speaking, and writing.

There is provision for selection of reading materials by the children themselves.

Scheduling of the reading period is flexible, so that children may read at different hours and for varying lengths of time.

[2] Charles F. Reasoner, *Where the Readers Are* (Dell, 1972), pp. 8–9.

There is more uniform emphasis on an individualized reading program.

Reading groups are rarely fixed.

There is less emphasis on graded standards of achievement—for example, less pressure on the six-year-old to read if he is not ready and more acceptance of the five-year-old who is already reading.

Reading is viewed less as a series of exercises and more as an activity with a purpose: enjoyment, reference, discovering information. Emphasis on content is greater, in order to interest each child in the material that he is reading.

Various kinds of reading matter, including poetry, literature, and informational materials are considered a valid part of the reading program.

Teachers accept as goals of instruction the establishment of an appreciation of reading and of the habit of reading independently.

These differences can be illustrated by analysis of reading instruction in open classrooms at three different points in the child's development: reading readiness, beginning reading, and "developmental reading."

Reading Readiness

There is no single age at which all children are automatically ready to read. Although this fact has been widely acknowledged, many traditional schools still seem to expect all children to be ready to begin formal reading instruction in the first grade. The effect on the child who cannot comply with this timetable is often tragic. All about him children may be successfully reading books, having negotiated their rites of passage into "real" school, while to him a page of type remains mysterious and frustrating. No matter how sensitive the teacher is, it is difficult for her to prevent a child from suffering the trauma of being a nonreader in a traditional class.

In an open classroom in which no common curriculum is prescribed for all, children are more relaxed about beginning reading. All of them are not expected to start reading the same book at the same time, and many additional readiness activities are available for those children who require a slower start. It has been noted that the child in an open classroom is less exposed, less "pegged." This point is significant in connection with beginning reading. A child who requires a longer "readiness period" is not in the unenviable position of being left out when most of the other class members receive their copies of the first hard-cover reader—as may well happen in a more traditional class. In the absence of this kind of social pressure, there can be more consideration for his individual style and pace of learning.

The reading readiness activities in open classrooms may include many that are also used by teachers in traditional classrooms. There are some however which arise from the environment of the open class. Reading readiness is related to language development. A child who has had little exposure to speech will encounter difficulty in reading. Many aspects of the open classroom facilitate language development: freedom to talk with other children, play, classroom discussions, dialogues between teacher and child, making and listening to tape recordings. In fact, the entire organization of an open classroom, with its provision for interaction among members of the class, is designed to encourage practice in the use of language: a particularly crucial aspect of reading readiness for those children who reach school with limited vocabularies.

Books without words are also used for language development. Children are given books that contain only "pictures"; they are to supply the stories themselves. Many such books are available, but even more valuable are picture books made by the teacher or the class. The teacher may take a series of photographs of the class engaged in an activity or of children acting out a story. Props can be used to stimulate these skits. For example, in one first-year class a teacher used a broken doll as a stimulus. The children were encouraged to create short stories about the doll. Some chose events preceding the discovery of the doll, others proceeding from it. Groups were encouraged to act out their stories, which were photographed and made part of a book. The children then "read" the books to the class. Others chose to tape-record their "scripts."

Children may be encouraged to cut out pictures from magazines, to arrange them in story sequences, and then to "read" the stories to the class. Preparation of movies and film strips is another technique for facilitating language development and "sequencing," both of which are essential to reading readiness. These activities can be inspired by a television program, a story that the class has heard, or a wholly original story. (See instructions for making films and film strips in Chapter Three.)

Another aspect of language development is hearing the spoken word. For this reason, in addition to engaging in conversations, teachers read to children regularly and provide opportunities for older children or volunteers to read to smaller groups of children during the school day. Children are urged to handle books, and they often "reread" their favorite books themselves, turning pages and repeating some of the words from memory. In the process they are establishing left-to-right progression and beginning to distinguish a few words.

Listening includes a heightened awareness of sound. Children may listen to music and to tapes. In one school the teacher taped a special story each week, which children could enjoy whenever they wished. Sometimes a tape was coordinated with an actual book, which the children followed as they listened. Musical instruments can be constructed and played, to arouse an awareness of pitch. Children are encouraged to listen to sounds: the

Children listen to a story taped by the teacher. (Photograph courtesy of Merrick Public Schools, New York.)

clock's ticking, water running, coins jingling. They begin to discriminate among the sounds of different words or letters.

Readiness for reading also requires ability to distinguish between certain pairs of concepts—right and left, big and small, before and after, and similarity and differences—as well as perceptual skills and ability to classify materials. For this reason many concrete materials must be available for children to sort and rearrange. Activities that help to establish motor control, coordination, and body awareness are appropriate. Folding, cutting, pasting, solving puzzles, weaving, sewing, making pegboard designs, bead stringing, woodwork, tracing, and physical exercises are a few such activities. Children can make jigsaw puzzles themselves by either drawing or mounting cutouts on cardboard; irregular lines are drawn on the back of the cardboard and the picture cut along these lines.

Readiness also requires exposure to varied experiences, by means of both materials and people in the classroom and through trips into the "larger environment." There can be walking trips in the vicinity of the school or longer bus trips. Reactions to the trips may be discussed: Writing stories summarizing them provides further experience with relations between language and words.

The classrooms of young children should furnish constant exposure to words. Although most teachers of "prereaders" do label the door, closet, sink, and so on, it is more helpful to write these labels in sentence form:

"This is a door"; "This is a closet. We put coats here"; "This is a sink. We wash here." Using the children's names in signs not only develops reading vocabulary but also "personalizes" the room. For example: "This shelf is for John, Paul, Brian"; "Molly painted this tree." Necessary information should be written so that a child is motivated to read. The lunch menu or directions ("Please put the scissors here") may be posted.

Children should be helped to become familiar with letters of the alphabet and simple words. Many experiences are used: play with alphabetical letters (for example, matching lower-case and capital letters), cutting out letters and words, tracing letters that the teacher has written on paper or on the board. Children can make letters in sand or dough, perhaps baking cookies in those shapes. They will learn to identify letters by touch: on sandpaper or in sand, salt, or sugar poured on a flat tin. They can even create letters from jello by writing the outlines in mucilage and pouring dry jello powder on them.

The relation between letter and sound can also be established through readiness activities. Children can cut pictures from magazines to fill folders with words that begin with similar sounds. Sound boxes can be established for objects whose names begin with the same consonants: for example, pen, pencil, pit, popcorn, peanut.

Some games help to develop auditory discrimination. "I Spy" is one example. The teacher places some objects on a table. He and the children then take turns saying, "I spy something that begins with a _____." The other children must then point to the appropriate object. After a while they may be able to point to any object in the room that starts with the specified letter.

Some children enjoy writing jingles together:

> I found the bug
> It was on the _____. (rug)
> Run to the hall
> Find your _____. (ball)

Other children supply the missing words and also invent their own. Some set jingles to music, using familiar tunes or composing their own.

There are also activities for first writing experiences. Children learn to write their names, to label colors and objects, and to recognize other children's names, identifying which ones begin with the same letters.

Beginning Reading

There is no clear-cut point at which developing readiness for reading terminates and actual reading instruction begins. The child may continue to require some readiness exercises and may only gradually indicate that he is able to identify some written words. A bridge between readiness activities and early reading can frequently be constructed through creation of a series of books by the child himself. This method is very popular in British informal schools, and these books constitute the child's "beginning readers." Each child is given a small notebook with about twenty blank pages. Each day he draws a picture in it and is encouraged to tell the teacher about it. The teacher helps him learn to communicate his thoughts by listening to his descriptions and discussing his book with him. His first book may have only pictures and no words. In his second book he dictates to the teacher a short sentence to accompany each picture. The teacher writes the child's exact words under the picture: for example, "This is my dog, Rover." The child is then encouraged to copy the words himself, either tracing the teacher's writing or repeating it underneath. Some children will write each sentence a few times. The next day each child again draws a picture, but this time the teacher asks him to read what he has previously written and then to dictate another sentence to be written in the book by the teacher. This procedure helps the child to build a core vocabulary. It is important that the teacher use the child's exact words. If the child says "Here am mommy," the teacher writes that sentence, because that is what the child "reads" as he copies it.

After a while the teacher puts some of the words in the child's book on cards and asks him to read and match them to the writing on the pages. Eventually the child will be able to write parts of the picture captions himself, coming to the teacher only for a word or two. The goal is to enable the child to read and write sentences in conjunction with his drawings.

Four steps are involved: tracing the dictated words written by the teacher, copying the words below the teacher's writing, matching cards to written words, and finally writing sentences alone. Although the first sentence written in the notebook may be quite short and easy to read, Doris Nash, headmistress of a school in Bristol, England, insists that it is an "insult" to children if teachers insist on translating their thoughts into redundant, simple sentences. In her school young children develop quite impressive language facility through dictating and eventually writing long passages of descriptive prose.

The child's books may also express his feelings or responses to nature, rather than merely describing his drawings. An incident, a leaf, a picture, or an animal may evoke from the child a statement that he may wish to incorporate in his book. When the child is personally interested in the contents of his "beginning readers," the words become easier for him to read and comprehend. For this reason provision should be made for children to build their own vocabularies, which they will want to use in their writing. One child's vocabulary may include "astronaut" and "president," that of another "school" and "teacher," and that of still another "robber" and "police." Each child may keep track of such words in an envelope, box, folder, or notebook.

The child may also dictate stories. When a typewriter is available, a volunteer or aide can record the child's dictation. This procedure helps children to organize their ideas and to make them more aware of the relation between printed and spoken words. Frequently, a child may choose a story to be reproduced for the rest of the class. A collection of children's early stories can become part of the class library.

Another activity involving writing and drawing is slightly different. The teacher writes a phrase in a child's notebook, perhaps "This is a tree with green leaves." The child copies the phrase and illustrates it. The teacher continues to write phrases, encouraging the child to read and illustrate them and reinforcing his basic vocabulary until he is ready to write his own sentences.

The integration of writing and reading in beginning reading instruction is typical of many open classrooms. Donald Moyle has noted the relation between writing and reading: "Writing is undoubtedly the best training for left-right orientation in reading."[3] He has also suggested that writing helps children to recognize familiar words in different contexts, thus consolidating their learning of vocabulary words by sight.

In Great Britain a fairly new reading scheme called Breakthrough to Literacy[4] links writing with beginning reading completely. Children in the initial stages of reading are supplied with "sentence makers," which include common words on cards, blank cards for additional words, a folder to store the cards, and a plastic stand. They first learn the words on the cards and then construct sentences on the stand. The sentences are read to the teacher and finally copied into a notebook. This notebook becomes the child's first reader.

Teachers in some open classrooms may use basal readers for beginning reading instruction. Those who do frequently attempt to introduce characters from the early books as "living people." The child plays with cutouts of these characters and matches names to them. Cardboard figures can be obtained from publishers or made by teachers and children. Before the book is actually given to a child the words used in the first stories are put on cards, and the child is helped to arrange them in sentences and to read them. The goal is to prepare the child for success when he is actually presented with a printed page. Flash cards and games help to reinforce his vocabulary.

Class or group experience charts have their uses too. Several children who have shared an activity—for example, baking cookies or building a

---

[3] Donald Moyle, *The Teaching of Reading* (London: Ward Lock, 1968), p. 136.
[4] Breakthrough to Literacy is the work of the Initial Literacy Project of the Programme in Linguistics and English Teaching at University College, London.

fort—should be encouraged to record their experiences with the aid of the teacher. These records, too, should at first be in the children's own words, and each participant expressly credited: "Mary said, 'It is raining today.' Jim said, 'I got all wet coming to school.' "

The teacher also writes personal notes to children, commenting on pieces that they have written or other work. The following intriguing interchange was found in the notebook of one six-year-old in a London classroom; the child had written a story about his Uncle Dave. Underneath it the teacher had written, "Is that the Uncle Dave who lives on the moon?" The child had replied in writing, "No, it is not."

The important point about beginning reading instruction in open classrooms is that it can include many kinds of activities in which children can participate without feeling inadequate if they are not ready for printed books. The teacher respects each child's pattern of growth and guards against uniform expectations. Her lack of anxiety and her confidence in each child are communicated and help to prevent development of many blocks. Obviously, the teacher does not ignore the child or simply wait for reading to "catch on." She is aware of the child's interests, his style of learning, and the materials with which he seems to have most success. Some children may benefit from general books, others from more structured basal textbooks, some from language-experience activities, and others from programmed linguistic series. The teacher is responsible for being familiar with available materials and assisting children to find those that will enable them to achieve success.

Developmental Reading

Goals of Reading Instruction   Once children have mastered the beginning stages of reading, the goals of reading instruction are two: to develop each child's ability to decode printed words into meaningful symbols and to develop an appreciation of reading. Both rest on the assumption that reading without understanding is insufficient. It is possible to teach children to read isolated words, but isolated words can be said to have the same relation to reading as have a few fallen leaves to the whole tree. Words must be decoded as parts of statements of meaning to constitute reading.

It is possible for comprehension exercises to ignore meaning. As an extreme example, a child can be asked to read a few sentences and then to answer some comprehension questions:

John was a *dunt*.
He liked to eat *patz*.
He only ate this at *miltz* time.

What was John?
What did he like to eat?
When did he eat this?

It would not be difficult to score 100 percent on "comprehension" of this exercise.

Reading with understanding requires that the child be able to relate to the words encountered. It therefore necessitates continued vocabulary development, exposure to varied reading experiences, and concept formation. E. Brooks Smith, Kenneth S. Goodman, and Robert Meredith have stressed these requirements in relation to reading readiness, but they are equally important at all stages of reading instruction. These authors have noted: "Particular attention must be given to concept development. Teachers need to assure themselves that children have sufficient background to deal with the new concepts that they will encounter in reading." They have called attention to the need to "verbalize the concept," in order to ensure that the child "acquires the language to express" it.[5] In this sense, the many opportunities for discussion and the rich variety of experiences provided in open classrooms are an integral part of reading instruction.

An appreciation of reading was posed as a goal of the reading program of open classrooms. There are two aspects of reading appreciation: purpose and pleasure. Appreciating its purpose implies recognition that there is information available in print that is not obtainable elsewhere and development of the habit of turning to printed material for such information. Successful training in these points of view ensure that reading will become part of a child's life in and out of school.

One method of fostering an appreciation of reading is to permit children to select reading material for themselves. The classroom should contain books on many subjects, both fiction and nonfiction, from among which a child may select. Rarely does the teacher regard particular books or exercises as necessary for all children. A child who reads books in pursuit of an interest, whether in science or in history, may consider these books part of his reading curriculum, as may the child who is on a spree of sports stories. The teacher helps a child to expand his interests in literature gradually, but she respects the child's choices and does not press him to balance his reading over a short period of time.

Materials for Reading Instruction There is no single preferred method of reading instruction in open classrooms, nor are there preferred materials. Teachers in open classrooms may use basal readers, paperback books, library books, reading kits, skill texts or a combination of all these materials and many others.

[5] E. Brooks Smith, Kenneth S. Goodman, and Robert Meredith, *Language and Thinking in the Elementary School* (New York: Holt, Rinehart and Winston, 1970), p. 277.

An appreciation for reading is encouraged by providing many reading areas in the classroom. (Photograph courtesy of Columbus School, New Rochelle Public Schools, New York.)

Basal readers may be preferred by teachers who find security in their sequential structures or feel that they have value as anthologies of short stories. When these readers are used in open classrooms, however, teachers are much less concerned that children read the stories in sequence. Rarely do they insist that each child read the same number of pages every day. Recognizing that some children have difficulty in finishing one story and that others can easily read more than one, teachers usually permit children to read as many pages as they wish. A weekly minimum may be established if it seems necessary. In some classes, children are permitted to choose stories from different basal readers. The stories that a child has read are discussed with him in reading conferences, just as individual books would be. Occasionally children who have read the same story are called together for a group conference. If the teacher wishes to assign workbook pages, she indicates which are related to each story and expects the child to complete them as he finishes the corresponding story.

Basal readers should never constitute the complete reading program by themselves. They offer only a limited diet of short stories, sometimes written in a uniform style. Children are entitled to more varied reading experiences.

Another problem with basal readers is their size. Children confined to a basal reading series for an entire year may actually read no more than two books in that year. They miss the sense of accomplishment in completing book after book. We note that the graded reading scheme most common in Great Britain is Ladybird, which consists of three parallel sets of twelve graded readers for ages five to nine. Each of the books measures 4½ by 6 inches and contains twenty to twenty-five pages of copy.[6]

The increased availability of paperback books is a boon to teachers, enabling them to establish classroom libraries fairly inexpensively. A recent study of fifth-grade children who were permitted to select books from among both paper and hard-cover books found that children preferred the former, associating them with "enjoyment" and finding them "shorter and easier to understand."[7] Because of their comparatively low cost, paperbacks offer a means of enlarging the choice of reading materials available in the classroom. It is essential that teachers who rely on individual books for their reading programs provide selections that are broad both in difficulty and in interest—and also that they furnish multiple copies of some titles so that children can read books together if they wish or discusss books with others who are reading them concurrently. There are several good sources of paperbacks for the classroom. Some individualized commercial reading kits include them. Books clubs offer paperbacks to students at low cost and often provide free books for the class when a certain number have been purchased. A class library can be built from these books and from books that individual students have bought and are prepared to exchange for others.

Class libraries can be further supplemented with books borrowed both from school and public libraries and even with donations. One group of classes sharing a common hall used it for a special library of donated books. Children were free to borrow these books, to take them home, and to return them—without any restrictions. No one was on duty, no sign-out procedures were required, and there was unlimited access to the books. It was hoped that this library would encourage children to read books at home, and it was most successful. The number of books "lost" was more than offset by the additional books that were constantly being received.

Reading kits such as S.R.A. (published by Science Research Associates, Inc.) may also be part of the reading program. Skill texts are used selectively by individual children who require the particular exercises.

Interest in reading can often be stimulated by provision of many different kinds of materials in addition to those described above:

Cartoons
Radio and television schedules

[6] The Ladybird Key Words Reading Scheme (Wills & Hepworth, Loughborough, Eng.).
[7] Beverly S. Sirota, "The Effect of a Planned Literature Program of Daily Oral Reading by the Teacher on the Voluntary Reading of Fifth Grade Children" (Unpublished doctoral dissertation, New York University School of Education, 1971).

Sports scores
Newspapers and magazines
Catalogues
Pamphlets
Instructions for making and playing games
Jokes books
Recipes
Maps
Charts
Puzzles
Letters
Song sheets

These are frequently kept in the reading corner.

Grouping for Reading Instruction Children may be grouped for reading or read individually. Usually there will be instances of each in open classrooms. However, the rigid groups that often form the basis for reading instruction in traditional classes are rarely found in open classes. Such groups tend to impose a common reading pattern on all members of each group and often create a classroom hierarchy based on membership in specific groups.

In contrast, reading groups that do exist in open classrooms tend to be flexible and to have varied purposes. For example, a teacher may call particular children together for instruction in a specific skill. They remain together as long as they have similar needs. The composition of the group changes as some master the skill and leave the group and as others join it. A group may also be formed on the basis of interest: for example, in reading biographies. Another group may meet because its members are reading the same story or book and wish to discuss it among themselves. Some stories are rich in ideas and subject to many interpretations. Children will want to share their reactions to such a story with one another, as well as with the teacher.

Oral reading may take place in groups. Children listen to one another read interesting passages or dramatize stories while reading them together. In vertically-grouped classes it is common for older children to read to younger ones or to listen as the younger ones proudly read a few pages. There is rarely a "round robin" of the type encountered in many traditional reading groups however. The usual purposes of round-robin reading are to help a child to develop oral-reading skills and to enable the teacher to assess these skills. Round robins may be a quite inefficient means of accomplishing these purposes. It probably takes no more time to hear children read one at a time than to have them sit about waiting for their turns, particularly when we consider the time lost while the teacher calls upon different children or admonishes others to be quiet and keep their places in the book.

More important, the round robin imposes a reading rate on children that may not be comfortable for all of them.

Individualized Reading The reading program in most open classrooms is individualized. At one time each child may be reading a different book or a different page of the same book. For the most part children select their own reading materials and the pace at which they read them. Many of the reading activities in which they engage are chosen by them, and most skills are taught as they are required for more effective reading. Each child's individual needs are diagnosed and an individual program developed with his participation. Children keep records of their reading and meet with the teacher to discuss it.

Several questions about individualized reading programs can be addressed from the point of view of the teacher in the open classroom.

How can the teacher be sure that a pupil is reading at his level? Actually it is not essential that a child read books at a consistent "level." There will be times when a child enjoys an easy book, others when he seeks the challenge of a more difficult one. There is probably a "frustration point" for some children, when too many unfamiliar words are encountered in a book; to avoid this frustration they can be taught to screen a book by reading one passage before they decide on the book. Publishers grade many books for difficulty.

In some classes teachers have color-coded books as "easy," "medium," or "hard." This coding could have undesirable connotations if the classroom atmosphere were competitive. But in the absence of this element in open classrooms, pupils are usually quite judicious about choosing books that coincide with their reading abilities and moods. There is no stigma in choosing an "easy" book and no credit in choosing a "hard" one. For their part, teachers are aware of each child's choices of books, noting which children may need encouragement to choose either more difficult or easier books or require direction in selecting books.

How can the teacher be sure that the child is learning a basic vocabulary? There really is no one basic vocabulary for any child. Basal readers are written in words most familiar to particular groups of children, but they may not be the words most commonly used by other groups. Even words like "mother" and "father" are not universal and may sound strange to children who use others terms of address for their parents. A child who selects his own reading material undoubtedly acquires a vocabulary that is appropriate for him. If there are words with which he has difficulty, the teacher helps him to learn them.

Does the teacher have to be familiar with the contents of all the books that children read? This notion is much more typical of classes in which teachers must function as all-knowing authority figures. Children in such a class are not permitted to read books unless the teacher has screened them and possibly developed a series of questions to go with them. In open classrooms teachers do not try to be familiar with the contents of every book. They personally read as many as possible, to help them in reviewing and recommending them. As children read and discuss others, teachers will become more familiar with them too. The pupils' knowledge of books can also be used in other ways. If a child is discussing a book unfamiliar to the teacher, another child who has read that book may be invited to join the conference. Other techniques help to eliminate the necessity for teachers' personal familiarity with every book in the classroom. As pupils complete a book, they can write short introductions so that others who wish to read these books can have an idea of their contents. A card file of such introductions can be maintained. If questions about a book seem desirable, they can be composed by students as well as by the teachers.

How can the teacher be sure that children are learning necessary skills in an individualized program? Individualized programs do not rule out instruction in skills. As the teacher observes a pupil's reading, she will note those skills in which he needs practice; frequently she will arrange a period of group instruction for children with common needs. Some open-class teachers have devised skill checklists. Instruction is then geared to these lists. It is desirable but not always possible that a child's training in skills be conducted in conjunction with his actual reading in order that he may recognize the need for the skill and practice its application.

Not all children follow the same pattern of skill development. In fact no single sequence of instruction has been agreed upon. Some series, for example, present long vowels first, and others begin with short vowels. Kenneth Goodman has refuted the notion that there is one defined sequence of skill development, denying that reading "involves exact, detailed, sequential perception and identification of letters, words, spelling patterns and larger language units."[8]

The reading program must include many types of skill instruction. Decoding skills (including phonics) will be taught, along with comprehension (drawing inferences and making generalizations) and research skills (taking notes, outlining, skimming, and summarizing). The last are frequently introduced as they become necessary in research projects.

How can the teacher be sure that the child is really reading a book? The teacher meets with each child regularly, and it becomes fairly clear which children finish their books, and which tend to skim them. Some children may have to be encouraged to choose easier or shorter books. Some may have to have their interest in particular books and "how they come out" aroused. The quality of the anticipated discussion of a book often determines whether or not a child will actually read it. If he is likely to be

[8] Goodman, "Reading: A Psycholinguistic Guessing Game," *Journal of the Reading Specialist* (May 1967), p. 126.

asked only whether or not he liked it and why, the answer "Yes, because it was funny" may suffice for any number of books and may encourage superficial reading. But if the child anticipates a dialogue (either with the teacher or with other children) about some of the ideas in the book, he may be motivated to read it carefully.

The goal is not to produce "quantity" readers. A child who has read one book with real pleasure, who has learned to treasure it and to reread it, may be the more "successful" reader than is the one who has raced through five books. For this reason, competitions—Who Can Read Twenty Books First, Reaching the Moon by Reading, and the like—detract from the pleasure of just reading.

There are many ways in which children can report on books that they have read. They may write reports, plays, "coming attractions," book jackets, questions and summaries; make films, dioramas, puppets, sculpture, collages; paint murals or illustrations; or organize quizzes, using charades or questions. Although there may be room for all these activities in the classroom, we do not expect a child to react to every book that he reads. For example, it is one thing for a child who has just finished reading about Helen Keller to decide to investigate Braille, facilities for blind people, or how seeing-eye dogs are chosen and trained. It is quite another to expect every child who has finished the same book to pursue one of these activities.

Children sometimes have the feeling that they must "pay" for every pleasant school experience. If they go on a field trip, they have to write about it. If they read a book, they have to write a report. If they hear a poem recited, they will be asked to write poems themselves. Reading a story should have an intrinsic value, should be savored for itself, and not necessarily as background for completing workbook pages, comprehension questions, or reports.

An individualized reading program may include basal readers and general books. The child may be expected to read a minimum number of pages from his basal reader weekly and to choose other books as well. Or he may be permitted to choose his reading material freely. Much will depend upon the individual child's pattern, interests, and growth. The teacher will want to be certain that the reading material is contributing to his overall progress in reading. If it does not, the teacher may suggest a more structured program or different types of materials. An individualized reading program does necessitate regular reading conferences with each child.

The Reading Conference   An individual conference is held regularly with each child, in order to assess his reading progress. Appointments for such conferences can be initiated by either teacher or pupil. Pupils should have opportunities to sign up for conferences when they have finished books, need help, or just want to read to the teacher or discuss certain stories. The teacher will also want to schedule conferences with children.

The conference is primarily diagnostic, rather than evaluative. This approach sets the tone. The child is not "marked" on his reading, nor does the teacher choose difficult words out of context and ask him to define them. The teacher is interested in the child's reading behavior: which books he chooses (Do they form a pattern? Are they varied?), whether he is reading superficially or gaining meaning from his reading, and his reactions to material. The teacher notes whether or not the child is growing in ability to read independently and what instruction is necessary to aid him. The conference need not be a teaching period. Skills that the child requires may be noted and later taught to several children with similar needs in a group.

Conferences can include discussion of the meaning derived by the child from a book, to develop concepts; oral reading for diagnosis of reading behavior, building vocabulary, and development of skills; recording of reading progress; suggestions for future work. Not every conference will necessarily incorporate all these elements. Some conferences may be focused on single facets—like discussion or oral reading—but over a period of time all facets will be covered.

In discussing the book, teachers want to know what children are gaining from their reading. Are they drawing inferences, identifying important ideas? Questions about trivial details ("What was the color of the uniforms?") should be avoided. Instead open-ended questions should be posed; for example, "Can you describe someone you know who might have behaved as Karana did?"; "Tell me about a time in which you had an experience similar to Bill's." When asking an open-ended question a teacher should be aware that a child may need a few minutes time to think before he replies. Teachers often ask important questions but then become uncomfortable when children require moments of silence to organize their thoughts. It is also well to realize that the closeness of a conference can be difficult for a child; the shy child may be unable to think freely in such situations. Much depends upon the quality of the relationship between teacher and child. If it is open and trusting, if the child feels accepted and there is mutual respect, then discussion about a book can be a treasured interchange of ideas leading to intellectual growth.

In some conventional classrooms oral reading has been stressed out of all proportion to its value in reading instruction. It is in fact a skill rarely used outside the classroom. When reading instruction focuses on oral reading, it may even lead children to form bad silent-reading habits. It can nevertheless be invaluable, when used selectively in the conference, as a means by which the teacher can diagnose a child's reading progress.

Aaron Lipton has observed that the manner in which a child reads aloud is an indication to the teacher of his feelings about reading:

> Some children read rapidly, without feeling, omitting words, substituting words and generally rushing through their material. They may be saying, "I don't really want to do this, but I will, and try to get over with it as

fast as I can." They may say this because they are either afraid to fail, bored with the material, or just not in touch with the feelings the author has tried to set down in print. Other children may read word by word, hesitatingly and in a staccato manner. . . . Still others may read with feeling, and with reasonably accurate perception. . . .[9]

In each instance the child reveals through his reading behavior how he feels about reading. This attitude, as well as the specific skills that the child uses in his reading, is what the sensitive teacher seeks to discover. The teacher will also note what cues the child uses in reading words. Are they phonic or contextual? What kinds of errors does he makes? Does he substitute words for those in the text? Do the substituted words change the syntactical structure of the passage? Do they change the meaning? Each of these cues tells us something about the child's reading pattern. It is through careful attention to his oral reading that the teacher can assess his needs.

As he listens to the child read, the teacher may wish to check his comprehension of some of the vocabulary. The authors of some individualized reading programs recommend that each child keep a dictionary on his desk or jot down unfamiliar words as he reads. This requirement could easily slow the child's reading and interfere with another important reading skill: learning to grasp unfamiliar words from their contexts. Occasionally a child may wish to stop reading to seek the definition of a word that is essential to the meaning of the passage—or he may even make note of a particular word. But the goal of reading instruction is not to force the child to shift back and forth constantly from the reader to the dictionary. Such work is appropriate to a dictionary exercise and not to a reading experience. For this reason, when the teacher discusses certain words with the child, in order to check his comprehension, she chooses words that are basic to an understanding of the story and permits the child to read them in context as he defines them.

Records are kept by both teacher and child. The child lists the books that he has read, the dates during which he has read them, and any comments that interest him (including vocabulary words). The teacher records details about the child's reading, diagnoses, and any assignments scheduled. All the records may be combined in a reading folder. (Specific suggestions for reading records are included in Chapter Five.)

As a result of the conference the teacher may suggest specific exercises for practice in skills or may recommend specific books for the child to read. Children are not expected to be familiar with the contents of all the books available to them. For this reason, free selection by a pupil should not be accompanied by benign neglect from the teacher. Books should be discussed both with individual children and with the entire class; they

[9] Aaron Lipton, *Reading: A Psycholinguistic, Psychodynamic Point of View* (New York: Bellwether, 1972), p. 6.

should be recommended or assigned to children when appropriate. Frequently the teacher will suggest that a few children read the same story so that they may discuss it or pursue a common follow-up activity.

Phonics in the Reading Program   Many children benefit from a consistent program of phonic instruction, which does have a place in the open classroom. Phonics are less apt to be taught as an isolated skill in such a classroom. Nonsense words, for example, or words that have no meaning for the child should be avoided. Phonic instruction should, whenever possible, be tied to the child's vocabulary and reading material. For this reason, teachers in many open classrooms institute instruction in phonics only after children have acquired some verbal recognition of vocabulary.

Although the value of phonic instruction has been established and children should receive such instruction, too much reliance on phonics may discriminate against those who have problems learning in this manner. Some children have difficulty in distinguishing sounds, or their dialect patterns do not match those used in standard phonic material. To drill these students on short-vowel sounds, for example, year after year seems a waste of time.· The sensitive teacher recognizes this, and that there is no single way of teaching reading. There are several "cues" that a child uses to derive meaning from print: phonetic cues, structural analysis, and configuration of words; syntactical and contextual cues like the positions of words in sentences and the contexts in which they are used; experiential cues, drawn from the child's own background, and concepts that enable him to interpret specific material.

Viewed from this perspective, phonics provides but one approach to teaching reading. The teacher will help a child to use a number of cues as he searches for meaning in his reading.

Games   Games are particularly useful in practicing word recognition and reinforcing phonic skills. Some games provide practice in reading and following directions. Whenever possible written instructions should accompany each game; they may have to be rewritten by the teacher so that children can read them independently. Although innumerable commercial games like Scrabble, anagrams, bingo, and kits for all kinds of phonic skills are available, teachers and pupils can easily devise their own. Children should be encouraged to do so.

Fun with Language

In an environment in which language is rich, words have a fascination in themselves. Children become interested in the origins of words, strange and unusual words, long words, short words, and word games. This interest should be encouraged. In addition to the etymology of words, children will be interested in biographies of people whose names have become the basis for new expressions—as in Pasteur and "pasteurization," Hippocrates and "Hippocratic oath," and Hobson and "Hobson's choice." Some children will want to investigate new words that have been added to dictionaries only in the last decade. They will be intrigued by palindromes, words or phrases that read the same backward and forward: "madam," "radar," "mom," "sis," "pup," "a man, a plan, a canal, Panama," "Madam, I'm Adam," and so on. Other children will compose and discover new palindromes or search for words that make other words when read backward: "stop" ("pots"), "keep" ("peek"), "ton" ("not").

Children can also write "Tom Swifties." Tom Swift is the hero of a series of stories, by Burt L. Standish, in which adverbs are used freely. In a "Tom Swifty" the adverb is shifted to another word in the sentence to make a play on words. Here are some examples composed by sixth-grade youngsters: " 'I'm going to measure the room,' he said squarely"; " 'Please pass the sugar,' she said sweetly"; " 'I have no jacket,' she said coldly."

Crossword puzzles, Double-Crostics, and cryptograms can also be constructed by students. They will enjoy unscrambling words or messages like "pahyp yabihrtd" ("happy birthday") and attempting to make as many words as possible from the letters in a word like "mathematics." These puzzles can be posed by teacher or children on the bulletin board every morning, just for fun.

Other activities related to reading involve cutting words or cartoons from magazines. These clippings are then placed in a box, and children paste them on paper to construct messages. Newspaper comic strips (like *Peanuts* by Charles Schulz) can be cut out without their texts; then children can write their own words to go with the pictures.

Secret codes offer practice in reading and spelling. Some, like the one in Figure 10.1, are also useful in reinforcing visual perception. The message is spelled out in the shapes shown in the key; the presence or absence of a dot indicates which of two letters associated with a given shape is intended. Older children will enjoy this one as much as younger ones do.

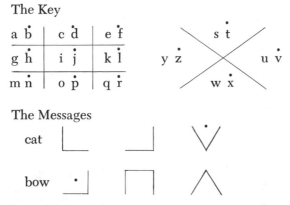

Figure 10.1   A Secret Code

The language activities outlined here should not be treated as isolated tasks; rather, they should help children to become familiar with the English language, its structure and patterns. Language should be presented as a rich resource for imaginative expression in both speech and writing. Children should be helped to become sensitive to the beauty of a picture painted in words; frequently they will respond with a special interest in writing. This phase of the curriculum in the open classroom is discussed in Chapter Eleven.

Chapter
ELEVEN
Writing

One of the most dramatic differences between traditional and open classes is the quality and profusion of children's writing in the latter. The Plowden committee recognized this difference when it visited informal schools in England. In its report the committee commented on the "revolution" in the "amount and quality of children's writing."[1] The same situation is readily observable in open classrooms in the United States.

In the open classroom writing is viewed as an extension of spoken language; just as children are encouraged to communicate freely through speech, they are also encouraged to express their thoughts freely and often in writing. A consciousness of language, a sensitivity to the richness of ideas that can be conveyed by words is developed. Writing becomes a natural way of indicating and responding to sensations and feelings, a means of communicating personal thoughts and of recording significant information. The result of this emphasis on writing is that even very young children produce imaginative pieces of poetry and prose in open classrooms.

Writing is also integrated with every other area of the curriculum. We have already noted that much early reading is taught in conjunction with writing, but so are many other subjects. Spelling, for example, is often taught through writing. Rather than expecting a child to memorize lists of words, the teacher selects a few words that he has misspelled in his writing and makes them the basis of his spelling curriculum. Instruction in English grammar and punctuation is also frequently coordinated with writing. Rather than offering formal grammar lessons in which parts of speech are defined and punctuation skills introduced, teachers in open classrooms teach these skills as the need for them arises in a child's writing.

[1] Lady Bridget Plowden, *et al.*, *Children and Their Primary Schools*, I (London: H.M. Stationery Office, 1967), p. 218.

Handwriting—manuscript, or cursive, writing—is also developed in the course of "functional" writing. Copying paragraphs from the blackboard for handwriting practice is rare. Children may be shown how to form certain letters of the alphabet in this way, but basic handwriting practice occurs as children engage in meaningful writing.

A child in an open classroom may spend a major portion of his day writing. He may write his "readers," keep a diary, compose a poem or story, record some scientific observations. He may also write in conjunction with many other activities. For example, when he bakes, he is urged to record recipes and procedures. When he completes a construction, he may prepare a written statement about it. Writing accompanies his work on topics and projects and on mathematics.

Children write letters. They compose greeting cards and set words to music. They may participate in publishing a class newspaper or magazine in connection with which they may interview people in the school or neighborhood. Much of their writing is a source of personal pride and is frequently carefully illustrated.

Children and teachers who view writing as an extension of speech also communicate through written messages. We have noted that teachers and children may exchange personal notes. A teacher may write a comment about a child's work or suggest a resource. The child may reply in writing, or may simply send a message about an incident that he wishes to share with the teacher. There is a special satisfaction in organizing thoughts on paper and in the personal interaction between student and teacher that results from an exchange of private notes. Some students can express their emotions more freely in writing than in direct speech. Once children have become accustomed to writing, they will require little encouragement to start. In the beginning, however, certain techniques for stimulating prose and poetry writing may prove helpful.

STIMULATING PROSE WRITING

Children in open schools often keep series of writing notebooks. Some serve as diaries, others are for pieces of creative writing. Some children may start the day by writing in their diaries; entries may vary from a few words to a detailed account of an experience on the previous day. Frequently children use this forum to enter reactions to television programs or sports events. One London headmistress who encourages daily diary entries explained: "Every child comes to school eager to talk to the teacher, to share an experience. The teacher cannot listen to each child, so instead we encourage him to write it down. In that manner he is still receiving individual attention from the teacher." She added, "And if he has a great deal to say, we don't rush him."

The creative-writing notebooks can be used in different ways. They may be viewed as collections of special original pieces—selections of poetry or prose that the child especially treasures—which have been corrected before being copied into them. Or they may contain uncorrected daily work. Some children enjoy keeping writers' notebooks, in which they enter their thoughts, phrases that intrigue them, or descriptive passages. A child may include a one-sentence statement like "It rained so hard today, the clouds must have failed their math tests." Or he may write a few words that he enjoys ("squishy, squashy, squirmy, squeezy") or a reflection on nature ("The icicles are long earrings hanging from the tree"). Another child may note interesting antonyms or synonyms ("Instead of big: tremendous, swollen, mammoth, corpulent, colossal, elephantine"). The purpose of the writer's notebook is to encourage sensitivity to language, to descriptive words that convey images or thoughts. Some children will jot down phrases that they have discovered in their reading and wish to remember. The notebook serves as a resource for the child and as motivation for further writing.

Trips away from the classroom provide background experiences necessary to enrich a child's writing. There should be many opportunities for children to explore their environment and to express their reactions. A trip to the country, the seashore, an old building, a debris-strewn lot can evoke written images. Similarly, a ride on a train, a subway, or a boat or just a walk through a park can stimulate writing. Sometimes merely examining a familiar object with a view to recording observations can produce exciting prose. For this purpose a piece of fruit, a vegetable, a bit of meat, or a glass of bubbling soda held to the light can be used. Many people go through life with their eyes "half-closed." They may have difficulty recalling the pictures that hang over their desks or the colors of friends' eyes. To set the stage for writing, teachers help children to become more observant. They may ask them to close their eyes and then to describe familiar objects in the room, urging attention to details. The children may go on "silent walks" and then return to the classroom to describe what they have observed.

Children are encouraged to explore the world through their senses. Objects with special smells—perfume, freshly baked cookies, deodorant, camphor flakes—are collected. Children can shut their eyes and feel a rose petal or a piece of sandpaper and then describe their sensations. They may be shown a conglomeration of bright colors, a painting, a rainbow; they may taste salt, lemon, or ice cream. An ice cube can be handled. Music is played loudly softly, rapidly, slowly. Cardboard eyeglasses with colored cellophane lenses can be constructed so that the children can view the world in different colors. They are encouraged to become aware of a variety of words that can convey their thoughts.

Sensitivity to a stimulus is developed on many levels. For example, in a light rainfall children may go for a walk under umbrellas, in order to listen to the sound of the rain, to *experience* it. On a windy day young children in one class walked about silently and then were asked to describe the wind. Here are some of their comments:

> The wind is like a big fan.
> a horse running wild.
> a dog's bark.
> It roars like a lion.
> pushes the sun.
> blows houses around.
> is whispering secrets to the trees.

As snow falls, children may be encouraged to describe how it feels, tastes, looks. They can be asked: "Can you hear it falling? Can you smell it? What shapes does it take? What do the shapes remind you of? What associations do you have with snow? If you were an ant, a bird, a polar bear, a leaf, a snowman, a tree, how would you feel about snow?" They should be pressed for detailed answers. They can also be helped to understand and express emotions. Pictures of people can be cut from magazines and the children asked: "How do they seem to feel? Why do you think they feel that way? Have you felt like that?" If a child is happy, he may be asked: "how happy? As happy as. . . .? On what other occasion did you feel as happy?"

An important feature of the open classroom is the writing corner. In Chapter Three we discussed methods of organizing this corner and some of the materials to be included. We shall review them here, together with some specific suggestions for their use. It was noted that the writing corner should include both lined and unlined paper, as well as paper in colors like green, pink, yellow, and blue. Different colors often seem to express different moods. Some children will enjoy writing mysteries on dark paper, sad stories on blue paper, cheery ones on yellow paper. For other children, the same colors may symbolize entirely opposite moods. Paper should come in various shapes too. The teacher may supply some, but children can also be encouraged to cut paper to suit their writing. They can cut tall, thin pieces for "tall" tales; short, round pieces for a few lines of prose; animal shapes for stories about animals; and shapes to fit holiday moods (hearts for Valentines, Christmas trees for greeting cards, turkeys for Thanksgiving stories). And, of course, standard sizes of white paper should be available for children who find the other approaches unnecessarily distracting.

There should be abundant materials for illustrations; pens, pencils, magic markers, crayons, felt-tipped pens. In addition to the usual illustrations apart from the text, techniques for including small illustrations in written texts, as well as for illuminated or historiated initial letters, should be demonstrated. Decorative borders may accompany some pieces of writing, or light crayon illustrations may be superimposed on them.

There will be many suggestions for writing in the corner in the form of illustrations, activity cards, and resource boxes. A writing resource box can contain story starters:

> It looked like an ordinary house, except for the strange package on the porch.
>
> John knew that his mother had told him not to . . . but . . .
>
> I knew something strange would happen today from the minute I got out of bed.

Story starters should be supplied by children, as well as by the teacher. Another possibility is activity cards on themes. They contain the spellings of words that children may need to write on the themes:

> *Football*
> touchdown
> goal post
> referee
> field
> penalty
> offside
> huddle
> scrimmage

A group of children may enjoy writing stories on a common theme. For example, some may organize a mystery-story workshop. They may read mystery stories together, studying how writers set moods and develop and resolve plots. The children then share ideas for their own stories, write them, read them to the group, and discuss one another's stories.

Historical fiction also lends itself to this approach. A group may study a biography, that of Harriet Tubman, for example. They then write about different days in her life. Other members of the group may wish to discuss these stories and whether or not they appear consistent with the person's reported behavior. In this manner children benefit from constructive criticism of their stories in a sort of "writers' workshop."

In many schools older students enjoy writing stories for younger ones. Occasionally they use characters familiar to the younger children and place them in different situations. Another impetus for writing is a group of "you were there" cards. On each card a historical incident is listed. The child is asked to pretend that he is a person or thing present on the occasion mentioned: with Christopher Columbus on his voyage, with Abraham Lincoln as he wrote the Gettysburg Address, with George Washington when he chopped down the cherry tree. Using these cards, children have pretended to be "a bird on the mast of Columbus' ship," "a hair in Lincoln's beard," "a cherry on the tree" and have described their imaginary experiences.

Autobiographical details, real or imaginary, can also be used as topics for writing: for example, "My Favorite Person," "My Best Day," "A Trip I

Took," "My Preferred Size," "My Greatest Invention," "My Hideout," "My Secret Wish," "Rotten Thoughts," "Magic Powers," "Things I Do Best."

An interesting addition to the writing corner is a collection of empty book jackets, which can usually be obtained from the school library. Children can staple a few blank pages inside each jacket, and, without having read the actual book, they can write a version inspired by the jacket. Later they can read the original book and compare it with their own.

A display in the writing corner of everyday objects—a tea strainer, an eggbeater, a pair of pliers—can stimulate writing in many ways. Children may be asked to devise unusual uses for the objects or to write stories in each of which one object plays a central role. This display should be changed frequently, and both teacher and children should contribute to it.

A collection of pictures—either reproductions of art masterpieces or pictures clipped from magazines—can provoke interest. Children write about what happened before or after a picture was produced, what the depicted character is thinking, and so on. A roll of inexpensive white shelf paper can be hung in the writing corner. Children compose and write on it: joint birthday messages, poems, or descriptions of accompanying objects.

All stimuli in the writing corner should be changed regularly. In addition to those already listed the following instructions for activities can be included:

> Pretend that you are an object—a potato chip, a ball, a pencil, a star. Place yourself in a situation and write about it. (As a variation, a stimulus box with actual objects can be provided; the child can pick one and write its story.)
>
> Observe a leaf, a tree, a sunset, a flower, a blade of grass, an ant. Write about it.
>
> Write a tall tale, a fairy tale, a fable, a "just so" story, an imaginary tale of a visit to a planet or an imaginary place.
>
> Invent a strange animal (perhaps with the head of a dog and the body of a fish). Write about it.
>
> Write a telegram to anyone in the world. Limit it to fifteen words (or other stated number of words).

As children become accustomed to writing and experience the satisfaction of expressing themselves in this manner, they will require less stimulation from the teacher.

STIMULATING POETRY WRITING

A child who is introduced to poetry in an open classroom acquires a special appreciation that may last a lifetime. In the past poetry lessons usually meant copying, memorizing, and analyzing poems or listening to sermons in the form of poetry. In a classroom where the teacher truly enjoys poetry, however, the children too may learn to prize it. A poem should be read to the class as if a special personal possession were being presented. Both teacher and children will want to read poems that have special meanings for them. The class should have many poetry anthologies, with many examples of lyric poems, humorous poems, city and country poems, narratives, and ballads.

A particular poem may just fit the mood of the moment. It may be a humorous poem like one of Edward Lear's limericks or Carl Sandburg's "Arithmetic," or it may be a serious poem like Langston Hughes' "City." Children who are exposed to poetry in this manner will want to write it themselves. Such writing provides a uniquely satisfying means of expression.

Poetry can be defined simply: It is the language of the emotions, words that convey feelings, a special mode of expressing sensation and moods, of describing experiences. Many children speak in poetry without realizing it: "I was so full I thought I would burst in a thousand pieces"; "The fog was so thick you could cut it with a knife"; "Just once, I wish we had a week of all Sundays." These expressions are poetic.

Children have to understand this definition of poetry, to view poetry as a means of dealing with emotions. To the child who is bursting with excitement over the first snow storm of the season, responding to a piece of music, or brooding over his failure to hit the softball, poetry offers a release, a means of clarifying and expressing his feelings. Too often poetry writing in schools becomes a stilted search for rhyming words. By emphasizing our definition of poetry, teachers can make it clear that poetry need not rhyme. A poem like Carl Sandburg's "The Fog" can be read as an illustration of this point.

As awareness of the environment and heightened sensory perceptions stimulate prose writing, they also inspire poetry writing. Sensitivity to language and to sensory experiences will as often lead children to create poems as to create prose. The teacher encourages consciousness of smells, sounds, tastes, sights, tactile impressions. There is attention to beauty, to color, to arrangements of materials, to displays.

A table in the classroom may contain a collection of different materials assembled by the pupils; chosen because of varying textures, colors, shapes, and patterns; and arranged attractively. Another table may contain all similar materials—for example, bottles. Bottles of many shapes, colors, and sizes can be collected and displayed. Sometimes objects of one color are collected. Children can be encouraged to describe their reactions to colors in poetry. Red is . . . Blue is . . . Black is . . .

Suggestions for writing poetry can be entered on activity cards kept in the writing corner. As with prose writing, children should require fewer such aids as they come to appreciate poetry as a natural way of communicating their feelings. Some children at first appreciate structured forms for writing poetry, though others find compliance with prescribed forms limiting. The first group can be introduced to forms like haiku, cinquains, and limericks. These forms also offer means of introducing poetry writing for the first time.

Haiku are three-line poems, usually on nature themes, each totaling seventeen syllables; the first and third lines have five syllables, the second seven:

> A flaming sunset
> Glowing in a red-streaked sky
> Quickly gone from view.

Cinquains are one of the easiest forms of poetry for children to write. Each is composed of five lines, the first line of which is the one-word title of the poem. The second line contains two words amplifying the title, the third three words describing action associated with the title word, the fourth four words expressing feelings about the title word, the fifth one word that is a synonym for the title:

> Halloween
> Strange costumes
> Trick or treat
> Spooky, haunted, scary, dark
> Pumpkin

A limerick has five lines; lines one, two, and five rhyme with one another, and lines three and four rhyme with each other and are usually shorter than the other three.

> There once was a young man from Kirk
> Who hated to do any work.
>   As for cleaning his room
>   Just the thought brought such gloom
> That it drove him completely berserk.

Other poetry starters can be placed in a poetry resource box by both pupils and teacher. Here are some examples:

Misery is	School is
Happiness is	Sisters (brothers) are
Beauty is	Friends are
Quiet is	Babies are
Noisy is	Smooth is
Patience is	Rough is

| Spring is | Sweet is |
| Christmas is | Sour is |

Sometimes poetry, like prose, can be inspired by a trip, a walk, or a collection of unusual objects. For example, children may wish to take a walk on the first day of spring, on a hot day, on a cold day.

Alliteration is fun for children to play with. They may write phrases like "five fickle friends fighting furiously" and then poems in which each line contains a different alliterative phrase. Alphabet games also lend themselves to alliteration ("S is a silly, soft, stylish letter; T is a tiny, tipsy, taut type").

Kenneth Koch has successfully used the following poetry starters: "I wish I were . . ."; "I used to be . . . but now I am . . . ."[2] Using these leads, children devised outlandish completions for them: "I wish I were an astronaut eating green cheese on the moon"; "I used to be a purple pickle, but now I am a green hot dog." Unusual definitions may be the subjects of humorous poems. Ruth Krauss' *A Hole Is To Dig* offers several examples.[3] Children will enjoy completing definitions such as: "A dog is to . . ."; "A pencil is to . . ."; A mother is to. . . ."

A child who has difficulty in writing his thoughts on paper may dictate a poem to the tape recorder, listen to it, and revise it before asking an older child or an aide to transcribe it. In this manner children who may have limited mechanical writing skills can thus nevertheless dictate imaginative poetry.

Once children have formed the habit of writing poetry, they will require few poetry starters. A change of season, a sudden storm, a trip, an object, a mood, or any special feeling will evoke a poem. As they continue to write, they will experiment with many forms. Some will enjoy rhyming their lines occasionally; others may concentrate on rhythmic patterns. All children who have experienced the satisfaction of creating poetry have added a special dimension to their lives that they will long treasure.

The words of songs, particularly of some popular, folk, and rock songs, constitute poetry that most young people enjoy. Pointing to the relation between music and poetry may lead children to set their poems to music or to write poems to fit original musical compositions. The rhythm of a poem may also lead a child to accompany his reading of a poem on a musical instrument, using it to highlight the beat or emphasize the mood.

STIMULATING FUNCTIONAL WRITING

Teachers have found that as children improve their ability to write in any one area, all their writing—creative and functional—is affected.

[2] Kenneth Koch, *Wishes, Lies and Dreams* (New York: Chelsea House, 1970).
[3] Ruth Krauss, *A Hole Is To Dig* (New York: Harper & Row, 1952).

A. B. Clegg, who studied children's writing in Great Britain, has written:

> It is sometimes held that a pupil's ability to use words well does not
> apply generally to all his work and that if he writes poetry or expressive
> prose really well it does not follow that he will be able to give a clear
> account of a scientific experiment. . . .
>
> All the evidence . . . leads to the belief that this is in the main false
> and that the ability to use words well is an indivisible achievement which
> once learned will be used effectively in whatever kind of writing the child
> does. . . .[4]

Functional writing is frequently required in open classrooms in connection with the work of the class; it is rarely assigned out of context. One
example is the writing of letters. Many a teacher has spent hours teaching
children the proper forms for business or friendly letters—with only limited
success. The elementary school child usually sees little need for this skill.
Teachers in open classrooms therefore provide opportunities for their students to write *real* letters to serve the children's own purposes; these letters
are actually mailed. As a result, letter writing becomes an important activity
in these classrooms.

There are many ways to stimulate letter writing. Stationery is a
permanent feature of the writing corner. Some children enjoy making
their own stationery by painting designs on papers. In some classes stationery is created and reproduced on a ditto machine. Envelopes are provided. Directions for both business and friendly letters should be available
on activity cards. Other useful resources include:

1. *Addresses of the publishers of children's books.* Children may write to
   authors or illustrators in care of their publishers; many such authors
   and illustrators appreciate hearing from children and are gracious
   about replying.
2. *Addresses of the President, the Governor, senators, legislators,* and so
   on, noting their birthdays when available. Children may wish to write
   about local issues, request photographs or information, or send birthday greetings.
3. *U.S. Government Printing Office bulletins.* Many free publications
   are available and will be sent upon request.
4. *Books listing free or inexpensive material.*[5] These books list companies
   that will send materials to schools upon receipt of written requests.
5. *Lists of pen pals with whom children may correspond.*

[4] A. B. Clegg (ed.), *The Excitement of Writing* (London: Chatto & Windus, 1969), p. 5.
[5] Several guides are available: Patricia H. Suttles (ed.), *Elementary Teachers Guide to
Free Curriculum Materials* (Randolph, Wisc.: Educators Progress Service), published
yearly; Thomas Pepe, *Free and Inexpensive Educational Aids* (New York: Dover, 1972);
Joe L. Jackson (ed.), *Free and Inexpensive Learning Materials* (Nashville, Tenn.: Division of Surveys and Field Services, George Peabody College for Teachers, 1972).

6. *Home addresses and birthdays of all members of the class.* This list encourages letters when a child is ill and also birthday greetings.
7. *Local lists.* In some communities patients in hospitals and nursing homes appreciate correspondence from school children.

CORRECTING WRITTEN WORK

The policy on correcting written work can be guided by the purpose of the writing. If a child has written a creative piece for himself alone, it seems unnecessary to correct his spelling or punctuation. If the teacher wishes to use the piece to make a point, he can xerox it or make notes on a separate piece of paper, rather than mark up the child's work. Creative work should never be graded, nor should concern for spelling or punctuation be permitted to distract from the content of the material, the thoughts that the child is expressing. The teacher hardly wishes to limit a child to writing only those words that he can spell or those phrases that he can punctuate. Reacting to a child's writing only by correcting his punctuation is like refusing to listen to an important message unless it is delivered in well-phrased sentences. The child may be tempted simply to give up.

There are occasions, however, when written work is to be displayed, to be made part of a permanent collection, or to be mailed. This work should be expected to meet standards of accuracy; if necessary the child should be asked to rewrite it to correct his errors. It is often a mistaken kindness to exhibit a child's incorrect work. It may prove embarrassing to him if other children call attention to his errors; it is kinder to help him correct them before the work is displayed, filed, or mailed.

There is a difference between accepting errors in a child's writing because they represent the best that he can do and setting no standards for written work—creating an impression that spelling is unimportant. On the contrary, children should be encouraged to acquire habits of careful spelling. Provision, from the moment when the child first begins writing, of dictionaries geared to his reading level will help.

DICTIONARIES

In addition to commercial dictionaries, many classrooms contain dictionaries made by the teachers and children.

Children may maintain personal dictionaries in small notebooks, with a single page for each letter of the alphabet. When a child requires the spelling of a word he turns to the page for its initial letter, and then the teacher, an aide, or another child supplies the word that he wants to add.

Cards with individual words can be filed under each letter of the alphabet; they can be kept in individual envelopes tacked to the wall, in pockets of fabric shoe bags, or in shoe boxes with dividers for different letters. The child may take a card back to his seat or copy it into his personal dictionary.

A group of commonly used words may be displayed on large cards in the writing corner. Special reference books for spellings of words on specific subjects may be maintained: for example, holidays like Halloween, Thanksgiving, Rosh Hashanah, Yom Kippur, Christmas, Easter, Fourth of July, Chanukah.

For young children, illustrating words with pictures helps them to read the words as they need them for writing.

Children may be encouraged to add words to the word files. In some open classrooms the teachers encourage children who use certain words frequently to make their own card files for such words. Each teacher reviews the class word file regularly, eliminating words that are no longer generally needed and distributing them to children who may need particular cards.

Children have to be helped to use dictionaries properly. They should be guided to a balance between too little use of dictionaries and too much reliance on them for words that children can spell themselves. A child who needs frequent help with spelling words may have to be encouraged to organize his thoughts and put them down on paper; corrections can be made later. Constant jumping up to consult dictionaries inhibits writing. The teacher will have to find a pattern for encouraging each child to be conscious of proper spelling while still permitting him to express his ideas freely.

BOOKBINDING

Children's writings are enhanced by being bound into books. Binding is a simple process and provides a ready means of collecting a group of favorite poems or organizing a report or story. The bound volume can be illustrated and added to the reading corner, donated to the school library, given to a class of younger children, or presented as a gift.

Materials required for binding books include fabric or contact paper, masking or binding tape, oak tag or cardboard, construction paper, and glue or rubber cement. Pages to be bound together, including pages for the title, dedication, contents, and the like, should be stapled down the left-hand side.

Two pieces of oak tag or cardboard should be cut a half-inch longer and wider than the pages. One piece of fabric or contact paper is cut one and one half inches longer and wider than the dimensions of the two pieces

Children write and bind books for the reading corner. (Photograph courtesy of Merrick Public Schools, New York.)

of oak tag laid side by side. The oak tag is laid on the fabric, with a gap of about a quarter-inch in the center for the spine of the book. The margins of fabric are folded around the edges of the oak tag and glued. Corners should be glued diagonally as in Figure 11.1. Two pieces of construction paper are cut about a quarter-inch shorter than the oak tag but large enough to hide the edges of the fabric; they are glued over each side of the cover so that they mask the edges of the fabric, with a minimum of glue—usually a little around the edges is sufficient. The book is attached to the covers by means of two pieces of tape, one for the front of the book and one for the back: One edge of the tape is attached to the edge of the book so that it covers the staples and the other to the center of the oak tag.

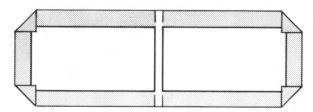

Figure 11.1 Folding Fabric around Book Covers

Chapter
TWELVE
Mathematics

Much of the effort of the curriculum-reform movement in the United States during the 1960s was directed at revising the mathematics curriculum. Until then mathematics, as taught in primary schools, consisted largely of arithmetic: numbers and computations. The emphasis was on learning tables and manipulating numbers, without attention to underlying concepts. Children were taught that the rule for dividing fractions is "reverse and multiply" and for multiplying by ten is "add a zero." Work consisted mainly of pencil-and-paper exercises involving automatic responses and memorization. If the child had forgotten the answer to the problem 3×6, for example, he was unlikely to solve 6×3 instead, for the commutative principle was rarely taught. Even when "story" problems were posed to children, they were designed for arithmetical computations and rarely required much thought. It was not unusual to hear a child who was struggling with a "story" problem ask the teacher, "Do I have to add or subtract?" Learning how to solve the problem was secondary to finding the right answer.

The "new math" was introduced to enlarge the scope of the curriculum and to facilitate understanding of mathematical concepts. Set theory was used to explain mathematical relationships. Although the need for concrete experience was acknowledged, in practice textbook illustrations of concrete objects were more common than were opportunities for actual handling of materials. Although the language of the "new math" did express significant mathematical concepts, it was often too difficult for young children to grasp. Attempts to distinguish between number and numeral or between association and distribution, for example, sometimes led only to semantic exercises, rather than to real mathematical understanding.

194

Most important, mathematics was still taught through pencil-and-paper exercises. In most traditional classrooms today the entire mathematics curriculum may consist of teachers explaining concepts and students practicing them in workbooks or on paper. Teaching the underlying relations among numbers may appear a waste of time when emphasis is still on facility with mechanical computations.

In a curriculum in which abstract exercises that must always result in exact answers are emphasized, many children find mathematics a strain, a subject that reinforces their feelings of inadequacy. In schools it is socially acceptable to "hate" mathematics—especially for girls, because of sex stereotyping in our culture. The question "Why teach mathematics at all?" has even been raised, as it has with reading. The fact is that most people rarely require more than simple computations in everyday life. For more complex operations inexpensive computational devices are becoming widely available.

Yet mathematics can be one of the most exciting and creative areas of the curriculum, and it is rapidly achieving this status in open classrooms. Mathematics, as viewed by open educators, is more than simply a study of abstract symbols; it is also a search for patterns and relationships, for underlying order in the world. It provides a means of classifying objects in the environment into manageable units. Its practice can lead to development of scientific attitudes and can encourage the growth of logical thought.

The difference between the mathematics curriculum in open classrooms and that in more traditional ones can be seen at a glance by even the most casual observer. An open classroom is equipped as a mathematics workshop with abundant materials: aids for computation, devices for measurement, shapes, and instruments. Children are actively engaged in mathematical activities. In the traditional classroom there may be no visible evidence of the mathematics curriculum.

In order to understand the open educator's approach to mathematics, we must review some of the ideas of Jean Piaget[1] that constitute its theoretical underpinnings. Piaget has found that children actually learn mathematical concepts much more slowly than we had recognized. Young children may, however, demonstrate a misleading verbal facility with numbers. They may be able to count to 100 and even to tell which number comes before or after another, but in the sense of actual quantity the concept of 100 may not be established at all. Piaget experimented with concepts of "conservation" and "reversibility," which he found develop slowly in children. Con-

---

[1] For short but clear expositions of Piaget's views in these respects, see David Elkind, "Giant in the Nursery, Jean Piaget," New York Times Magazine (May 26, 1968); also Richard E. Ripple and Verne N. Rockcastle (eds.), Piaget Rediscovered. (New York: Cornell University Press, 1964).

servation is the principle that a given quantity of liquid or other matter remains the same, no matter how it is arranged. For example, when water (or beads) is poured from a wide jar into a narrower jar, so that its level is higher, children who have not acquired the concept of conservation (up to age six or seven) insist that the narrow jar contains a greater quantity than the wider one did. Reversibility is the principle that performing a mathematical process in reverse will yield the original quantity, for example, if two beads are subtracted from a set of ten and then the two are added to the remaining eight, the total sum will then be ten beads again.

Without the concepts of *conservation* and *reversibility*, young children cannot understand the notion of number, the notion that, regardless of how a set of objects is arranged, divided, or combined, the number of objects in the original set remains the same. It is not obvious to children, for example, that $10-3=7$ can be "proved" by adding $7+3$. The child requires many experiences with concrete objects—matching, sorting, and pouring quantities into different containers—before he can appreciate the invariability of a given quantity of objects or liquids. Not until the age of eleven or older, according to Piaget, are children able to reason abstractly. Until then they have to work with concrete materials, in order to solve problems with comprehension. A teacher who overlooks these facts of development can unfairly cause children to feel inadequate, when in fact they are not yet capable of mastering the exercises that they are assigned. Teachers sometimes worry that permitting children to use concrete objects in their computations may lead to their reliance on such objects as a "permanent crutch." Actually, as in any stage of a child's development, when the child outgrows the need for concrete objects and becomes able to reason abstractly, he will do so.

In no area of the curriculum is the open educator's definition of learning as a process requiring active involvement of the child more pertinent. The mathematics curriculum in an open classroom permits constant participation by the learner: in formulating hypotheses, making estimates, and checking results. Mathematics is also frequently integrated with other subjects. Measurements are rarely taught out of context but rather as they are required in constructions, play, cooking, or analysis of the environment (the classroom, the yard, the corridor, or the child's own personal dimensions). Graphs are drawn to present information. Computations are made for many "real life" purposes: in conjunction with a class sale or fair, with collection of milk and lunch money, with a trip, or with shopping lists. Experience with proportions and relationships is gained through comparing the heights of children or of shadows or the weights of different objects. Mathematics is thus linked with science, social studies, writing, and reading.

Teachers do not, however, leave the learning of mathematics to chance. They are generally guided by a list of skills that are appropriate at different ages. Their role is to ensure that children have opportunities to master these skills both through "life" experiences and systematic practice.

The mathematics curriculum in an open classroom therefore includes paper-and-pencil exercises, as well as work with concrete materials, the former usually to reinforce notions that have been grasped while working with materials.

THE MATHEMATICS PROGRAM IN OPEN CLASSROOMS

There are three main sources of mathematical experiences in open classrooms: mathematics textbooks, workbooks, or commercial mathematics kits; activity cards; and general activities. The mathematics program, particularly in the early stages of its organization, will probably include all three. Each can be used in a variety of ways.

Mathematics Textbooks, Workbooks, or Kits

Some teachers in open classrooms prefer the structure of a sequential mathematics book or a commercial kit. These materials have a place in the program but cannot constitute the entire program itself. In addition, there must always be provision for children to engage in practical mathematical experiences. Time for the latter can be made available through a somewhat different approach to using the textbook.

The mathematics book is not assigned a page at a time to a large group simultaneously. Instead, children are permitted to work independently at their own rates. The teacher may indicate which pages she expects a child to complete, permitting him to skip pages that are redundant if he does not require so much practice. Furthermore, each child is not necessarily expected to complete every problem on every page. It may be just as effective for a child to solve six problems on a page as to solve twelve. Sometimes the smaller assignment may be more effective because, if a child makes an error, for example, $7+6=14$, repeating that computation may simply reinforce his error.

When a teacher has assigned a book to a child, she will indicate those pages that require some prior instruction—perhaps by placing "red flags" on them. The child then works independently until he reaches a page that is "flagged." At that point he signs up for a conference with the teacher or waits for the teacher to schedule an instruction period for a group of students with similar needs. Usually pupils check their own work, but the teacher may indicate particular pages that she wishes to review, in order to satisfy herself that the work has been understood.

There is another approach to using mathematics textbooks. Some teachers prefer to designate several topics for a child to complete in a given period of time. These topics need not necessarily be covered in sequence.

For example, a unit on geometry and one on decimals may not have to be studied by the child in the order in which they appear in the book.

In some classes basic mathematical experiences are provided through activity cards, and textbooks are used only selectively to afford practice in pen-and-pencil exercises. Instead of texts teachers may also construct their own mathematics kits by filing pages from various textbooks. Children are expected to complete some of these pages for practice.

Activity or Work Cards

Activity cards are used to furnish practical experiences in mathematics.[2] They are very popular in open classrooms. They can be correlated with topics that are being studied or can suggest general mathematical investigations. (Examples of activity cards will be given later in this chapter.) Cards can be employed in conjunction with a basic textbook or as the main focus of the mathematics program.

When a basic textbook is used, activity cards offer a means of ensuring practical experience. The child may be expected to complete several activity cards regularly. Many will inspire further work on the textbook topic that he is studying, in order to ensure an opportunity to explore the topic more actively. Usually there are enough cards so that the child can choose among them.

In some classrooms activity cards constitute the entire mathematics program. Cards are devised to correspond with each of the topics to be included in a particular year. A child may be expected to work through a series of cards in sequence (as in some British schools); the cards may also be color-coded for different concepts and levels. Providing a large variety of cards in each area permits children some choice.

Mathematics activity cards can be quite directive, leading children to the same abstract exercises presented in textbooks, but then there is little justification for their use. On the other hand, they can encourage children to investigate mathematics actively. The contents of each card are thus decisive. Whenever possible, cards should encourage children to formulate hypotheses and to devise further activities to test their findings. For example, the following extract from a card on the concept of time suggests a variety of experiences:

> How long is a minute?
> How many times do you breathe in a minute? Estimate; then find out.
> Do you always breathe the same number of times each minute? Can you prove your hypothesis?
> What other things can you do in a minute?

[2] See Chapter Four for suggestions for constructing activity cards.

General Activities

Mathematics instruction in the open classroom is not limited to work on discrete topics. There are ample opportunities for children to engage in broad mathematical experiences frequently related to other areas of the curriculum. Beside open-ended activity cards, materials in the mathematics corner—pendulum, trundle wheel, blocks, games, string, and so on—provide such opportunities. Still others can arise from a child's project work: drawing plans for a toy house, investigating a plot of ground, building a geodesic dome. Such activities lie at the heart of the mathematics curriculum because they ensure that the child can use the competence in mathematics that he is acquiring.

THE SCOPE OF THE MATHEMATICS CURRICULUM

Although a teacher encourages an active approach to mathematics and frequently teaches mathematics skills as the child needs them in his projects, she does not leave the learning of mathematics to chance. Teachers must have a knowledge of the scope of the mathematics curriculum in the elementary school and of what learning is appropriate for their youngsters.

A trundle wheel is frequently used to measure a corridor. (Photograph courtesy of Merrick Public Schools, New York.)

Most mathematics textbooks, regardless of grade level, provide for work in the following categories:

> Number and numeration: counting, reading and writing
> Sets: language and symbols
> Operations on whole numbers
> Operations on fractions
> Problem solving
> Measurement
> Geometry

In practice these categories frequently overlap, but each does involve sequential skills, with which teachers must be familiar. Many school districts provide lists of the skills in each of these categories that must be taught. The teacher can construct her own list after screening a number of textbooks for each grade. As in other areas of the curriculum, the sequential teaching of skills by grade level may not provide the most fruitful approach to teaching in an open classroom. Familiarity with such lists does, however, offer a reference by which teachers can ensure that sufficiently diversified experiences are being provided for each youngster, and also a basis for assessing a child's progress in mathematics.

SUGGESTIONS FOR MATHEMATICS ACTIVITIES

Activities in each of the listed categories can be devised. Many will in fact encompass more than one category. An exercise in measurement, for example, may include practice in numbers, operations on numbers, and problem solving. For the purposes of illustration, however, we shall discuss a number of activities corresponding to each of the categories identified. In the classroom the teacher will certainly not attempt such fine distinctions. The suggested activities have been numbered, but the numbering does not imply that they are to be based in sequence. Each activity is meant simply as an example of many others that can be devised. Grade and age levels have not been noted; one activity can be adapted to many different age levels and easier or more difficult computations substituted for the ones suggested.

Numbers and Numeration

The very young child needs experiences with concrete objects to establish his understanding of basic mathematical relations: similarities, differences, "bigger than," "smaller than," "greater than," "less than," "heavier than," "lighter than." In order to comprehend such concepts, children have to handle objects, sorting, classifying, weighing, matching, and counting them. Here are some examples:

Similarity and Difference

Activity 1   Containers are filled with different objects: at first two different ones (perhaps peas and beans), then various different ones (peas, beans, seeds, nuts, pebbles). The child is asked to sort them according to type.

Activity 2   Several activities with these different objects are suggested: counting the number in each set of objects and noting which has more and which less; weighing each set and noting which is heavier and which lighter; arranging the objects in each set in order of size.

Activity 3   Counting boxes can be created from egg cartons, with the pockets numbered from one to twelve; the child places the proper number of objects in each pocket.

Activity 4   Containers are filled with similar objects like buttons; the child is encouraged to devise as many different ways of classifying them as possible: by shape, color, size, number of thread holes, and so on.

Activity 5   To reinforce the notions of "similar" and "dissimilar" the child is asked to collect five or ten objects that are similar in one respect: color, size, weight, shape, function, or the like. He should be encouraged to vary the criteria of similarity beyond the two most frequent ones: color and function. Another person in the room can be asked to surmise how the objects have been classified.

Comparisons of Weight and Number

Activity 6   The weights of materials like wet or dry sand, water, and beans can be compared; the child guesses and then tests his hypotheses.

Activity 7   Quantities of different objects having the same weight are compared; the child determines how many nails weigh the same as five screws or how many pebbles, buttons, beans, wooden rods, nails, and so on weigh the same as one rock.

Activity 8   Children can compare combinations of items: how many pebbles and buttons weigh the same as one rock, how many wooden rods weigh the same as six pebbles and four nails, what has the same weight as five nails and five buttons.

Place Value   Commercial mathematics devices (like Stern blocks, Unifix cubes, and Cuisenaire rods), pennies and dimes, and also different number bases or number systems are useful in activities related to the concept of place value.

Activity 9 The Egyptians used different symbol to present powers of ten.

Symbol		Equivalent Numeral
Vertical stroke		1
Arch		10
Scroll		100
Lotus plant		1000

Each symbol could be written nine times; for the tenth another was used.

(The child is asked to write the following numerals in the Egyptian manner: 9, 46, 78, 97, 562, 5555. He also determines how to subtract with Egyptian numerals.

Activity 10 The child devises a number system using the same principle that the Egyptians did, without revealing the number that he is assigning to each symbol; he writes some symbols, and then a friend tries to discover his code.

Large Numbers   The notion of what constitutes a set of 100, 1,000, or even 1 million has to be established. Many teachers secure numbers of similar objects: 1,000 plastic spools or sticks or 100 pennies or nails. Children sort them, pile them, weigh them. The following activities aid in developing this notion:

Activity 11 The child is asked what he can do in 100 hours, what he can buy for 100 pennies, what he knows that is more than 100 inches long or more than 100 feet long, what weighs more than 100 pounds, whether or not there are 100 words on a page of his reader, and how many pages he requires to assemble 100 words.

Commercial devices like the "100 board" are excellent for teaching counting and sense of 100. These activities can be duplicated for 500 and 1,000.

Operations on Numbers

Activity 12 The child is instructed to find out how many breaths he can take in a second and then how long it would take him to breathe 1 million times.

Activity 13   He determines "how much" 1 million pennies are and com-
putes how long it would take, if each child in the class
were to give one penny a day, for the class to save 1 million
pennies.

Activity 14   The child writes his name on a piece of paper and then
determines how long a piece of paper and how much time
he would need to write his name 1 million times.

Activity 15   The child is asked how he would find out how much 1
million peas, beans, books, nails, and the like would weigh.

Estimation   Estimation helps to develop number concepts. For each
of the activities described so far, children should be asked to estimate the
answers before actually making computations. Children can gain practice in
addition and subtraction by computing how their estimates vary from their
actual findings. Estimation can be further practiced in the following activities:

Activity 16   A jar of peas is provided, and the child is asked to estimate
how many peas he thinks are in the jar and how many
ways he can check his estimate without actually counting
the peas.

Activity 17   The child estimates how many grains of rice are in a pound
and tells how he will determine this quantity. Will he need
a pound of rice to do so? How much do 1 million grains of
rice weigh?

Activity 18   The child estimates the weights of ten pencils, five books,
twenty-five buttons, and so on; then he checks their actual
weights and compares his estimates with his results, recording the differences.

Graphs   There should be many opportunities for the child to illustrate his mathematical findings, which also provide a means for him to
visualize his experiences. Children can construct many kinds of graphs. The
first ones may be pictograms illustrating one-to-one relationships.

Activity 19   The child is asked to make a picture of himself and to add
it to the appropriate month column on the class birthday
graph. Each child uses a similar-size piece of paper for the
picture and pastes it on to a large mural chart that has the
months noted on it.

Activity 20   The child cuts a strip of paper two inches wide and the
same length as his height, puts his name on it, and decorates
it as he wishes. The pieces of paper should then be pasted
side by side in a class-height graph.

Activity 21   The child is asked to find out the favorite colors of the
people in his classroom and to show the results on a graph.

Other graphs can be constructed to reflect the results of surveys. Bar graphs are generally used to show frequency, pie graphs to show percentages of a total unit.

Sets: Language and Symbols

Many of the activities described so far help to establish the concept of set. Children can be aided to visualize a set by using hula hoops or embroidery hoops to enclose sets. For example they can be asked to place a hoop around the members in the set of children with green stockings in the class.

Shared characteristics of different sets can be described by means of Venn diagrams.

Activity 22   The child constructs a diagram to show how many members of the sets of boys and girls in the class have blue eyes (see Figure 12.1). Similar diagrams can be used to represent boys and girls who are only children, have common interests, were born in the same month, and so on. Even very young children can construct them.

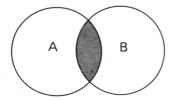

Key
A: Set of boys in class
B: Set of girls in class
▓ : Set of boys and girls with blue eyes.

Figure 12.1   Venn Diagram Showing Set of Boys and Girls with Blue Eyes

Operations on Whole Numbers

It should be emphasized that children in open classrooms still need much practice in computation. Flash cards, games, and mental-arithmetic problems should be part of the mathematics program. There are also many activities that require mathematical operations. They should be encouraged, not only because of the practice involved but also because they help children to understand the different processes and require children to apply their computational skills.

Structural blocks, sticks, disks, rods, cubes, and number lines are valuable aids in understanding operations on numbers. The child who works with such aids can clarify the concepts of addition and subtraction, can visualize multiplication as repeated addition and division as repeated subtraction, and can grasp what a remainder in division is.

Many activities that require operations on numbers involve measurements.

Activity 23   The child is asked to find out' how long it would take him or a particular pet to walk a mile, without actually walking the whole distance.

Activity 24   The child determines the thickness of one book and how high a pile of 100 similar books would be; he is asked where he would store them.

Activity 25   The child finds the weight of 100 gallons of water without weighing one whole gallon.

Activity 26   The child divides a pile of 100 beans into eight equal piles without counting them; then he counts each pile to determine whether or not they are equal. He is asked, "If each pile were to have the same number of beans, how many would be left over?"

Activity 27   The child cuts a length of string so that each of six children will have an equal piece.

Activity 28   The child takes one short length of string and one much longer one, then determines how many of the shorter lengths can be cut from the longer one and whether or not any string will remain.

Operations on Fractions

Cooking and baking (see Chapter Thirteen) offer excellent opportunities for manipulating fractions. Other activities involving fractions include:

Activity 29   The child is asked to measure the thickness of a ream of paper (500 sheets) and then to determine how thick one, five, ten, or fifty sheets of paper would be without opening the pack.

Activity 30   The child is asked how many feathers, peas, or sheets of paper he must weigh before he can calculate the weight of one feather, pea, or sheet of paper.

Activity 31   In one exercise with diminishing fractions the child measures and cuts out a large square of paper. He then folds it and cuts it carefully in half, pasting one half on a long roll of wrapping paper, wide adding machine tape, or pieces of paper taped together. He labels this piece "1/2." He folds the remaining half and cuts it in half, pasting one half onto his roll and labeling it "1/4." He repeats this process, labeling each piece in turn "1/8," "1/16," and so on. The object is to discover whether or not there is a limit to how often he can repeat the process.

Operations with money can also be considered fractional operations.

Activity 32   The child is asked to plan a weekly shopping list or a meal and then, using supermarket advertisements, to figure out how much it will cost.

Activity 33   This problem is posed: "If you had $5 to plan a party for the class what would you buy?"

Activity 34   If a collection of foreign coins can be obtained, children can calculate how much different objects would cost in each currency. They can also make a chart, using a picture from an advertisement, noting the price of the pictured object in Spanish pesetas, English pounds, Russian kopeks, French francs, and so on.

A class store, cookie sales, juice sales, and opportunities for children to keep class funds or to manage lunch or milk money all contribute to practice in using money. Children should also be encouraged to acquire a notion of the costs of items.

Activity 35   They can be asked to guess the prices of a pair of boots, a child's coat, a specified game, a specified car, and so on. They write down their guesses, then check them against newspaper advertisements for these items, noting how the average price of each item compares with their estimates.

A class store offers practice in computations. (Photograph courtesy of Merrick Public Schools, New York.)

In some classes the students print their own currency, which they use in many classroom transactions, including those at their class stores. But some teachers have found that children learn about money more easily if they can handle real currency. A fund of about $10 in coins can be used for work with problems involving money.

Problem Solving

All the mathematics activities described so far are in fact "story" problems, requiring a problem-solving approach to mathematics. Conventional mathematics textbooks usually have a few pages of story problems, usually requiring computations. One conventional example: "If there are 24 children in a class and 2/3 have brown eyes, how many have brown eyes?"

In an open class, children would approach this question from a different angle. They would be more likely to conduct their own survey to determine how many children have brown eyes and then to perform a variety of mathematical operations to determine the percentage of children with brown eyes. In an open classroom the same problem might therefore be posed in this way: "Do you think that there are more brown-eyed or blue-eyed children in this class? What is the proportion of brown-eyed children to the total number in the class?" The advantage to this approach to problems is that it often suggests further investigations. In a class in which this particular problem was posed a group of children became interested in determining whether or not the proportion observed in their class was typical of another class as well. They finally extended their survey to the entire school.

We reiterate that the emphasis in open classrooms is on solving meaningful problems rather than on presenting abstract verbalizations. Children are permitted to use concrete materials freely to help them to visualize and to comprehend the mathematical concepts involved.

Measurement

Measurement is used in many aspects of a child's work. Those described here offer additional practice in some kinds of measurement. Children should also have experience with liquid measurements: in water play, in serving juice to the class, in computing the prices of different containers of milk. The use of scales in many activities helps to reinforce understanding of weight measurement.

Activity 36   The child makes a book entitled *All About Me*, in which he records as many of his own measurements as he can. For example, he traces his feet and measures their length and width. He measures the length of each finger and the span

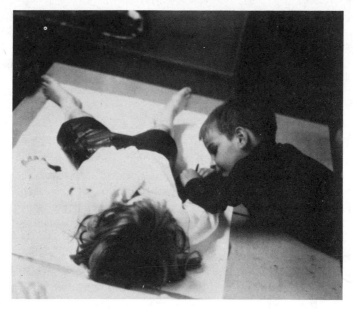

Life-size figures are constructed by one child tracing the outline of another. (Photograph courtesy of Sullivan Primary School, London.)

between the tips of his thumb and little finger when his fingers are spread. He measures the circumference of his waist and head, his height and his weight. This book can can also contain other information that he considers pertinent: perhaps the ages of his brothers and sisters (and their total ages) and the numbers of people in his family.

Activity 37   One child lies down on a large piece of paper so that another child can trace around him. Then he cuts out the figure and paints it as he wishes.[3] He can then try to determine what valid measurements he can take from this cutout.

Activity 38   A child is asked to find out whether or not anyone in the class weighs the same as he does and, if so, whether or not the second child also has the same height. Measuring the heights of all the people in the room and determining which height is most common can help him to grasp the concept of average.

Activity 39   The child is asked to check as many different measurements of people as he can, as in Activity 36, and then to determine whether or not there are any relationships between certain measures: height and length of feet or fingers, for example.

[3] By cutting out two such outlines, stapling them together, and stuffing them with shredded paper he can make a life-size image of himself.

Activity 40   To establish the concept of standard measure the child puts his foot on a piece of paper, traces it, and cuts it out. He then determines how many paper feet he needs to "walk" across the room and whether or not others in the room need the same number. In order to find out, he traces the feet of as many different people as he can.[4]

Activity 41   The child determines how many ways he can measure the length of the room without using a ruler. He can substitute string, paper, boxes, cards, toys, feet, and so on.

Activity 42   Children can find out how large a brontosaur was and whether or not one would fit in the classroom. They can try to think of places to put one if they were to keep it in school.

Activity 43   A yardstick is set against the wall; then the child bounces a ball and measures the heights of the bounces when the ball is dropped from different heights. He can make a chart of his results.

Activity 44   The child measures his shadow on a sunny day. He can ask a child who is taller or shorter than he to do the same and then can compare the corresponding measurements.

Activity 45   A large piece of paper is placed on the ground and one child traces the shadow of another child. The tracing of the child's own body (see Activity 37) can then be compared with that of his shadow; the two shapes should also be compared.

Activity 46   A row of sticks three, four, and five feet long is placed in the ground and the shadow cast by each is measured every hour of the day. The child records his findings, draws conclusions, and tests them by inventing other experiments.

Measurement activities should also include measurement of time and temperature. Temperatures can be recorded at different times of the day at different places for several months. Records are kept, and various computations and generalizations about temperature should result.

Activities involving measurement of time include those emphasizing the concepts of seconds, minutes, and hours, as well as those involving computations of time.

Activity 47   The child is asked to list what he can do in one second, one minute and one hour respectively. Then he calculates how many times he can write his name, write the alphabet,

---

[4] Rolf Myller, *How Big Is a Foot?* (New York: Atheneum, 1962), describes humorously the problems resulting from failure to establish a standard measure in building a bed for a queen. Young children will enjoy the story.

breathe, blink his eyes, run a mile, and so on in each unit of time, without actually doing it.

Activity 48   Railroad or bus timetables can be used to make up a trip and to calculate how long it would take to go from one itinerary to another.

Children can be asked to construct different instruments for telling time.

Activity 49   They can construct a sun dial by mounting a stick in the earth or hammering a large nail into a wooden board. Then they note where the shadow of the stick or nail falls in each hour, writing that hour at the shadow line each time. Observing the sun dial at various times of the day for several days, they can determine whether or not it is always accurate.

Activity 50   A child is asked to try to construct an instrument for telling time from a candle and from sand or water and two containers. He draws diagrams illustrating his results, and tries to devise other timepieces.

The teacher should make certain that children understand that their measurements are only approximations and that a mathematician using more precise instruments would obtain more accurate results. Estimating dimensions before actually measuring them helps to fix the concept of the measure.

Activity 51   The child draws lines one inch, one foot, and three feet long by estimate, then measures them to determine his accuracy. Then he repeats the experiment, drawing *wavy* lines of similar lengths and devising a means of measuring these.

All measurement-activity cards can include instructions that the child estimate his results before conducting his measurements. He may be asked to keep a chart with the headings "My Estimate," "Actual Measure," and "Difference." As has been stated, this also provides practice in computations.

Geometry

Experiences in geometry range from recognition of simple shapes to determining the properties of geometric figures. At first activities may involve cutting and matching shapes or listing objects in the room that have specific shapes: circles, squares, rectangles. In a further attempt to familiarize children with shapes, teachers can suggest that they identify them by touch. Different shapes can be placed in a bag; the child is asked to feel one, name it, and then draw it on paper. He then compares his drawing with the original.

The child can also be asked to construct shapes.

Activity 52   He can be asked, "In how many different ways can you cut an apple? What shapes have you formed?"

Young children also require many opportunities to work with sand and water, in order to develop a sense of volume and capacity.

Activity 53   Using jars or liquid measures of different capacities the child determines how many smaller containers are equivalent to one larger one.

Activity 54   The child estimates, then tests, which of several jars of different shapes will hold more.

Geoboards, which help to familiarize children with geometric concepts can be bought commercially or made by the children. Nails are pounded into a board at equal distances from one another. In one convenient arrangement twenty-five round-headed nails are spaced one inch apart to form a five-inch square. Shapes can be formed by winding rubber bands or strings around the nailheads. These boards lend themselves to a variety of geometrical experiences, ranging from fairly simple to more complex ones.

Activity 55   The child constructs a rectangle with three units on one side and four on the other. He then determines its area and its perimeter. He increases one side, a unit at a time, noting how the area and perimeter change. After repeating this experiment with rectangles of different dimensions, he can try to predict the effects of changing one dimension without using the geoboard.

Activity 56   The child constructs as many different figures having equal areas as he can. Then he is asked which has the smallest and which the largest perimeters.

Activity 57   Using graph paper the child constructs as many different shapes as he can, using first four squares, then five, eight, and eleven squares. He is then asked which covers the most surface.

Constructions of three-dimensional figures helps children to understand cubes; they can make cubes from flat sheets of paper. Two other notions, those of symmetry and tessellation, can be developed through work with sheets of paper. Activities in tessellation are frequently coordinated with examination of beehives or crystals.

Activity 58   The child folds a sheet of paper in half and cuts a piece from one folded corner. When he opens the paper he is asked what kind of shape he has formed and what he infers about the angles flanking the fold.

Activity 59   The child gathers as many different geometric shapes as he can and determines which ones can be fitted together so that no space remains between them. He pastes those shapes together.

Another activity that furthers the understanding of geometric relationships is "curve stitching," which demonstrates that the intersection of straight lines joining sets of points arranged in reverse order on two axes will form curves (see Figure 12.2).

Activity 60   The child draws two lines to form an angle on a piece of cardboard. Then he marks off ten equally spaced units on one line and numbers them from one to ten; he marks off the other line in the same way but numbers the units in reverse. Using string he then connects the corresponding numbers as in Figure 12.2. Although only straight lines have been used, the result is a curve. The angles and arrangements of points can be varied and the resulting variations in shape noted—and some attractive designs created.

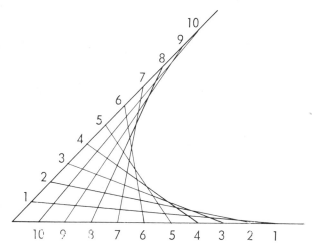

Figure 12.2   Construction Based on Curve Stitching

THE MATHEMATICS CORNER

Many objects in the mathematics corner—an egg timer, old wheels, springs from a clock, calendars, wire, string, ribbon, wool, wood, tape, rope

—will suggest further investigations. One class was able to persuade some-one to donate a used cash register for its mathematics corner. Many stores are discarding older machines in favor of more modern ones, and the discards can be purchased relatively inexpensively. As children become aware of the possibilities for mathematical experiences inherent in objects, they themselves will contribute many more to the mathematics corner. In one class a waffle iron generated a number of experiences with geometry. In another children collected samples of fabrics that had geometric designs. Many artists use geometric shapes in painting; Piet Mondrian is an example.

The mathematics corner may also include activity cards with suggestions of broader scope—perhaps directions for building a pendulum or a spring scale. Many valuable experiences can arise from such activities.

Activity 61   A pendulum is an object suspended from a fixed point so that it moves freely through the action of gravity and momentum. A string can be suspended from a hook screwed into the middle of a bar, which is suspended across two chairs or a doorway, from a ceiling, or the like. A weight is attached to the free end of the string and set swinging. The children can count the number of swings in a minute under varying conditions: different weights, varying lengths of string, different kinds of string. They record their results and draw conclusions.

An attractive mathematics corner invites experimentation with materials. (Photograph courtesy of Merrick Public Schools, New York.)

Activity 62   To construct a spring scale, the children attach one end of a spring to an upright board. On the lower end of the spring they attach a jar top or some other container for objects. Using different weights (perhaps one, two, and three ounces) they mark off a scale on the board. They can check its accuracy by weighing objects on it and then on a commercial scale.

Probability is another mathematical concept that can be developed in the mathematics corner. A package of pennies, dice, colored disks or playing cards is all that is necessary. The children try to find out how often heads will appear when two coins are tossed and the frequency of each combination when three coins are tossed at once. They determine how often each combination of the dice appears or the chances of drawing a particular card from a deck. Results can be recorded and compared to standard formulas of probability.

THE USE OF MATHEMATICAL ACTIVITIES

Each of the activities discussed in this chapter can be modified for a particular group and put on an activity card.[5] It is often best to have only a limited number of cards available at first, so that the children do not simply "thumb through," try a few, and discard them—but attempt to explore the ramifications of each. In weighing two objects, for example, the teacher does not want them to stop with a computation ("three pebbles weigh as much as one rock"). She seeks to illustrate relations between size and density, to foster ability to estimate and a grasp of the concept of number, and to stimulate children to pose their own questions ("If these three pebbles weigh as much as one rock, how would another three compare?"). At first the teacher can suggest that a student complete one activity from a card and then devise one of his own, but this suggestion should soon be unnecessary. If mathematics activities succeed in instilling an experimental approach to mathematics, children will not be limited to problems raised by the teacher but will use them as a starting point for many explorations of their own invention. One teacher recently cited an example. A jar of pennies had been provided along with an activity card asking that children first estimate the number of pennies in the jar and then accurately determine the total number without counting the pennies. One group of

---

[5] There are two excellent British sources of suggestions: the Teachers' Guides of the Nuffield Mathematics Project, a series of soft-covered books on the following topics: *Computation and Structure, Shape and Size,* and *Graphs Leading to Algebra* (New York: Wiley, 1967–1972). *Mathematics in Primary Schools,* Schools Council Curriculum Bulletin No. 1 (4th ed.; London: H. M. Stationery Office, 1972).

children decided to weigh ten pennies on a postal scale; they found that the ten pennies weighed one ounce. They emptied all the pennies into another container, weighed the empty jar, then returned the pennies and weighed the full jar. They then computed total weight of the pennies alone as fifteen ounces, multiplied by ten, and concluded that there were 150 pennies in the jar.

But they did not stop there. Some of them decided to verify their results by counting the pennies. To their surprise, there were only 132 pennies. For the next few weeks the entire class was absorbed in trying to find the "missing" pennies. First they rechecked the weights but found their original calculations to be accurate. The problem was not solved until children thought of weighing different pennies individually; they found minute differences between the weights of new and old pennies, for example. They tested this result by securing new pennies from the bank, wrote to the U.S. Treasury for verification, and finally reached a resolution of the problem.

Many commercial activity cards are now available from mathematics textbook publishers and British educational suppliers. They vary in quality. The teacher should guard against simply providing an entire set of cards for a class. It may be necessary to screen them, choose a few that seem relevant at a particular time, and introduce them gradually as certain concepts become interesting to the students and can be applied. A collection of miscellaneous mathematics activities does not constitute a mathematics curriculum. Teachers have to keep in mind the scope of the curriculum and the extent to which the activities are contributing to children's acquisition of concepts and skills.

Recording Findings

In working with activity cards children should be expected to record their findings either in narrative form or in mathematical or pictorial representations. Such recording helps to establish the relationship between concrete experience and the mathematical symbols used. It is, of course, unnecessary that a child record every aspect of his work. He may need time to absorb a concept or to verify a theory by performing numerous activities. In some instances recording may facilitate his work; in others it will distract him from the exercise at hand and can be delayed until he has completed his experiments.

Even a young child who is limited in his ability to record his experiences in writing may need an opportunity to express his conclusions. He can do so in an oral presentation to the teacher, a group, or even the whole class. Such opportunities may help him to generalize from a few specific activities and to recognize the significance of his work.

To stimulate interest in the recording of information, students may be encouraged to maintain both personal and class books of facts. All kinds of statistics can be entered in them, so that they become personal and class almanacs.

Maintaining a Class Book of Facts

As a student obtains information, he enters it in the class book, with the date on which he has discovered it and his signature. As other students make similar findings, they sign his entry, indicating that they are verifying the data that he has collected; they may also challenge his statistics and ask that they be checked by other students. The problem is then entered on a "challenge" page.

The book of facts may be in narrative form or may consist mainly of pictures. It can be divided into sections for different kinds of entries: information on class members (likes, dislikes, favorite colors, favorite television programs, eye color, hair, height, weight, month of birth, average pulse rate, and so on), similar information about the total school population; information about numbers (100, 1 million, the smallest fraction to which one piece of paper can be folded, and so on), information about measurements (numbers of tiles in the hallway, of dots on the wall, of blades of grass on the playground, and so on), and information about people, places, and materials (average age of American presidents when they were elected, weights of various objects, heights of trees, numbers of men and women in different countries, population densities of different states, and so on).

COMPUTATIONS

Students will require practice in basic arithmetic operations. Instruction can take the form of a few minutes' practice each day with a group, of one child's testing another, or of the teacher's assigning computation exercises to be completed in writing. Teachers can also help children to perceive the *order* in arithmetic—the patterns in multiplication tables, for example. Children who discover that the digits in the products of multiplication by nine always add up to nine or to a multiple of nine will have less difficulty remembering these products; they may also be impelled to search for such order in other tables. Computations can be more than mere mechanical exercises.

Commercial and homemade games and mathematical puzzles also furnish useful practice in computations: ring toss, dominoes, bean-bag games, bingo (using different numerals), magic squares, puzzles, and race tracks. Some children are intrigued by mathematical puzzles (like discovering functions) and may wish to post a few on the bulletin board for others to solve.

In this chapter we have focused on mathematical experiences as primary activities in themselves; but some of the most productive mathematical activities are those encountered by the child in other facets of his daily work: planning his projects or topics, measuring materials for his scientific experiments, noting the growth of plants and animals in the classroom, and engaging in creative activities like painting, printing, building, weaving and dance. Mathematics is also intimately connected with cooking and baking, to which we turn our attention in Chapter Thirteen.

Chapter
THIRTEEN
Cooking
and
Baking

Cooking and baking are regular and accepted components of the curricula of open schools, for both boys and girls. In many schools a few classes share small ovens; if ovens are not available, children cook on small hot plates in the classroom or, as a last alternative, prepare dishes that do not require cooking (see recipes at the end of this chapter).

Many areas of the curriculum can be integrated in cooking and baking experiences. Children read and write recipes, learn to follow specific directions, discuss and record results. To cook, they must measure and weigh ingredients, often adjusting quantities to conform to classroom requirements and the times that such adjusted dishes must remain in the oven. Scientific principles can also be derived from cooking and baking. Observing changes produced by heat and by products like baking powder and yeast often leads to investigation of chemical change. Children taste and smell food and are thus motivated to discover more about taste buds and vapors: why certain foods have distinct flavors and odors. Interest in cooking can result in the study of nutrition, digestion, food groups, and the sources of various animal and plant foods.

In one class popping corn suggested a number of science and mathematics activities. Before the corn was popped, children were asked to estimate how many cups of popped corn would result from one cup of fresh corn; how much fresh corn would have to be provided and at what cost if each member of the class was to have three-fourths of a cup of popped corn; whether or not a cup of popped corn will weigh the same as a cup of fresh corn; and the total weight of the popped corn. After the corn was heated, the children were encouraged to observe what made the corn pop and puff out. They determined that, when popcorn kernels are heated, the moisture inside turns to steam, which expands, builds up pressure within the kernel, and finally bursts the shell of the corn permitting the starch within to puff out. Several children then became interested in starch itself. They floated it in water and discovered that it is insoluble, tested different foods to ascertain whether or not they contain starch, and noted the effects of saliva on foods containing starch. This study led in turn to an investigation of enzymes.

Here is an example of the direct use of mathematics in baking, from a school in England. This school had secured the services of an aide, who was assigned to help children bake. (Adult volunteers, particularly retired people, frequently serve in this capacity; see Chapter Eighteen). On one day a group of six children was working with combinations of six. Each had baked six cookies on which he had placed four raisins and three bits of chocolate. As they completed their baking, the children wrote a book about six, with illustrations. They totaled the number of cookies baked by the group and the numbers of raisins and chocolates used by each child and also by the total group. At the end of the day the children sold some of the cookies for six cents each and recorded the total value of their sales. The aide explained that in this school baking was often used in this manner for practice of mathematical computations.

An interest in food can result in study of the diverse eating habits of people. In some classes children are encouraged to prepare and sample foods from other countries. One group of children undertook to cook a dish associated with a different country each week. They selected recipes and made Spanish rice, Italian pizza, Brazilian candy, French omelets, and Saudi Arabian basbusa. In another class a group studying Japan organized a Japanese tea party for the class. They inverted corrugated boxes, cutting out the sides in order to simulate legs, painted them, and used them as low tables. Rectangles of wrapping paper were stuffed and painted for pillows. Children who attended the party were asked to leave their shoes outside the door and to don kimonos that the children had made. The group then partook of Japanese tea and cookies. This experience led other groups to reciprocate by organizing French and Russian meals.

In some classes children coordinate their study of United States history with the cooking of regional dishes or of those identified with particular states. Children may also bake dishes associated with holidays. One class made Pilgrim butter, cranberry relish and corn bread for Thanksgiving as part of a class project on the Pilgrims. The children wrote the menus on "hornbooks," which they constructed by stapling black oak tag to flat sticks and writing on the oak tag with chalk. They dressed in Pilgrim costumes and served the meal on long Pilgrim tables. Before eating the children washed their hands with "Pilgrim soap" (oatmeal covered with cheesecloth) and brushed their teeth with "Pilgrim toothpaste" (baking soda and food coloring).

Baking and cooking can appeal to many senses, not only to taste and smell. Children hear the hiss of steam, see the deep yellow of egg yolks, and feel various textures: the graininess of sugar, the brittleness of corn-flakes, the softness of fresh dough, the hardness of raw rice, the fuzziness of peaches. They also learn to use utensils and tools and to share materials; these activities thus also serve as important social experiences.

It is possible to correlate baking with study of literature also. Members of one class decided to make some of the dishes mentioned in stories that they had read. They made Pinocchio's poached egg, Captain Hook's poison cake, Heidi's toasted cheese sandwiches, and Uncle Ulysses' dough-nuts.[1] In another class a group baked gingerbread cookies (see recipes at the end of this chapter) after reading "The Gingerbread Man." A number of related activities were then undertaken. Some children became interested in spices and the origin of ginger. They decided to grow some spices in the classroom. Others constructed a huge "gingerbread man" and wrote extremely imaginative adventures for him, locating him in strange sur-roundings from which he kept running away as in the original story. A bound book of these stories was presented to the school library.

Several special cookbooks are available for use in classrooms. Children may wish to compile their own, collecting recipes from books, teachers, parents, and chefs. Work on this topic can lead to a lasting hobby. Classes that wish to engage in frequent cooking and baking may find the expense of ingredients burdensome. Some of it can be defrayed by selling part of the finished product. Various fund-raising events—perhaps a fair or a white-elephant sale, for which children may repair old toys to sell—can also be organized. Such events, in addition to providing funds, are in themselves valuable learning experiences.

Children should, if at all possible, participate in shopping for the ingredients of their recipes and should list in advance what they will need and how much it will cost. This preparation not only offers good mathe-matics practice but also makes children aware of food prices and perhaps even of consumerism. In one class this approach had an interesting by-product. The children shopped regularly at a neighborhood store for supplies for their cooking corner. As prices mounted each week, they became concerned about inflation. During the price freeze they organized Operation Price Watch, monitoring the prices of various key food items weekly and matching them against published ceiling prices. At one point they wrote to a government agency complaining about a violation.

The cooking corner should be stocked with basic ingredients, and children should be permitted to decide which recipes they wish to use and

[1] Recipes for these dishes can be found in Carol MacGregor, *The Storybook Cookbook* (New York: Doubleday, 1967).

to make sure that the necessary ingredients are available. In some classes groups rotate responsibility for keeping the cooking corner stocked: deciding which foods to buy and sometimes raising the necessary funds. As in other areas of the curriculum, the teacher seeks to extend children's learning and interest through cooking: posing questions, suggesting written reports or creative writing about their results, and taking advantage of many possible facets of a cooking and baking experience.

Recipes to be used in the classroom should require minimum adult supervision. There are many children's cook books, which can be kept in the cooking corner. The teacher and children may also collect recipes and put them on activity cards or in an index file. Some examples of appropriate recipes are included here; several require no cooking or baking, others can be baked on a hot plate, and still others require an oven.

No-Bake Recipes

Peanut-Butter Kisses

1 cup peanut butter   1 cup jam or honey
2 cups dry milk solids

Mix all ingredients together. Shape into a long roll. Cut into bite-size lengths.

Children choose recipes from books available in cooking corner. (Photograph courtesy of Merrick Public Schools, New York.)

Cream-Cheese Cookies

1 3-ounce package cream cheese
½ cup plus 2 tablespoons
   confectioner's sugar
1 drop vanilla extract

3 tablespoons sugar
1 tablespoon cinnamon
Chopped nuts, chocolate sprinkles,
   shredded coconut, or other topping

Soften cream cheese. Mix in confectioner's sugar and vanilla extract. Roll into balls, approximately one inch in diameter. Combine sugar and cinnamon. Coat cheese balls with this mixture. Then sprinkle on topping.

Chocolate-Sprinkle Delights

2 ounces butter
3 heaping teaspoons cocoa mix
1 teaspoon confectioner's sugar

1 tablespoon chocolate sprinkles
   or other topping

Combine the first three ingredients. Roll into balls. Roll balls in chocolate sprinkles.

Hot-Plate Recipes

Crunchy Pretzel Bits

1 6-ounce package semi-sweet
   chocolate pieces

2 cups pretzel sticks or rings

Melt chocolate over hot water. Crumble pretzels. Add to chocolate. Stir until pretzels are thoroughly coated. Drop by spoonfuls onto waxed paper. Refrigerate.

Peanut Brittle

1 teaspoon butter
1 cup salted peanuts

2 cups sugar

Grease a 9-inch square pan with butter. Spread peanuts over the bottom. Heat sugar in a frying pan, stirring constantly until it forms a light-brown syrup (about 15 minutes). Carefully pour hot syrup over peanuts. Cool. Break into pieces.

Oatmeal Cookies

6 cups sugar
1 cup shortening
¾ cup dry milk solids
1½ cups water

9 cups rolled oats
¾ cup cocoa
1½ cups peanut butter
1½ teaspoons vanilla extract

Combine the first four ingredients. Heat until the mixture boils. Remove from heat. Add remaining ingredients. Drop by teaspoonfuls on waxed paper. Cool.

Oven Recipes

People Cookies
Makes about 3 dozen

½ cup shortening
1 teaspoon salt
1 teaspoon flavoring
1 cup sugar
1 egg
2 tablespoons milk

2 cups flour
1 teaspoon baking powder
½ teaspoon baking soda
Food coloring
Candies
Raisins

Combine the first four ingredients. Add the egg and milk. Then blend in the next three ingredients. Divide dough into four parts. Blend in food coloring for different skin tones. Flatten each part into a round. Decorate the "faces" with candies and raisins. Bake at 400 degrees 8–10 minutes.

Paint-a-Shape Cookies
Makes about 5 dozen

⅓ cup shortening
⅓ cup sugar
1 egg
⅔ cup honey
1 teaspoon flavoring
2¾ cup flour

1 teaspoon baking soda
1 teaspoon salt
Food coloring (optional)
1 egg yolk
¼ teaspoon water

Grease cookie sheet. Combine the first five ingredients. Then add the next three. Blend in food coloring if desired. Roll out dough to ¼-inch thickness. Cut into shapes. Place at least an inch apart on greased cookie sheet. Combine egg yolk and water, and paint designs on cookies with mixture. Bake at 375 degrees 8–10 minutes. Do not let cookies become too brown, or colors will not remain clear.

Gingerbread Boys

2 teaspoons baking soda
3 tablespoons water
⅓ cup shortening
1 cup brown sugar
1½ cup molasses
½ cup water
7 cups flour

1 teaspoon salt
1 teaspoon allspice
1 teaspoon ginger
1 teaspoon cloves
1 teaspoon cinnamon
Raisins, candies, nuts, and other
    toppings

Before beginning draw the shape of a boy, about 4½ inches long, on cardboard. Dissolve baking soda in 3 tablespoons water, and set aside. Combine the next three ingredients. Add the next seven ingredients and baking-soda solution. Divide dough into twelve parts. Roll each part out to ¼-inch thickness. Press the cardboard pattern onto each part, trimming off excess. Use raisins, candies, nuts, and so on for the features. Bake at 350 degrees about 15 minutes.

Chapter
FOURTEEN
Creative Arts:
Arts and Crafts,
Music,
Dance and Movement,
Drama

Creativity takes many forms in open classrooms. Children respond
to music through art, movement, poetry, or drama. One child discovers
the intricacy of a piece of coral, another perceives the order among
multiples of nine. Creativity can be expressed in various ways: spinning
about in order to "feel" the rotation of the planets, constructing a dome,
creating a picture from plant seeds, and so on.

Creativity has been defined as *new ways of perceiving things or
relationships* and as *originality of thought.* An individual's "new way of
perceiving" or his new thought is original to him, even though others
may have enjoyed similar perceptions or thoughts before. As open
classrooms are dedicated to children's dicovery of relationships for
themselves, they are especially suitable climates for fostering creativity.
Arthur Foshay, in discussing creativity, practically defines an open-
classroom setting: "The first requirement for creativity is that one
deliberately open one's self to new experience. . . . What is required
is that one learn to take an open, unstructured look at the data
available. . . . One must suspend habitual judgments, habitual
interpretations, in order to be open to experience."[1]

Throughout history people have expressed themselves through
various art forms. Primitive man decorated his water jugs, painted
pictures on cave walls, made jewelry, and built huge structures. Young
children have an innate desire to create. The preschool child plays with
crayons, paints, and blocks; he dances to music. There is growing
awareness that the work of young children may in fact constitute
primitive art of high quality.

[1] Arthur W. Foshay, "The Creative Process Described," in Alice Miel (ed.), *Creativity in
Teaching* (Belmont, Calif.: Wadsworth, 1961), p. 24.

Many of the child's creative urges are stifled by the structure imposed on them in conventional schools and by the devaluation of creativity in the curriculum. In many traditional schools art and music are treated as *special* subjects in which children engage only once a week. This weekly activity may be the child's only opportunity to use art materials or to listen to music. Frequently the experiences themselves are highly structured; the whole class is expected to participate in the same lesson. Because art and music are not incorporated into the child's daily work, he comes to perceive them as insignificant, having no relation to the "real" work of school. This attitude may be particularly unfortunate in an epoch in which people must be educated to use leisure for more than watching television.

In contrast, teachers in open classrooms do not view creative activities as separate facets of the child's school experiences. They are not considered "frills" to be cut from the budget when finances are low or pursued only as relaxation from "important" work. Open educators find emphasis on creative activities in school consistent with their objective of educating the whole child and encouraging him to reach his full potential and to become an individual with varied interests. When appropriate materials are readily available in the classroom, it is as natural for children to react to an event by producing a painting or a dance as it is to produce a written report.

Children are encouraged to express themselves in art. (Photograph courtesy of New Rochelle Public Schools, New York.)

Children are encouraged to communicate their feelings in various mediums. A classroom display, a walk in the school neighborhood, or a field trip to a more distant place can stimulate sensitivity to the surroundings and many creative expressions.

In England F. A. Haddon and H. Lytton have studied the growth of "divergent thinking" in formal and informal schools. They have found that, on five out of six tests, children from informal schools had significantly "higher divergent scores" than did those from more conventional schools and that, on the sixth test, they also had higher scores, "though it did not reach statistical significance."[2] A follow-up study four years later revealed that: "In spite of the differing school experiences of the intervening four years, the effect of the type of primary school the children had attended was still clearly and significantly noticeable, the children from informal primary schools outperforming those from formal primary schools (on tests of divergent thinking)."[3]

Creative activities in schools are generally identified with subjects like arts and crafts, music, dance, movement, and drama. Although these activities can be integrated into the work of open classrooms, each deserves separate scrutiny in a discussion of the curriculum.

ARTS AND CRAFTS

Each open classroom is stocked with abundant art materials: paints, colored inks, clay, yarn, wood, string, boxes, blank film, plastic, straws, crayons, fabrics, various kinds of paper, and innumerable other materials for constructions, sewing, and collages. There should be a collection of "junk," natural materials, and dried foods: bottles, egg cartons, tubes, styrofoam packing, feathers, buttons, pine cones, rocks, nuts, sand, seeds, bark, macaroni in different shapes, dried cereals, corn chips. Children are encouraged to view all objects in the environment as potential art materials and to contribute to supplies for the arts-and-crafts corner.

The art corner should be tastefully designed with careful attention to display and storage of materials. Displays that call attention to different characteristics—shape, color, pattern, texture, density—engender sensitivity to detail. For example, a display may include a collection of objects of one color, or shape, or a group of fabrics with varying textures—perhaps velvet, fur, burlap, wool, and nylon. The corner must be maintained neatly despite

[2] F. A. Haddon and H. Lytton, "Teaching Approach and the Development of Divergent Thinking Abilities in Primary Schools," *British Journal of Educational Psychology*, 38 (1968), 171–180.

[3] Haddon and Lytton, "Teaching Approach and Divergent Thinking Abilities—Four Years On," *British Journal of Educational Psychology*, 41 (1971), 136–147.

the profusion of supplies. Children should be expected to care for the materials; brushes should be washed, open jars of paint sealed, and objects returned to clearly marked storage areas.

Care of materials reflects a sense of their worth as art supplies, rather than simply as a pile of meaningless junk. A box of rocks stored with jars of paint may suggest to children that they decorate the rocks, whereas rocks tossed at random among a pile of other materials will rarely do so. There are many possible storage containers for art supplies: cans, boxes, drawers, dishpans. Boxes divided into separate areas by pieces of cardboards can be made into chests to hold small items like buttons, seeds, pine cones, and nuts. An indoor clothes rack is useful for drying paintings. Or a clothesline can be strung in a convenient area. Pictures can be attached with clothespins for drying or display.

Art and craft activities in open classrooms fall into three categories. The first includes illustrative or expressive work undertaken as an adjunct to other activities: for example, illustrating a story. The second category is appreciation, study of artists and their work. The third might be labeled "art for art's sake." Work in this category is unrelated to other activities and exists solely for the pleasure and stimulation that it yields. Each of these categories has a place in the curricula of open schools.

Illustrative and Expressive Work

Art is a dimension of all activities in open classrooms. When children write stories, poetry, or reports they naturally tend to illustrate them. Construction may become part of almost any class project. Similarly, models are built and costumes designed for a play; textiles can be hand-printed for curtains for the classroom or a toy house; photography can be used to illustrate reports; and children can be encouraged to represent mathematical findings pictorially. Children may mount leaves, press flowers, and design pictures from leaves and flowers as part of a broader study of nature. They can examine the properties of different hard materials by taking rubbings from them.

Art activities are closely correlated with reading too. Children who have read a book and wish to report on it often choose to do so by designing dioramas, film strips, puppets, murals, posters, or book jackets. Collages are popular for biographies. In one school some children were interested in biographies. As they finished each book they made a collage of items representing significant aspects of the subject's life. A famous nurse or doctor, for example, might be represented by absorbent cotton, a tongue depressor, Band-Aid, and so on. These collages were displayed on a special bulletin board, and the rest of the class was urged to guess whom each collage depicted.

A British headmaster who had visited United States schools insisted on this fundamental difference between the approaches to art in American schools and British informal schools: "In the United States technique appears most important. The aim seems to be to create pretty pictures. Art is separated from the rest of the curriculum. Here, art is an expressive activity. We look at art as a means for children to express their intellectual activities." When pressed for an example, he continued, "A young child may wish to say something about garages. Art is one way in which he can express his ideas. We will show him technique as he requires it." He explained that he had observed an art teacher in an American school teaching potato printing to an entire class. This activity, he claimed, would be most unusual in his school; potato printing would be taught only to a small group if they were seeking an appropriate way to express an idea.

This view of art as expression of "intellectual activities" is especially appropriate for open classrooms. It has been noted that children learn through concrete experiences, through experimenting, touching, and observing. Art offers such opportunities. As a child seeks to recreate an experience, he becomes aware of its details and learns more about it. Artists who wish to paint the human body recognize that they must also study anatomy. This same attention to detail may enrich all of a child's school work. The child who illustrates a story must examine the period in which the characters live, their ages, and their environment, in order to gain deeper understanding of the story. The child who mounts leaves must learn about how to preserve them, the brittleness of different ones, and the permanence of their colors.

Art Appreciation

An appreciation of the works of the masters develops naturally in children who are attuned to beauty and sensitive to art forms. Open-classroom teachers believe that children should have opportunities to become acquainted with our rich artistic heritage. They therefore hang reproductions and whenever possible encourage visits to museums to see the originals.

In one class the teacher introduced an "artist of the month" program. Each month she set up an exhibit of reproductions of the works of a different artist; books and film strips about his life and work were also available. Children who wished to study the "artist of the month" were encouraged to do so in various ways. Some did research on his life, others on the period in which he lived, others on the techniques that he used in his paintings. Many children attempted to imitate the artist's painting style: using geometric shapes to produce "Mondrians," wide brush strokes for "Van Goghs," dots for "Seurats" and "pop" objects for "Oldenburgs." Other children expressed their reactions to the paintings in music, movement, and poetry. They wrote about the pictures, the moods created, the implications of the scenes, and the characters depicted. In one instance, a rather involved dramatic presentation resulted when children decided to reenact a scene in a print, making their own costumes to match those in the painting. The result of the "artist of the month" program was not only a growing appreciation of art but also an introduction to many methods of manifesting such appreciation.

Some open classrooms include museum corners for the display of reproductions. Each exhibit is well cared for and the selection is changed regularly. For interested children, material for further exploration is provided. They are encouraged to choose the works to be displayed, and sometimes parents will lend genuine works to be exhibited. The museum corner can be a very special area: a quiet corner, a setting for soft music, a retreat to a special kind of beauty.

These approaches to art appreciation are particularly appropriate to open classrooms because they stimulate new interests in children. Many children who visit museums to see originals works by "their" artists develop lasting appreciation for the work of the masters.

Art for Art's Sake

Art and craft activities are also valued as creative experiences in themselves not necessarily related to other facets of work. The environment can inspire many activities. Children can go on sketching trips to interesting landmarks, scenic spots, or only just outside the school building. In some instances they later reproduce the scenes in the classroom in paint, clay, or cardboard constructions. Activities can be correlated with the seasons; natural objects like leaves, bark, shells, and acorns can be brought into the room to heighten awareness of seasonal changes. Leaf prints call attention to the different shapes and designs of leaves and also make interesting mountings. They can be made by tracing, lightly rubbing crayon on a piece of thin paper placed over the leaf, spatter printing with a small sponge or toothbrush around a leaf resting on paper, pressing carbon paper on to the underside of the leaf, or lightly painting the back of the leaf with shoe polish or paint and then transferring the design to paper. Children will discover many other techniques of leaf printing.

Other forms of classroom printing are possible. Children may wish to print stationery for their own correspondence or designs for the outsides of folders. Potatoes and other vegetables, stones, pipe cleaners, crumpled paper towels, pieces of rubber matting, sponges, blocks of wood, and string can be used for quick printing. A "print shop" can be part of the art corner.

Mosaics of one color or many are also popular. Crushed eggshells dipped in paint or simply pieces of colored paper cut in different shapes from old magazines can serve as raw materials.

A pile of different-sized paper bags can be used to make puppets. Two large, supermarket-size bags can be stuffed, decorated, and attached at the openings to create a life-sized figure. Or else the bottom of a smaller lunch bag can be stuffed with rags or old socks and tied off with string for head and neck; the rest of the bag forms the body. Arm holes can be cut for the puppeteer's fingers. The head may be decorated with button eyes, wool hair, and felt mouth and nose.

Although an art activity may be originally designed as an experience in itself, it frequently leads children to other explorations. In one class puppet making led to an extensive project. Children read stories about puppets, did research on different methods of making puppets, and kept notebooks on specific procedures. They wrote stories featuring the puppets' tape-recorded conversations, and maintained diaries indicating the times of day that the puppets woke up, played, ate meals, went to bed, and so on. They planned and also recorded different puppets' measurements in these diaries. The project culminated in a show that included dialogue and music written by the children.

Paper animals can easily be created from brown wrapping paper or old newspapers. An eight-page section of newspaper is folded in half along the natural fold. Then an animal or object is drawn on one side and cut out. Three of the sides are stapled together, leaving one side open. The open side is liberally stuffed with small strips of newspaper, then stapled shut. The resulting figure is then painted and decorated.

In some classes the use of old newspapers and other waste materials for art can inspire an interest in ecology. There are many uses for "waste." Empty milk containers can be covered with paper and made into blocks for constructions. They can also be used for "roller movies."[4] Sticks are inserted through the top and bottom of the carton. Scenes are painted on adding-machine tape, one end of which is attached to each stick. A viewing hole is cut in the front of the carton, and the tape can then be rolled back and forth from one stick to the other. Old matchboxes can be used to make toy furniture, cotton spools for animals, bottles and old tin cans for vases. Contact paper transforms old cans and boxes into colorful pieces. Steel wool, covered with felt and stuffed into empty tuna-fish cans that have been sprayed and decorated, produces pincushions. Beads may be crocheted together for rings or earrings. A class can make a patchwork quilt for its quiet corner from scraps of fabric that the children have stuffed and sewn together. Scraps of wool can be woven on looms constructed by the class, and many durable objects like trays, small tables, and waste-paper baskets can be built from discarded cardboard. Remnants of muslin can be silk-screened, printed with linoleum blocks, spatter painted, stenciled, or painted free-hand. They can then be sewn into aprons, curtains, or hangings.

---

[4] A container or box of any size can be used for roller or "television" movies. Dialogue can be taped to accompany them.

Other activities also rely on scraps or easily obtainable materials. In one class the teacher set out some clay and some inexpensive plastic straws. The children learned that the straws could be held together by pieces of clay, and some really imaginative constructions resulted. In another class toothpicks and raisins were used with similar results. Pieces of burlap can be stitched or woven into a wall hanging. One edge of the burlap can be rolled around a rod and stapled. Then the rod can be hung from the wall with cord. An entire group can make a burlap hanging, each child contributing a portion.

Visitors with special talents can provide the classroom with additional art experiences. A parent or other adult versed in flower design, tie dyeing, jewelry making, macramé, needlework, or any other craft will often agree to visit and instruct an interested group. Children, too, should be encouraged to share their talents and hobbies. A survey of the class or school at the beginning of the year will generally produce a list of talented youngsters and parents.

Teachers are less concerned about specific activities than about awareness of the possibilities for creativity. They may help children to find appropriate techniques for using materials. There are many "how to do it" art books in libraries; sometimes the appearance of such a book can serve as an impetus to new kinds of exploration. In one class a book on architecture[5] led to a long-range project that culminated in the children's building a replica of the Parthenon.

There may be an art-activity box, with directions for specific projects like making toy animals, but it should also contain cards that will stimulate less structured experiences. Some open-ended questions help youngsters to view their environment from a fresh vantage point:

> What if the world were composed only of lines?
> What if everything were round?
> What if parts of animals and people got all mixed up?
> How would the world look if everything were red? Or green? Or black? Or upside-down?

When teachers consider art activities worthwhile they set appropriate standards. Some children tend to paint the same scene over and over, fail to notice details, or generally produce work inconsistent with their abilities. As in other areas of the curriculum, helping children to recognize that they are capable of meeting higher standards of work can reaffirm their confidence in their own abilities. Emphasis on painting in British informal schools and the high standards set for children's work have led

[5] Forrest Wilson, *Architecture: A Book of Projects for Young Adults* (New York: Van Nostrand & Reinhold, 1968).

to marked improvement in the quality of work produced, lending credence to one headmistress' claim: "We are not just interested in our children playing at art; we are producing artists!"

One further point about art in open classrooms should be made. The appearance of the classroom is related to a class' appreciation of art. Children's work should be carefully labeled and exhibited. Respect should be accorded to both individual and group efforts. Drapes can be made for windows and pillows for lounging; parts of the room can be color-coordinated; and old furniture can be painted and decorated—all to create an aesthetically pleasing environment.

MUSIC

Music is also a regular part of the work in open classrooms. Children sing together, learn to read and compose music, play instruments individually or in groups, listen to music, and express their reactions in a variety of ways. They hear a wide range of compositions, from those of classical composers to those of more modern ones. They interpret the moods of the pieces in art, poetry, writing, movement, and dance. Children become sensitive to the particular faculty of music for reflecting moods or actions. They can be urged to compose tunes that "sound" happy, sad, or "giggly"; that "sound" like someone walking slowly, running, or going up and down stairs; or that remind them of smooth or bumpy objects.

Inexpensive instruments like recorders, harmonicas, auto harps, and xylophones are available for daily use. In the music corner (sometimes set up in the hall, so as not to disturb other members of the class) children can experiment with sound and can play and compose pieces. Music can also be combined with other activities like poetry; children can be encouraged to compose scores for their original poems. Once the habit of music is established in a class, it will seem natural to accompany a skit with music, either as a background or to introduce changes of scenes and moods.

Mathematics can be studied through music: Fractions can be taught by means of musical notation, and counting songs help children to memorize the number sequence. If the teacher plays an instrument there can be many occasions for teaching through songs. In some classes children sing together. Duplicating song lyrics offers reading practice as well. Some classes have enough musicians to staff class bands, sometimes with homemade instruments.

In some classes soft music is played at times throughout the day. It may have a relaxing effect on the class and often tends to lower the noise level as children try to hear the music.

Some class members or their parents may be musicians. They should be invited to demonstrate particular instruments and how their characteristic sounds are produced. Many musical instruments can be made in the classroom. For example, thin pieces of rubber can be stretched over the open ends of wooden kegs (like those in which lumber yards ship nails) or other containers to make drums. They can then be painted and decorated.

A few small metal bells can be attached to a piece of elastic that has been sewn into a "bracelet" to fit a few fingers or a wrist.

For a harp a rectangular hole about 3″ long by 2″ wide is cut in the center of the lid of an old cigar box. About five individual pieces of wire or nylon fishing line of varying lengths is strung between hooks placed at intervals across the top of the box so that the strings are parallel and descend gradually in length. Filling similar bottles or glasses with different amounts of water produces a kind of celesta.

Clay pots of different sizes can also be used for bells. A piece of string is passed down through the hole in the bottom of each pot and then through an empty thread spool. A knot is tied below the spool to prevent the pot from slipping. Then cup hooks are screwed at intervals along a large stick or broom handle, and the pot strings are tied to the hooks.

Old plastic lemon- or lime-shaped containers make good maracas when partly filled with rice grains, split peas, or sand. The tops should be securely fastened with strong tape.

Old salt boxes partly filled with similar materials also make good musical shakers. They can be decorated. For a different kind of shaker, inverted bottle tops can be loosely nailed to a piece of wood, so that the tops rattle when shaken.

Different lengths of tubing or wood can be attached to a bar so that they hang freely. (Holes may have to be drilled in the tubing so that it can be attached to the bar with string.) The result is a set of chimes.

To make a zither, a child can stretch different-sized rubber bands across a cigar box whose lid has been removed.

In making these instruments, children should be encouraged to experiment with shorter and longer containers, shorter and longer strings, thicker and thinner cases, and sound boxes of different materials like wood, metal, and cardboard. They will find that they can invent many of their own musical instruments.

DANCE AND MOVEMENT

Closely related to music in open classrooms are dance and movement. Movement is the expression of moods and feelings through body motions; movement may be structured in dances. For young children movement is a natural form of expression. They jump up and down when they are excited, and they cower when frightened.

Like other forms of creative activities movement develops a child's sensitivity to his enviroment. It forces him to become aware; helps him to perceive how other people and objects look, feel, act; and permits him to respond to them freely as in dance. Through movement a child explores his world; he learns about distance, height, and space. Children can be asked to stretch to the space above, to tiptoe through the space "in the middle," and to "feel" the area near the floor.

Movement is also closely related to language. Children may express their reactions to different words, frequently onomatopoeic words like "crashing," "banging," "clanging." Movement can heighten their sensitivity to sounds. Loud, shrill sounds evoke different actions from those in response to soft, gentle sounds. Children may interpret letters of the alphabet by imitating their shapes, as well as their sounds. On the other hand, they may use language to describe how they feel as they move about in accordance with their own inner rhythms.

They may use numbers in their movements, perhaps making up step sequences (two forward, four backward, two sideways) and putting them together in dances. Frequently after an exercise in movement children are inspired to engage in different forms of creativity; painting pictures to capture their moods or staging a drama. Movement may take many other forms. The teacher can read a story and ask the children to interpret the actions of different characters through movement.

Frequently, a teacher will play an instrument like a drum or tambourine or a recording and encourage the children to respond actively. Rowen has noted that young children are amazingly sensitive to musical qualities:

> Playing strange-sounding Oriental music to nursery-school children will often elicit movement responses that closely resemble Oriental dance. This is not because of exposure to concert dance or to television. Children of this age have not seen enough to imitate it. Their delicate, undulating motions are sincere reactions to the quality of the music they are hearing.[6]

Children may also be asked

> To move like a bird, like the wind, like a hard rainstorm.
> To express how a person (a monster, a witch, a giant) makes them feel.
> To "be" an object: the sun, a cloud, a tree, a machine, a train.
> To "become" an animal.
> To act out the dripping of water, a burst of steam from a kettle, the whirring of a computer, the steady ticking of a clock.
> To pretend that they are balloons slowly filling with air and then to pretend to be either the air gradually escaping or the balloon taking a dizzy path as it loses its air.

[6] Betty Rowen, *Learning through Movement* (New York: Teachers College Press, 1963), p. 14.

Experiences in movement are a basic part of the curriculum. (Photograph courtesy of Merrick Public Schools, New York.)

Movement not only enhances the child's observation of his environment, but also serves as an emotional release for many children. M. Brearley has concluded that "movement is indivisible from life. . . . Every movement of man is expressive of himself, his aims, struggles and achievements, it reflects the inner activity of the person."[7] Viewed from this perspective, experiences in movement are basic to any school curriculum.

DRAMA

Children are natural actors and actresses. They are aided in their attempts to perceive their environment by assuming different roles. Young children play mother, father, and teacher, imitating important members of their environment as a means of expressing feelings about them, relating to them, and understanding their functions.

Drama can help children to cope with real life by enabling them at times to escape into fantasies in which they become other people. Drama, beside stimulating the imagination of children, is a great boon to language development and creativity in art, music, and writing.

Open classrooms include many materials for dramatic expression. For younger children there will be a playhouse and materials that will enable them to assume many roles. In every classroom, regardless of the students' ages, there is room for dress-up materials to inspire dramatic productions. Parents can be asked to donate old suits, dresses, gowns, and uniforms. A collection of hats and shoes is appreciated. Some classrooms have extensive wardrobes of costumes, many made by the children from donated fabrics.

In this environment skits and plays are frequently staged. They do not have to be based on prepared scripts but can result from outlines that the children have written; frequently they are short and spontaneous and are presented to small groups. They may be inspired by field trips, books, projects, or simply the urge to act. They help to make participants more perceptive about characters in books or in their environment.

A frequent form of dramatic expression is pantomime. Children can interpret situations like carrying heavy packages, two railroad trains meeting at a crossing, a young child walking in a fierce wind. They can also pantomime situations and ask others to guess what they are.

Although most children enjoy participating in "dramatic productions," for some children this experience is particularly significant, satisfying basic needs as they grow up. The open classroom can cater to such needs.

[7] M. Brearley, et al., *Fundamentals in the First School* (Oxford: Blackwell, 1969), p. 88.

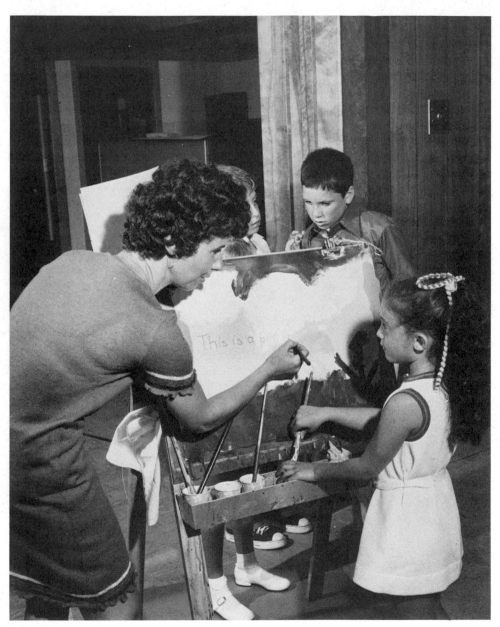

Photograph courtesy of Merrick Public Schools, New York.

Part
FOUR
Implementing the Open Approach

Chapter
FIFTEEN
Focusing on the Individual Child

There is an old children's game called "snake rope." The leader holds a long rope at one end, while a number of other children line up along the rope, pulling it taut in front of the leader. The leader then starts swinging the rope around faster and faster; the rope must remain taut so that it does not wrap itself around the leader. As the speed of the rope accelerates, the children must run to keep up; if a child falls behind he is "out." Those farthest from the leader, who have a longer distance to run, as well as the slower runners, begin to drop out until eventually only a few are still left holding onto the rope. They are declared the winners.

In some ways this game is an analogy for traditional teaching. The teacher is the leader. She stands in the center of the room presenting the lesson, but as she proceeds the "slow runners" drop out one by one so that only a few are left at the end of the lesson. They are declared the "winners" by our educational system.

INDIVIDUALIZATION OF INSTRUCTION

It was in recognition that all children cannot be expected to "run" or learn at the same pace that many educators came to emphasize *individualization of instruction*. Over the years the phrase has become almost a catchword for many different kinds of educational schemes. Such diverse approaches to education as "free schools," which oppose planned curricula, and "programmed instruction," which includes a very specific curriculum, have laid claim to it. In fact, individualization has been adopted as a goal of practically every educational reform movement of this century. It is the keystone of the philosophy of open education.

Individualization of instruction appears to be open to many inter-pretations, however. Education is not the only arena in which individual-ization and individual rights are emphasized in theory but remain somewhat shadowy in actual practice. American society continues to accept the value of the individual in a democratic nation, yet much of the dissatisfaction of our times is attributed to the accelerating degree to which the individual feels that he is losing his identity. One popular poster reads: "I am a human being. Do not fold, spindle, or mutilate." The inconsistency between emphasis on the individual and the growing impersonality of our society helped to spark unrest in the universities in the 1960s. Students expressed frustration over large classes in which their individual identities were submerged, over their inability to meet instructors as individuals, and over the general curriculum, which they found unresponsive to individual needs.

The elementary school teacher today, regardless of her teaching method, does not have to be convinced of the need for individualized instruc-tion. Her problem, as she sees it, is not the objective but the achievement of it in the average-sized class of twenty-five to thirty students. It may be that part of the difficulty lies in her conceptions of individualization. Many teachers think that individual teaching or the preparation of an individual curriculum is required for each child. Such tasks are obviously overwhelm-ing, probably even impossible.

On the other hand, some teachers have attempted to individualize instruction by adopting a common curriculum for their entire classes, with minor modifications either in content or in the rate at which it is covered for individual children. This approach has been less than satisfactory in ensuring individualization. An examination of the differing perceptions of individualization of instruction in traditional and open classrooms, as well as some of the practices resulting in each should clarify this issue further.

Individualization in Traditional Classes

Attempts to individualize instruction in traditional classes have been largely influenced by stimulus-response learning theory, which has domin-ated much of educational thinking in this century. More recently they have incorporated elements of B. F. Skinner's further modifications of this basic theory. According to stimulus-response theory, behavior consists of discrete acts that can be shaped by conditioning. Teaching is the process of conditioning a child to certain kinds of behavior. In translating this theory into classroom procedures, the teacher usually decides which responses (learning) she wishes to induce: the behavioral objectives. She then deter-mines which cues and stimuli will evoke and reinforce those responses. Instruction is thus determined by predetermined behavioral objectives. Individualization is interpreted as varying instructional cues to ensure that each pupil produces the desired response (learning a prescribed curriculum).

The teacher who adopts this approach assumes the responsibility for setting specific objectives for children in advance, for deciding what each child is to learn. Individualization—altering the path that each pupil travels in mastering this predetermined curriculum—is generally accomplished by one or more of the following methods:

> Varying the pace of learning for individual children.
> Varying the duration of learning for individual children.
> Varying the mode of teaching for individual children.
> Modifying the curriculum for individual children.

Although proponents of these methods have succeeded in calling attention to individual differences among children and have to some extent taken account of these differences, they have also generated many problems. Varying the pace of instruction without changing the content has often led to competition among children ("What book are you on?"). There have even been instances in which older children who are poor readers have been forced to use basal readers or mathematics books clearly intended for much younger children. Some may even endure the humiliation of being assigned to the same books as are younger siblings.

Varying the duration of learning by retaining children in grades for longer periods of time, though undoubtedly sometimes justifiable from a developmental point of view, is not generally accepted socially. It may do irreparable harm to a child's self-concept in a school in which age and grade level are clearly linked, particularly if the child is physically large for his age.

Varying the mode of teaching while recognizing that all children do not learn in the same manner takes no cognizance of the fact that all children may not need to learn the same material. As a result, children are often given "special" instruction to remedy school-defined deficiencies.

Modifying the curriculum has frequently led to ability grouping, which has created social problems and problems of self-esteem for members of the lower ability groups. Frequently groups at either extreme find themselves isolated, as the other children shun the "dumb kids" and the "intellectual snobs." Both groups certainly receive false notions of their places in society.

What these approaches to individualization have in common is the basic notion that all children must master a prescribed curriculum designed by the teacher or other school personnel. This notion places limits on individualization. Furthermore, schemes arising from this notion have often failed to achieve their purposes: "In circular plans based upon individual instruction, the individualization has been largely illusory. A considerable mechanistic quality has limited such schemes, and the fact that the individual students came through the successive turnstiles at their own pace has been made to signify more than it actually means."[1]

In assessing schemes for individualization based largely on guiding children along a single educational route laid out by the school, other effects should be considered. First, responsibility for children's failure to master the curriculum is frequently placed on the children. The curriculum is not open to question! Children who fail to travel the specified path are judged inadequate and often labeled in inappropriate terms.

Second, emphasis on the prescribed curriculum raises the need for frequent evaluation to determine how well children are mastering that curriculum. The resulting almost constant grading and evaluation of children lead to what Philip W. Jackson has called a "distinctly evaluative atmosphere that pervades the classroom from the earliest grades onward."[2]

Individualization in Open Classrooms

Individualization of instruction is also a key premise of open education, proceeding from emphasis on each child's unique needs, interests, and talents. But, when open educators speak of individualization, they speak in a different context from that of traditional educators. Their position rests on a different theoretical base: rather than stimulus-response theory, Gestalt field theory of learning and a humanistic point of view. Whereas stimulus-response theorists view behavior as discrete, Gestaltists seek to study it as a whole, as parts interwoven in an overall pattern. Whereas behaviorists tend to interpret the child's behavior mechanically, as entirely dependent upon proper conditioning, Gestaltists argue that the whole is more than the sum of its parts. Learning is not something that teachers can automatically elicit in a student as I. P. Pavlov induced salivation in his dogs.

Open educators consider behavior purposeful (involving the personal motivation of students) and education the process of developing new insights from experience. Each individual has his own "life space," his concept of reality, which he builds throughout his life. In order to learn he must actively participate in modifying his ideas and incorporating new ones into his existing mental framework.

Viewed from this perspective, students must collaborate in the formulation of their curriculum goals. Such involvement is considered prerequisite to effective learning. In open classrooms therefore individualization means *individual children sharing in the formulation of their educational goals.*

[1] Fred T. Wilhelms, "The Curriculum and Individual Differences," in Nelson B. Henry (ed.), *Individualized Instruction*, 61st Yearbook (Chicago: National Society for the Study of Education, 1962), p. 66.
[2] Philip W. Jackson, *Life in Classrooms* (New York: Holt, Rinehart and Winston, 1968), p. 20.

The teacher's responsibility is not to decide in advance exactly what each child will study but rather to provide a climate in which individual children can make choices about their curriculum and explore matters of concern to them. The teacher encourages each child to participate in establishing his educational objectives and to search for his own answers. Concomitantly, the teacher is freed from prescribing each child's exact course of study and from always having to know the "right" answers. The curriculum can thus be expanded to encompass many matters that interest students beyond those that are "covered' in graded textbooks. This philosophy does not imply a laissez-faire approach to the curriculum, one in which each child "does his own thing"; rather, it implies a freeing of the curriculum from predetermined constraints so that it can truly be adjusted to meet the unique needs and interests of each child. The child does not decide unilaterally what he will study, but neither does the teacher. The teacher recognizes the child as a participant who has a right to be considered and consulted. In this scheme of personal learning it is not necessary for each child to use the same book. His definition of what he "should" learn may well be as valid as the teacher's definition would be. The teacher no longer needs to prod each child along the same educational route. Individualization in open classrooms may well encompass an individual curriculum for each child, but it is no longer necessary for the teacher to design it personally.

This difference is not to be construed as implying that the teacher never sets learning objectives for the children. Particularly in reading and mathematics, teachers are conscious of the range of required skills in those areas and determined that their students will achieve competence in them. They are not left to chance. But even in these subjects there generally is provision for individual children to choose some materials for themselves and to choose some of their own modes of learning the required skills.

It is clear that individualization of instruction in open classrooms includes at least three components: the child's determination of some of his educational goals, his selection of materials to meet goals determined both by him and by his teacher, and his "self-instruction."

Closely related to individualization of instruction is the notion of freedom for children to pursue their own interests. A child's interests often determine which matters he wishes to explore (his educational goals) and the materials with which he chooses to work.

Individual Interests in the Curriculum

The use of topics and projects in open classrooms as a means of encouraging children to pursue their individual interests was discussed in Chapter Seven. Several considerations contribute to open educators' emphasis on children's interests as a significant component of the curriculum.

Initially these interests are singularly effective bases for individualizing instruction. Donald Nasca, for example, has surveyed individualization of instruction in 600 school districts in New York State and has concluded that diversified activities in a classroom that permit children to pursue their own interests constitute an "ideal individualized program."[3]

Much of what children study in traditional elementary schools is superficial; rarely is a subject pursued in depth. When children are not involved with the material to which they are exposed, uninterested in it, they tend to forget much of it. This superficiality is not conducive to developing habits of serious intellectual inquiry. On the other hand, a child who seeks to answer his own questions is more likely to pursue his study in depth. Rather than concentrating on a broad curriculum, he may specialize in an area that interests him. As a result he may develop a serious interest that an enrich his life outside school. Today, when people need to learn to use leisure productively, it is necessary to help children to acquire such interests. In fact, it may be more valuable to the child to gain a hobby than to learn a specific job skill that may rapidly become obsolete.

Teachers in open classrooms acknowledge that it is no longer possible to teach children everything about a subject or to anticipate what they may need to know in the future. There is therefore a wide range of choices for a particular child and much latitude to explore different areas. For example, the curriculum may include a unit on air. Rather than limiting himself to an examination of the physical properties of air, as suggested in many science textbooks, a child may prefer to study pollution. For some children a study of mushroom growing may hold more interest than does the unit on dairy farming suggested in the textbook.

The child's right to explore his interests in school can be justified from another point of view. When children are engaged in tasks that interest them, they are more productive. Success in tasks that they themselves have helped to formulate promotes a sense of accomplishment and self-confidence, which in turn leads to personal growth.

To stimulate significant work, however, the teacher may have to intervene at a number of points. The child may not pursue an inquiry to the degree of which he is capable. The headmaster of a London school has emphasized the importance of the teacher's assessing the work of a child in terms of his abilities: "I expect the topic in which a child is engaged to be a challenge to him and commensurate with his potential. If, for example, a young child of six is interested in cars and cuts and pastes pictures, or builds models, this might be acceptable. But for the child of nine or ten I would expect this interest to encompass more depth, such as research into car engines and their operation."

[3] Donald Nasca, "Individualized Instruction," Speech to Suffolk County Regional Education Center (Montauk, N.Y.: March 30, 1971).

It is also important for the teacher to recognize when the child has reached a point at which he needs help in finding new directions for his investigation or in deciding to go on to different pursuits. Otherwise the child may grow bored, and the quality of his work may deteriorate.

Furthermore, in emphasizing children's interests, it is easy to overlook the fact that children do not come to school with an already fully developed range of interests, which they are simply awaiting permission to explore. It is not intended that children's interests be limited to those they already have. On the contrary, the teacher must provide an environment that will stimulate new interests in many areas. John Dewey recognized this necessity when he urged that teachers offer "the environing conditions which are requisite to start and guide thought. . . . It is certainly as futile to expect a child to evolve a universe out of his own mere mind as it is for a philospher to attempt that task."[4]

The teacher exposes children to many materials, media, field trips, and books. A trip to a butterfly farm, to a mushroom farm, or to a state capital can spur a variety of new interests. A television program about Stonehenge, an article about whale fishing, a film about an archaelogical excavation, a marine biologist's talk on the discovery of coelacanths off the coast of South Africa—all can contribute to setting children on new paths of investigation.

Dorothy Gardner, a leading British theorist of informal education, summarized the teacher's role in stimulating new interests: "In discussing freedom for children to pursue their interests in school, I am reminded of the philosopher Herbohn, who denied free will on the ground that 'one is not free to do what he has never thought of.' It is up to teachers to see that children think about different things."[5]

PROVISIONS FOR THE SPECIAL CHILD

The term "special child" is in many ways a misnomer. It originates from the assumption that there is an average child and that those who fall above or below this average are special.

As there are an infinite number of traits on which children can be measured, the "special" classification must actually be based upon a specific set of yardsticks: generally school achievement, intelligence, or marked physical or emotional disability. In conventional usage, the term refers to children of both low and high intelligence, those with learning problems and those who achieve particularly well, those with physical or sensory disabilities, and those with emotional problems.

4 John Dewey, *The Child and the Curriculum* (Chicago: University of Chicago Press, 1903), p. 18.
5 Dorothy Gardner, personal conversation with author, July 1971.

In practice, however, *the special child is the one whom the school has difficulty educating*. This definition of special children has to some extent been created by the schools and is a product of the schools' emphasis on conformity and application of general behavioral norms to individual children. The presence of special children tends to be more apparent in traditionally organized classrooms.

The Special Child in the Traditional Class

Most traditional classes are organized by grade level corresponding to chronological age spans, which are defined by arbitrary cut-off points—usually the beginning and end of the calendar year. With this organization comes the concept of average or normal behavior for each grade. Textbooks are identified as suitable for certain grades, and it is assumed that what is in the third-grade reader is what eight-year-olds should be capable of reading.

Other, similar judgments are made. Children in first grade are considered ready to read, whereas it is sometimes argued that children in kindergarten will be harmed if they are taught to read; for the child in second grade, not having learned to read is considered failure—even though there is sometimes only a few days' difference between the ages of children in two different grades.

Because of the dominance of this grade approach in schools, teachers tend to identify greater numbers of special children. The kindergarten child who already reads is "special"—and sometimes as difficult for the traditional teacher to cope with as is the "special" third grader who does not read.

Other aspects of conventional schooling also tend to emphasize the notion of special children. Seating arrangements and insistence on quiet in traditional classes tend to highlight any behavior that does not conform to established norms. A child is said to have a low concentration span or to be overactive if he has difficulty sitting in one place for long periods of time; the child who has to use the bathroom frequently is also considered "special." It is difficult for a child to conceal any problem in a traditional classroom. In a sense every child is exposed, "pegged," and graded.

It is possible to walk into any conventional classroom and from the children's behavior to identify the "dumb" and the "smart" members of a class. These distinctions are painfully obvious, for example, in a class discussion in which the teacher is seeking a particular answer: Everyone in the room knows which child will eventually supply it. The most blatant form of conditioning of children to their "places" in the intellectual hierarchy of the class is the establishment of ability groups. No matter what the apellation ("Bluebirds," "Mighty Mites," and the like), within minutes of their organization everyone knows which are the "low" and which the "high" reading groups. Teachers are often surprised at how quickly the children recognize the order of these groups. One child explained: "It's very easy. We know that whatever group John is in is always the dumb group, which-every group Nina is in is the smart group." Many an adult still bears the scars of having been in "dumb" groups in school.

It is also difficult to cope with feelings, or emotions, in a traditional class. The child who is frustrated by his work, angry, or threatened may become hostile or aggressive. In an environment in which quiet, order, and placidity are the rule there is no provision for absorbing and moderating his aggression. His aggressive feelings become threatening not only to the teacher but also to the whole class, which may then join with the teacher "against" the child—simply exacerbating the problem. The teacher is forced to "stand up" to the pupil because she fears losing face in front of the whole class, even though ignoring the behavior might be more effective.

There are other categories of special children in classes in which assignments are geared to the "average child." There are the children whose workbooks are never completed; there are those who seem to be champing at the bit, who would complete the entire mathematics workbook at once "if you let them." In this atmosphere both groups may develop special problems. The quick child may become bored, restless, or disruptive. The slow child may give up, turning instead to "doodling," "dreaming," "talking," or causing "trouble." Fear of inability to complete the work or of making errors may lead him to become "lazy." The "lazy" child is often one who cares a great deal, who may even be a perfectionist. He can cope with being criticized for laziness but not with the rejection that he fears when his "stupidity" is exposed. These decisions are rarely conscious. The child's laziness protects him and permits him to fantasize what he could achieve if he wanted to—though in reality he is paralyzed by feelings of inadequacy, which are confirmed by the unrealistic pace that the teacher has prescribed for him. It is easy to understand why one of the most important requirements of open classrooms is to make it comfortable for children to make mistakes.

In the atmosphere of the traditional classroom special children stand out, yet the school finds coping with them difficult. Societies have often mistrusted people who are different; school societies, too, mistrust special children and often treat them as outcasts. This attitude applies to the gifted, as well as to the slow, child. Albert Einstein was a poor student; Bobby Fisher dropped out of school.

The Special Child in the Open Class

In an open class special children are more easily integrated, less visible, and even to some extent defined differently. The child who lacks initiative or fears to take responsibility may require more special attention than does the one who would be considered overactive in a traditional classroom. The wide range of ages found in many open classrooms, some of which are organized to include two- or even three-year age groups makes it easier to include children with wide ranges of ability.

In England, though special schools for emotionally disturbed or mentally retarded youngsters do exist, many headmasters try not to send children to these schools unless absolutely necessary. As one London headmaster remarked: "We pride ourselves on taking care of our own. These children need the contact with normal youngsters, and in the informal atmosphere of our school we can absorb them."

Children work in small groups in open classrooms. Different children have opportunities to exert leadership at different times. The child who knows how to construct a wagon from wooden boxes is admired for this skill and may be considered as "smart" as the child who reads better. Because children move about with fewer restrictions, the active child finds more outlet for his energies. In a less evaluative atmosphere there are correspondingly less frustration and hostility. Teachers and children are not afraid to express emotion and in small groups they are more able to cope with members of the class who have problems. There is protection afforded by a small group: It offers security to the child who may wish to experiment with some materials or who cannot easily speak in front of a whole class.

Special children are thus less noticeable in many ways. In the traditional class the children who leave for remedial instruction are identified daily. The stigma may become unbearable for some children, who may suddenly and "inexplicably" refuse to go. With greater freedom to move in and out of the classroom a child's whereabouts in the open class can remain private if he wishes.

The Gifted Child   Open classrooms are uniquely suited to educating gifted children. In the open environment they are not limited to a common class curriculum and can more easily find stimulation, outlets for their talents, and opportunities to develop their interests. There are many examples. One New York ten-year-old was fascinated by biology. With the aid of the school nurse, she was soon typing and analyzing the blood of every child in the class and conducting a series of experiments on blood chemistry. Another child spent part of his day at the high school, working with computers. In a different school a musically gifted child had led a small group in composing an entire score for a class play.

The Plowden report suggests that the gifted child needs a "richer curriculum, not simply a quicker journey through the ordinary one." He needs "whatever contacts can be contrived with individuals outside the school who share his interests or can further them—the local museum curator, for instance, or any practitioner, architect, ornithologist, physicist, painter."[6] This kind of contact is possible in an open classroom. A parent, aide, or teacher can take a few children on a trip during school hours. In a conventional class children cannot be out of the room for any period of time because they will miss a class lesson. In an open class, in which there are few lessons for the whole class, the child can ask a classmate for help if he has missed some instruction or can join another group to make up work missed. As a result, arrangements for children to leave the room or even the building can more easily be made.

The Child Who Needs More Structure 'Another group of children may need special attention in open classes, particularly in the early stages of organization: children who find the diverse activities and freedom of open classrooms confusing, and who require more structure and direction. They should receive such help from the teacher uncritically. At times teachers have tended to treat such children as if they were inadequate or have adopted a punitive approach: "If you can't behave, I shall have to tell you what to do." This attitude is a violation of the concept of individualization in open classrooms. The teacher who respects the child will recognize that children's needs differ in many respects and will meet them without disparaging the child.

Some adults work best under pressure; some require direction, and others rebel against it. Children too do not all function in the same way. The child who needs to be told that at 9:00 he is to read a specific story, at 10:00 to do a certain page of mathematics, and so on is entitled to acceptance and attention to those needs. Such acceptance is consistent with the philosophy of individualization in open education. At the same time, the teacher encourages the child gradually to assume more responsibility and helps him to become more self-directed.

Different children require different degrees of direction: some to start reading, others to stay with an activity, others to care for material. The teacher must be aware of these varying needs. Freedom and direction are both components of open education, and both should be available to children in proportion to their requirements.

ASSESSING THE INDIVIDUAL

The production of educational tests is a major industry in the United States. Not only schools but also industrial firms, military services, government agencies, psychologists, and hospitals use them. Millions of tests are sold every year, most of them for the evaluation of individuals.

[6] Bridget Plowden, et al., *Children and Their Primary Schools*, I (London: H. M. Stationery Office, 1967), p. 307.

Testing has become a way of life in American schools, to the extent that some teachers speak of the necessity for teaching their pupils "how to take tests." Children are sometimes tested even before they enter school and then regularly throughout their school careers. There are intelligence scores, achievement scores in various subjects, and scores on class tests that the teacher may administer weekly. The instruction offered in school is often conditioned by test results. College acceptance depends upon College Board scores, and admission to graduate school on Graduate Record Scores. One educational psychologist recently described tests as "education's compulsive neurosis."

Open educators find the ubiquitous testing of children anathema, for both ethical and academic reasons. Ethically they are opposed to the constant evaluation of human beings. They question the standards used as measuring rods, the validity attributed to them, and the labeling of children as "inadequate" for failure to meet these standards. Futhermore, tests have become an important factor in the curriculum. The tail too often wags the dog: Instead of simply measuring the work of the class, the tests often determine it. An important deterrent to loosening the rigid curricula of many classrooms is teachers' and parents' concern that children will not be taught the specific kinds of material appropriate to the achievement tests administered in their school districts. Poor results on achievement tests, cannot be tolerated by the district, no matter how much the child has actually learned and grown during the period tested.

Because tests exert so large an influence on American education, the teacher in the open classroom must be aware of certain facts about them. They generally fall into two categories: ability or intelligence tests and achievement tests. Intelligence tests yield intelligence quotients, or I.Q. scores, that may remain part of a child's record throughout his school career and exert a pervasive influence on that career. Yet these scores are frequently misused and misunderstood.

The Assessment of Intelligence

Open educators recognize that intelligence testing, when administered selectively and when the results are used carefully, may help a teacher or psychologist to understand a specific child. But they reject the notion of intelligence as static and refuse to accept a child's I.Q. score at a particular age as necessarily indicating the educational level that he is capable of attaining. They see little point in administering group I.Q. tests to an entire school population, particularly because the results are likely to be endowed with more significance than is justified.

As the result of I.Q. scores children have been placed in special classes, have had their curricula altered, and have found their opportunities for higher education limited. Parents and teachers have frequently adjusted their expectations of a child's school performance to conform to this I.Q. score. The score thus tends to become a "self-fulfilling prophecy."

Despite numerous studies demonstrating the possible unreliability of I.Q. scores, these scores still affect teachers' thinking about children. We have even invented words to explain the disparity between classroom performance and intelligence-test scores: "under achiever" and "over achiever."

What precisely is an I.Q. score? It is based on the total number of a child's correct responses to a specific series of questions. When his total is compared with the average totals of other groups of people of similar age, an I.Q. score results. But there are a number of valid objections to dependence upon such scores.

First, the questions on an I.Q. test are specific questions chosen by one group of people. This choice may reflect the test makers' own cultural bias. Some of the words used, for example, may be more familiar to suburban than to urban children or may not be part of a particular child's experience. James R. Mercer, for example, has reported on his study of I.Q. tests: "What the I.Q. test measures, to a significant extent, is the child's exposure to Anglo culture."[7]

Second, it is not certain that the particular questions chosen effectively measure intelligence. Sometimes a kind of circular reasoning is followed. It is assumed that the tests measure intelligence; therefore, intelligence is defined as what the tests measure.

Several psychologists have argued that intelligence has different components, such as the abilities to think creatively, to evaluate, to foresee contingencies, and to memorize. J. P. Guilford who takes this view has suggested that there are "at least fifty ways of being intelligent" and that "to know an individual's intellectual resources thoroughly we shall need a surprisingly large number of scores." On the question of the relative influence of heredity and learning on intelligence, he has advised: "The best position for educators to take is that possibly every intellectual factor can be developed in individuals at least to some extent by learning."[8]

Third, the child's score on a test—whether a written test or a performance test—reflects his behavior on the particular day of the test. He may have been angry, he may have mistrusted the tester, the may have felt unwell, he may have misunderstood the questions, or the circumstances under which he was tested may have been unfavorable: The room may have been warm or drafty or noisy. Peter Watson has found that "when tested by whites, black subjects scored, on the average, several points below the level they reached if black persons tested them."[9]

Many group tests require reading skills that children possess to

---

[7] James R. Mercer, "IQ: The Lethal Label," *Psychology Today* (September 1972), p. 44.
[8] J. P. Guilford, "Three Faces of Intellect," *American Psychologist*, 1959, *14*, pp. 469–479.
[9] Peter Watson, "IQ: The Racial Gap," *Psychology Today* (September 1972), p. 48.

unequal degrees. Some children take more time to answer questions, some cannot or will not make guesses, some are motivated to take tests, some are frightened or tired or hungry on the day of the test, some have learned to copy answers, some have decided not to bother. (This last point was vividly illustrated during the scoring of some group I.Q. tests recently. The test had consisted of multiple-choice questions, and each child was to fill in one of four boxes to indicate his answer. One answer sheet caught the scorer's eye. This child had obviously decided against attempting to answer the questions and instead had chosen a pattern of answers. On the first question he had chosen answer box 1, on the second box 2, on the third box 3, and on the fourth box 4; then he had simply repeated this pattern through the entire test. Curiously enough, the resulting I.Q. score fell in the average range. How many children tire of tests and choose this or another manner of expressing their resentment or boredom over the whole "testing game"?)

Finally, a child's I.Q. score may vary from test to test. The author participated in a seven-year longitudinal study of seventy-one children, who were tested regularly from kindergarten to sixth grade. In the course of the study each child took between five and seven intelligence tests, two of which were administered individually by a school psychologist. Although the average scores for all the children on each test showed a high degree of correlation, for individual children there was in fact variability in test scores among all the tests, including the two tests administered individually and generally believed to yield consistent results. The findings of the study can be stated briefly: "A variability of 15 points on an I.Q. is considered significant. . . . Yet, if all the tests were considered, there were 80% (of the population studied) who had score variability of fifteen points or more, and 38% had variability of twenty-five points or more on the different tests."[10]

Other studies have confirmed the variability of I.Q. scores. Morris L. Bigge and Maurice P. Hunt have reviewed a number of these studies and have concluded that "whatever it is that an I.Q. test measures, it can be raised, or lowered, through a marked change in environment."[11]

The Assessment of Achievement

Most schools in the United States measure the achievement of their students regularly—every year, every two years, or more frequently. In addition to achievement tests administered to the whole school or school

---

[10] The Relation of Physical Factors to School Achievement (Port Washington, N.Y.: Unpublished report of the Flower Hill Kindergarten Study, 1968).
[11] Morris L. Bigge and Maurice P. Hunt, *Psychological Foundation of Education* (2d ed.; New York: Harper & Row, 1962), p. 137.

district, there are tests administered within state school systems. New York State, for example, tests each child in reading and mathematics, in third and sixth grades.

Although originally conceived as diagnostic instruments to evaluate the growth of individual children, achievement tests have become instruments for evaluating individual teachers, administrators, and schools. The New York State tests are an example. Results of the tests arranged by school district are published widely. Newspapers make comparisons among districts. Local school administrators are then judged by how well their children have achieved on the tests. Predictably, pressure for high achievement scores is so great that we occasionally hear reports of teachers coaching students on tests or of administrators "overlooking" a few low-achieving children during the test period.

Open educators do not reject accountability, nor do they reject assessment of children's accomplishments in the course of a school year. What they do reject is the limited range of learning at which tests are directed and the frequent misinterpretation of the results. Tests that emphasize paper-and-pencil exercises, superficial mathematical computations without understanding, or definitions of words without comprehension tend to encourage the same kind of teaching in the schools. The child who completes worksheet after worksheet full of isolated definitions or paragraph exercises need never read a book to score well on a reading achievement test. Tests may also discourage inquiry, for they teach pupils that knowledge can be divided into specific facts and that all questions have clear-cut answers.

Much of the criticism leveled against intelligence tests is also relevant to achievement tests: the selection of questions frequently reflects the cultural biases of the test makers; any given test score reflects children's behavior on only one day; a single child's results may vary from test to test; and certain tests may yield consistently higher results than do others.

Achievement-test scores are also contaminated by the degree of reading proficiency that a child has achieved. The child with reading difficulties or the one who reads more slowly generally scores low in *all* subjects.

The score on an achievement test is usually a combined score reflecting the average of scores on many different subtests. A reading achievement test may thus include sections on recognition of isolated words, comprehension of paragraphs, library skills, and reasoning ability. Two children scoring at a "third-grade level" on the same achievement test may have completely different patterns of achievement. One may have difficulty understanding individual words but be able to comprehend words in the context of a paragraph. Another child may be more proficient in defining vocabulary. Despite these obvious variations the creators of achievement tests appear to assume that there are children who can be described as "average" third graders, for example.

A final point involves the establishment of the norms to which children's performances are compared. The population used to establish these norms differs from test to test. It is valid to inquire of a particular test whether the child tested is to be compared with a group of his peers or with a vastly different group. It is conceivable, for example, that an urban school in a large eastern city may be administering a test whose norms are based on children in midwestern agricultural communities.

In addition many test makers establish a line below and above which certain percentages of the population are expected to score. It should not therefore be surprising that children do in fact fall below the dividing line. Yet this line is frequently construed as the "passing" mark for that test, and children who score below it are considered to have "failed." The result is that test makers "build in" failure for large numbers of children. As some children consistently fail to meet test standards, they may come to perceive themselves as inferior or unworthy—and finally as *failures*. This possibility is perhaps the greatest danger of the continual grading and testing of children in our schools, one which calls for a reappraisal of the use of tests; because it is to be hoped that all children could as a minimum be granted at least one freedom in school—freedom from being labeled failures.

Chapter
SIXTEEN
Grouping
for
Instruction

The first law requiring communities in North America to establish
elementary schools was passed by Massachusetts in 1647. This law decreed
that every town of more than 50 families had to organize an elementary
school and that every town of more than 100 families had to provide a
secondary school as well. The schools were to teach children to read and
to understand the laws of religion and of the secular government.
Attendance was not made compulsory, however, until two centuries later,
in 1852; again Massachusetts was the first state to institute such a
compulsory-attendance law.

Those early American schools had few problems of organization.
The children were generally housed in one room with one teacher. In some
towns pupils were so few that elementary and secondary schools were
combined. "Interage grouping" and "nongradedness" were realities in those
schools.

As the schools became larger and enrollments necessitated more
than one teacher and more than one room, problems of school organization
did arise; they have plagued educators ever since. As any system of
organization is in fact a method of classifying children, the criteria chosen
for grouping serve, in effect, as a statement of the school's values and
educational goals. A school that decides to segregate boys and girls in
different classes is making a statement about perceived differences between
the sexes. One that groups children according to I.Q.s is expressing its
priorities.

Nevertheless, schools confronted with a large number of children
are forced to devise some system of organizing them. By examining those
approaches that are most common in conventional classes more closely, we
can clarify the types of school organization preferred in open schools.

HORIZONTAL OR SINGLE-AGE GROUPING

The most frequent method of classifying children in schools is by age; each grade corresponds to a specific chronological age group. Children enter kindergarten at the approximate age of five and first grade at the approximate age of six. From then on, with a few exceptions, they proceed from grade to grade at the end of each school year.

This lock-step approach to school organization has come under attack from many quarters; critics point to the wide disparities—physical, emotional and intellectual—that may exist among children of approximately similar ages. Louise Bates Ames, for example, has argued that chronological age is an unreliable criterion for school placement and has suggested that "behavioral age" (how old a child *acts*, as determined by a series of behavioral tests) should be adopted instead. Ames attributes many school failures to the fact "that many children legally old enough to begin school are not old enough in their behavior to do so."[1] She claims that a majority of these students never catch up.

Although children may be assigned to grades in school according to their chronological ages, their actual placement within those grades is frequently based on such additional criteria as ability and achievement.

ABILITY GROUPING: HETEROGENEOUS VERSUS HOMOGENEOUS GROUPS

Ability grouping first started in the United States in the nineteenth century. It was originally conceived as a means of separating bright children and accelerating their progress through the elementary school, but it soon developed into a means of varying instruction for all groups of children: bright, "slow," and average. Grouping can be homogeneous or heterogeneous; that is, groups can be deliberately composed of either similar or dissimilar youngsters.

The word "homogeneous" is defined in the *Random House Dictionary* as "composed of parts all of the same kind . . . essentially alike." It is obvious that it can be applied to people only loosely, for no twenty-five children are "essentially alike." In schools, however, "homogeneity" generally means similar abilities or achievement in reading and mathematics, regardless of variation in other traits. "Heterogeneity" implies dissimilarity in ability or achievement.

Arguments about the wisdom of grouping homogeneously or hetero-

---

[1] Louis Bates Ames, *Is Your Child in the Wrong Grade?* (New York: Harper & Row, 1966), p. 7.

geneously have raged since this grouping first began. Those in favor of the former stress easier planning of lessons by teachers and more convenient tailoring of the curriculum to meet the varying needs of children with different abilities. Proponents of the latter speak of damage to the self-concepts of children in ability-grouped classes. The brighter children are said to acquire a false sense of superiority, whereas the slower ones are marked inferior. They also claim that, as the world is composed of many different kinds of people, children should learn in school to adjust to diversity rather than to sameness.

The practice of organizing classes into homogeneous ability groups runs counter to the philosophy of open education, which emphasizes the individuality of the child, respects his differences as well as his similarities, and assesses him on many dimensions beside academic achievement. Open classrooms have therefore tended to develop organizational forms that promote heterogeneity of groups rather than limit it.

GROUPING IN OPEN EDUCATION SCHOOLS

As school organization is an expression of the prevailing philosophy of the school, it is not surprising that schools organized for open education have different methods of grouping children. The concept of single-age classes may be eliminated; the traditional assignment of one class of children to one teacher may be modified; the graded approach to grouping and curriculum may be less rigid; or the school itself may be broken down into smaller units. Each of these possibilities represents an alternative form of organization for open education. Although none is indispensible in open education, they must all be understood as directions that open schools in the United States may well take.

Vertical or Interage Grouping

The antecedents of vertical grouping lie in the old village or rural school, where all elementary school children were grouped in the same room. Vertical grouping mixes children of different ages in the same classroom. The age range may encompass eighteen months or three years, but the most common span is two years.

Age groups in different classes overlap: sixes and sevens, sevens and eights, eights and nines, and so on. Or they may be distinct: sixes and sevens, eights and nines, tens and elevens, and so on. Schools can also combine vertical and horizontal grouping. Occasionally there may be reasons for keeping particular age groups together, especially those at either end of the school population: kindergarteners and the "graduating" class. These children are then placed in single-age groups and the rest of the school grouped vertically.

Vertical grouping is increasingly being adopted in open classrooms in the United States. Broadening the age range in a class tends to eliminate the grade-level approach to education and the corresponding stereotypes of what particular children should be "like" at given ages. It also inhibits teaching lessons to each class as a whole. Various other advantages, as well as disadvantages, have been suggested.

Advantages In most schemes of vertical grouping each child remains in the same class and with the same teacher for about two years. As a result the teacher starts each year with an established relationship with about half the class, which eliminates the need for some adjustments at the beginning of each school year. Particularly when the children are very young or entering an open classroom for the first time, the presence of a group of children already familiar with the structure, responsibilities, and limits of the open class can serve as a stabilizing factor. It also enables the teacher to become acquainted more quickly with the new children and to establish communication with their parents more quickly. Furthermore, longer-lasting relationships between the teacher and both children and parents cements understanding between home and school, a vital factor for open education.

A vertically grouped class is said to soften anxiety about learning problems especially among six- and seven-year-olds who are just beginning to read. As the teacher and child have two years together, the latter need not be considered a "failure" if he is still not reading at the end of the first year.

Within the class greater allowances for individual differences are possible because each child can relate to others in a much broader range of ages and presumably of intellectual and emotional development as well. The bright younger child may find intellectual companionship with older children easier but may feel more comfortable in physical or social activities with children his own age. Similarly, an older child may relate more easily, either intellectually or emotionally, to one who is a year younger. In addition, every child occasionally needs to experience or repeat activities associated with a younger age; he can do so without feeling conspicuous or inadequate in a vertically grouped class.

Perhaps one of the most important advantages of vertical grouping is the aid that older children can extend to younger ones. An important aspect of open education is provision for children to act as "teachers." A child can often learn more easily from another child than from an adult. In vertically grouped classes there are many opportunities for such contact. One child can listen to another read, can supervise or explain a game or activity, can instruct another in the use of materials, can administer a spelling test, or can help another child to practice some skills (as with flash cards). This kind of contact has been found to be beneficial to both participants; it is frequently the best method of reinforcing learning in the child who is teaching.

Disadvantages   The problems associated with vertical grouping generally revolve around meeting the individual needs of a more disparate group of children. Teachers may find it more difficult to provide the necessary materials and experiences for children with so broad a range of abilities and interests.

One of the declared advantages of vertical grouping is also viewed as a disadvantage by some teachers: The virtual elimination of lessons for the whole class can mean loss of an important time-saving device for the presentation of some material. Another difficulty is that vertical grouping may require more record keeping because so many children work on different activities.

Other charges are that older children tend to receive less intellectual stimulation in a class in which half the children are younger and that younger children demand disproportionate shares of attention.

Family Grouping   A pattern of vertical grouping that is increasingly popular in British informal classrooms is called "family grouping." This method is generally limited to younger children, those in "infant schools," ranging from about five to seven years old. Some British primary schools, however, have also been experimenting with family grouping in junior classes (ages seven to eleven).

Family grouping takes its name from a notion of the class as an extension of the family, with both older and younger children in the same room. The entire age range of the school is thus represented in each class. Several factors, unique to Great Britain, make this kind of family grouping advantageous.

In Great Britain most infant schools have a "staggered admissions" policy. Children are admitted at three times in the school year: at the beginning, after the Christmas holidays, and after the Easter vacation. Methods of coping with the new youngsters vary: Some schools establish "reception" classes for them; others are forced to accommodate them in already existing classes of five-year-olds, which are often just settling into routines, so that new children can be a disturbing factor. Sometimes older children have to be reassigned during the school year to make room for younger ones.

In family-grouped classes, however, new entrants can be dispersed among established classes; often they can be placed with older siblings, relatives, or friends. Rather than being placed with other immature children, the new entrant finds a stable environment in which the majority of the class, having been there for a year or more, is familiar with the routines. Other advantages are similar to those that we have described for patterns of vertical grouping in general.

The main disadvantage of family grouping in Great Britain seems to be the difficulty of meeting the needs of the older children, especially those who are almost ready to go on to junior school. Some British teachers believe that at this point they need special attention, which it is difficult to give them in family-grouped classes. A few teachers mention another disadvantage: They claim that many of the older children are burdened with the care of younger siblings at home and should therefore be relieved of this pressure at school. To meet these objections, several British informal schools have established a "transitional" form of vertical grouping; either the youngest or the oldest children are placed in a class by themselves, and the remainder of the infant or junior school is grouped vertically.

The decision on whether a class will be grouped vertically or horizontally depends, of course, on the particular teacher and children involved. The author's study of British schools has revealed that both patterns are used and that some schools include classes of each kind. (Details of the findings on British schools are reported in Appendix B.)

The School within a School

A significant element in the growth of open education in Great Britain has undoubtedly been the relatively small sizes of British schools. The Plowden committee has reported that a majority of state-maintained primary schools had totals of 100–300 pupils each.[2] British schools frequently house infant and junior classes in separate buildings. There is an attempt to limit infant schools to six classes and junior schools to eight.

In schools this small teachers and principals can know each child and his family, and the children can become acquainted with the entire faculty. Children can conveniently be permitted freedom to move through the buildings. The atmosphere undoubtedly engenders a closeness that is conducive to informal education. It is difficult to duplicate this atmosphere or to permit children the same degree of freedom in large American primary schools.

Richard A. Schmuck and Patricia A. Schmuck have reviewed studies of American school size:

> Students in small schools reported more personal kinds of satisfactions, for example, developing competence, being challenged, participating in activities they considered important, and achieving value clarity. . . .

> Students in small schools seem to make more efficient use of their facilities, at least in terms of group participation in educationally valuable activities. . . .

[2] Lady Bridget Plowden, et al, *Children and Their Primary Schools, Report of the Central Advisory Council for Education*, I (London: H.M. Stationery Office, 1967), p. 114.

Many activities can be conducted in the corridor. (Photograph courtesy of Merrick Public Schools, New York.)

The data on size give clear evidence that involvement and participation are not encouraged by large and impersonal schools.[3]

One solution to the problem of large schools in the United States may be to divide them into smaller units: "minischools" or "schools within schools." A group of classes spanning two or three age years can be housed in one wing of a building; these classes may be grouped horizontally or vertically. The teachers may function as equals, or one may be designated leader or deputy principal. The wing comes to have its own identity and certain common functions. For example, it may have a name, its own student government, and a newspaper. Classes work together on projects and common displays and meet together regularly.

Schools within a school lend themselves to team teaching or cooperative teaching. Certain joint activities can be conducted in the corridor. Speakers may be invited to speak to the entire "school." Parent volunteers and paraprofessional personnel can be shared among classes on the wing. Children may work cooperatively on various tasks, and, for the most part, they can be permitted freedom of movement through the wing.

A school may comprise several smaller schools organized in similar fashion. These minischools facilitate the establishment of an environment conducive to the growth of open education. They make it possible to en-

[3] Richard A. Schmuck and Patricia A. Schmuck, *Group Processes in the Classroom* (Dubuque: Brown, 1971), pp. 126–127.

large the physical space in which classes can function, to permit freedom of movement for children within defined limits, and to overcome the impersonality of the larger school. Teachers too may do a great deal more sharing. Many teachers now function behind closed doors, zealously guarding their own ways of doing things. Opening the doors of the classrooms while still limiting the open area makes it easier for teachers to share ideas, to plan joint activities, and to cooperate in solving the problems of individual children. A disruptive child, for example, may be more easily absorbed into another group during periods when his own class environment is especially difficult. In some schools the dividing walls between classrooms are removed, and an open space is established for the school within a school. In many ways these open spaces resemble open-plan schools.

Open-Plan Schools

An increasingly popular school design is the *open plan,* calling for large open areas and few fixed partitions. Instead, movable partitions can be used to create temporary rooms and hallways. The dividers can be removed to turn the entire area into a single open wing. A national survey of schools in forty-three states revealed that more than 50 percent of all the schools constructed in the United States between 1967 and 1970 were of this design.[4] Since then the trend has accelerated. The plan is becoming popular in other countries too. Ontario, Canada, for example, reported having built more than 400 open-plan schools between 1967 and 1972. Most primary schools now being built in England are also of this design.

In addition to the flexible use of space permitted by sliding or removable walls, these schools generally have other features in common. The floors are carpeted, and all furniture and equipment are movable. Internal space is organized so that central areas are available for use by all children: libraries; cooking areas; arts-and-crafts corners; areas for messy work, large constructions, or painting; small nooks for private work. It is important to include some "home" areas, where groups of children can meet, watch television, or engage in quiet work. Other small areas can be partitioned off for noisy activities like music and dance.

One inspector of schools from the Somerset Authority of Great Britain, which has built more than 100 open-plan schools since 1950 in order to keep pace with its expanding school population, insists that these home areas are crucial. He urges that they be furnished with a "domestic" feeling: perhaps with small chairs, curtains, and television sets. He thinks that they should also be enclosed to offer privacy but suggests that a wall

[4] *Open-Space Schools,* Project Bulletin No. 1 (Stanford, Calif.: School Planning Laboratory, School of Education, Stanford University, March 1970).

about 4 feet 6 inches high is enough to provide this sense while permitting teachers to observe the children.

In addition to the areas mentioned, there should be some provision for individual privacy—for teacher and pupil alike. One teacher may require a desk in a quiet corner, where he can work with individual children. Some children need a place where they can be alone or with one or two others at most. In one open classroom a small tent was pitched in a corner for this purpose.

Open-plan schools generally do not provide individual desks for children, but rather a variety of different seating areas: carpeted floors, wall benches, tables and chairs, stools, and some comfortable upholstered chairs. Architectural styles may vary widely. Most such schools are divided into large units that can accommodate 50–100 children each; others are like large boxes. A school in Connecticut has an interesting split-level design, with a winding staircase from the lower level to an upper level that is used for different interest areas.

Flexible design is stressed so that spaces can be reorganized to meet changing needs. For example, a series of wings similar to those in Figure 16.1 permits varying combinations of the 125 children accommo-

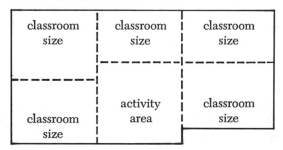

Figure 16.1   One Wing in an Open-Plan School

dated. The dotted lines represent removable partitions. A single class can be established for all 125 children, or there can be two classes of fifty and one of twenty-five, one of seventy-five and one of fifty, five of twenty-five, and so on. The possible combinations are many, and the space can be readily adjusted to the needs of the children.

Criticism of open-plan schools has been directed at the noise and possible confusion that can result from placing so many children in one undivided area. Some have stressed the problems confronted by children who require closer attention and more privacy. The difficulty of accounting for each child has also been mentioned, and indeed record keeping does require extra care in such a setting.

Proponents of such schools, on the other hand, stress the growth of pupils' initiative, freer use of interest areas and audio-visual equipment,

more flexible use of space permitting a greater range of activities, opportunities for children to interact with many more youngsters, and opportunities for team teaching, the specific advantages of which will be discussed in
Chapter Seventeen.

The relationship between open-plan schools and open education
requires clarification. The term "open plan" refers to the physical design
of a school. Other terms have been substituted: "open-space schools,"
"open-area schools," and sometimes just "open schools," which has caused
some confusion between the physical design of the school and its educational program. Actually, open education may or may not be practiced in
open-plan schools.

There is no doubt that the growth of open-plan schools is related
to the growing acceptance of open education, which has created a climate
for informality in schools. Teachers, too, have been amenable to open-plan
schools as a result of the opening of classroom doors in open education.
It is also true that open-plan schools lend themselves well to the practice
of open education.

But we must emphasize that open-plan schools are in no sense prerequisite to open education. Open classrooms can exist in various environments, including self-contained classrooms in quite traditional buildings.

Furthermore, the flexible arrangement of space does not by itself
create open education. Teachers in open-plan schools can continue to
teach in very traditional ways: lecturing most of the day to large groups

An open-plan school permits flexible use of space. (Photograph courtesy of Merrick Public
Schools, New York.)

of children, prescribing each child's curriculum, scheduling his day, and so on. In the process they can construct invisible walls around themselves, which are just as formidable as concrete partitions.

Team Teaching

Some open educators have questioned the use of the class itself as a basic unit. It had long been accepted that the best method of organizing elementary children in schools was in units of twenty to thirty children under the leadership of one teacher, who was responsible for teaching almost all subjects to the children and was expected to be expert in each. Debates generally revolved around optimum class size: What is the optimum number of children who can be assigned to one teacher while receiving the individual attention that elementary school children require? There have been many studies on optimum class size but little agreement on this question.

Some teachers have insisted that open education requires smaller classes, though this point has not been established. Most self-contained open classes are approximately the same size as are traditional classes.

Open educators have begun to address their attention to the validity of the class itself as a unit of organization. New approaches to classroom teaching have invalidated the notion that one teacher can be responsible for every aspect of a child's instruction. When lessons for the whole class are largely eliminated, there seems no further rationale for the class as the basic instructional group. Other units of pupil organization can be considered. Schools have grouped larger numbers of children together and made them the joint responsibility of several teachers or a team consisting of both professional and nonprofessional personnel. This approach, called "team teaching," will be discussed in detail in Chapter Seventeen.

GROUPING IN OPEN EDUCATION CLASSES

There are two perspectives from which grouping for instruction can be viewed. One is that of intraschool grouping, the organization of classes within the school; the other is intraclass grouping, the organization of groups within individual classes or teaching units. It is to the latter we shall turn in the remainder of this chapter.

Emphasis on individualization in open classrooms raises the question "Is there a need for groups?" This question highlights a misunderstanding of individualized instruction; the latter implies, not that every child works individually, but that each child's individual needs are taken into account. Frequently they can most effectively be met in groups.

Groups are a significant component of open education, essential to the functioning of the open classroom, even though they are often organized and operate quite differently from the way those in traditional classes are organized and operate. There are various kinds of classroom groups:

> Instructional or interest groups, formed around areas of the curriculum, whether reading, mathematics, or more specific projects like writing a play, painting a mural, or operating a store.

> Organizational groups, related to seating arrangements, administrative details, and the like.

> Social groups, formed for purposes of associative play and talking or working together.

In traditional classrooms most groups are instructional, highly structured, formed and led by the teacher, and fairly permanent. Movement of pupils among groups is rare. Most frequently the group is a reading group, chosen on the basis of reading ability. Pupils assigned to a reading group generally stay with that group throughout the term. A status hierarchy accompanies such grouping, the student's status reflecting his assignment to a particular reading group.

In open classrooms all three types of groups are common. In contrast to those in traditional classes, however, these groups tend to be flexible, loosely structured, formed and led by pupils as well as by teachers, and relatively impermanent. There is less likely to be an established reading group, for example.

Organization of Groups

Instructional groups organized by the teacher for specific learning tasks are usually temporary. As children are encouraged to work individually and do not depend upon constant instruction and detailed assignments, they tend to proceed at different paces and to engage in different tasks. Groups do not acquire permanence under these circumstances. For example, one group of children may begin by reading from the same book and may receive instruction in short vowel sounds. By the end of a month, however, it is unlikely that all the children will still be reading the same story in the same book or requiring the same phonic instruction. Some may need additional help with short vowels; others may need other kinds of help. Some may still be reading the original book, whereas others will have completed it. The teacher can now organize a new group, based on current requirements. In some instances, an instructional group lasts only for the course of an introductory lesson.

The same is true in mathematics. The teacher may select a group for instruction in a particular skill: perhaps multiplication of two-place numbers. Participation in the group may be open to others in the class as well. For example, some who have already received instruction in multiplication of two-place numbers may wish additional exposure. After a few days the teacher invites those who need further work in multiplication of two-place numbers to meet with her, omitting those who are now ready to proceed on their own. The latter may meet with her later in the week as part of a different group.

Beside mathematics and reading groups there are groups for project work, science, social studies, cooking, arts and crafts, and so on. These groups are most often organized by the students, though at times the teacher will suggest that certain children work together to ensure inclusion of particular strengths in the group or to place one individual with others. Social factors must be taken into consideration even in the organization of instructional groups.

Interest groups are not always distinct from instructional groups. A group of children working together on drawing up blueprints for a toy house may find it necessary to learn mathematical proportions and may approach the teacher for group instruction. Another group may want to learn punctuation, in order to write invitations to a presentation. Still other children may wish to analyze a book that they have read. Interest groups too are generally loosely structured.

The meetings of interest and instructional groups are often open to other members of the class, and for this reason they can be announced on the bulletin board. For example, other children may wish to participate in learning punctuation or mathematical proportions for reasons of their own.

Organizational groups are also common in open classrooms. When children are encouraged to accept responsibility for administrative and other chores, they may form groups to facilitate attendance taking, housekeeping, maintenance of bulletin boards, student government, selecting new learning centers, and so on. Students usually assume responsibility for choosing these groups.

Pupils in open classrooms form social groups too. The atmosphere of the class encourages them to talk and work together, so that, even when they are engaged in individual tasks, they may not work in isolation. There is a great deal of socialization as children sit and talk in groups while they work. Most often the group is busy with a common subject, perhaps mathematics or writing, but each with a different specific related task. Frequently they seek help from one another in solving problems.

The preponderance of groups formed and led by pupils deserves emphasis. Whenever possible, pupils are permitted to decide with whom they wish to work. Even in instructional groups led by the teacher she may on some occasions announce the topic and permit voluntary participation. The functioning of a group can be enhanced when the members are com-

Children in open classrooms frequently work in small groups. (Photograph courtesy of New Rochelle Public Schools, New York.)

fortable together. If one pupil feels insecure or threatened by others in a group, his performance is apt to be affected adversely.

Leadership of a group often resides with the pupils rather than the teacher, in instructional as well as in other groups. It has been noted, especially in vertically grouped classes, that older children often teach younger ones. But all students in open classrooms are encouraged to teach their peers. If a child has a problem he may consult the teacher, but he may just as frequently consult another student. It is common to see a student working with a spontaneously formed group—explaining how to use some material, demonstrating a craft, or even explaining a mathematical skill. Children often practice skills with other students, using flash cards or other devices or administering spelling tests to one another.

Working together in groups is important experience for the child. Apart from its instructional value, such work promotes his social development: his ability to work with others, to share experiences, to learn from others, and to exert leadership of his peers.

Chapter
SEVENTEEN
Team and
Cooperative
Teaching

Team teaching is an organizational device that is particularly interesting to open educators, though it first developed in line with other educational philosophies. Throughout history there have been isolated attempts to organize teams of teachers to work with large groups of students. Several educational experiments in the United States, dating back to the early 1900s, have partly incorporated the team approach—notably the Winnetka, Dalton, Gary, and Hosic cooperative plans. The term "team teaching" is, however, relatively new, in widespread use only since the late 1950s.

Team teaching received its major impetus in the post-Sputnik era in the United States. The growing use of technological equipment in that period seemed to stimulate different instructional patterns. The rationale was that presentations or lectures to individual classes were often redundant and that one teacher could as easily introduce a subject or show a film to a large group as to one class, thus freeing other teachers to work with smaller groups of students or even individuals during the same period. The emphasis was on efficiency: the more efficient use of teachers' time. The format in which teachers lecture to students was not basically altered by the shift to team teaching; only the size of the group listening to the lectures changed.

COOPERATIVE VERSUS TEAM TEACHING

The distinction between cooperative and team teaching must be understood. There are various channels for cooperative teaching in schools, most of which do not affect the basic organization of the class. For example, teachers in conventional schools may collaborate in developing work units or may exchange students for different subjects. Each teacher remains, however, primarily responsible for one group of students.

In contrast, team teaching implies that a group of teachers shares collective responsibility for all the students assigned to it. Judson T. Shaplin and Henry F. Olds, Jr., have offered this definition of team teaching: *"Team teaching is an instructional organization in which two or more teachers are given responsibility, working together, for all or a significant part of the instruction of the same group of pupils."*[1] We shall use this definition in our discussion.

Both team teaching and cooperative teaching are practiced in some open classrooms. In practice the distinction between the two is not always clearly recognizable, and much of our discussion in this chapter is applicable to both. Neither is a requirement for open education, but teachers will wish to be familiar with the possibilities of both.

COOPERATIVE TEACHING IN OPEN CLASSROOMS

Most teachers in open classrooms engage in some degree of cooperative teaching. The very movement toward open education entails openness towards others' ideas, sharing with professional colleagues, recognition of the talents of other faculty members, and desire to make these talents available to more than one group of children. Furthermore, as we have noted, teachers in open classrooms have opened their doors. In the process they have grown away from the "your student versus my student" approach that characterizes many traditional classes. Students from other classes are frequently invited through open classroom doors, and teachers exhibit mutual concern for all the students in the school.

Cooperative teaching takes many forms in open classrooms. Children in different classes may share interest centers or resource areas. They may work in a room or corridor accessible to several classes. An aide, a volunteer, one of the teachers, or all three may supervise this area. For example, one group of teachers may share the services of an aide in teaching cooking or crafts. Children from several classes may participate jointly. Sometimes a joint library is created; teachers pool their reference books and resource materials, and children from many classes have access to them.

There are other illustrations of cooperative teaching. Two or more teachers may decide to specialize in particular areas in their respective rooms. One may be more interested in music, another in dramatics. One

---

[1] Judson T. Shaplin and Henry F. Olds, Jr. (eds), *Team Teaching* (New York: Harper & Row, 1964), p. 15.

may equip her room with more science and mathematics equipment, another with pottery or other arts-and-crafts supplies. Students are permitted to pursue independent activities in either of the rooms. In this system teachers sometimes change rooms to work with children in particular centers. Cooperative teaching has the further advantage of permitting the sharing of talents among larger groups. In one school a teacher was a gifted musician. Through him the entire school population was exposed to rich musical experiences. Children were constantly composing pieces and running to "Mr. Oliver" to play them. Others were learning to play a variety of musical instruments. Still others were building and inventing new kinds of musical instruments under his supervision.

Teachers can also make joint plans for a group of environmental studies or projects, each taking responsibility for different ones. Children choose the particular ones in which they wish to participate and then work with the appropriate teachers.

Another advantage of cooperative teaching is the possibility of freer exchange of students between rooms. A child from one room can participate in some activities offered in another because he needs practice with some materials, has missed a particular discussion, or is simply interested. To facilitate this freedom of exchange, events in all the rooms are posted on a common bulletin board. Interest groups can also be drawn from all the cooperating classes, rather than from only one, which expands the children's range of possible choices. Finally, individual pupils with particular knowledge or hobbies can serve as resources in different rooms.

Cooperative teaching has many of the advantages of team teaching, whether or not it actually takes the latter form. These advantages will be spelled out in more detail in our discussion of team teaching.

TEAM TEACHING IN OPEN CLASSROOMS

In open classrooms team teaching has quite different emphases from those of traditional classrooms, where it has usually been adopted as a more effective means of organizing students for instruction. In open classrooms it can serve to increase the options open to both teachers and to pupils as they find their own paths to learning. For teachers interested in cooperative or team teaching, a more detailed review of some of the advantages and disadvantages is pertinent.

Advantages

Team teaching facilitates professional growth by providing teachers with opportunities to share ideas, plans, and observations in the classroom.

It also offers support and aid in attempts to solve many of the problems that may arise in the early stages of organizing open classrooms. It allows for wider use of expertise and the special talents of different teachers and children. Furthermore, it permits a greater degree of specialization by teachers. One may be more interested in art, drama, or science, for example and can assume leadership for all activities associated with his interest. The concomitant disadvantage—that teachers may tend to focus too narrowly on a particular subject—will be discussed later in this chapter.

Team teaching encourages children to develop broader ranges of interests, for more people with diverse interests are available as consultants or resources. It also facilitates use of a larger space in which varied learning centers can be organized: The result is a richer environment offering a greater choice of activities.

Team teaching permits organization of a larger group, within which a child is more likely to find companions close to him in abilities, interests, and needs. Children learn to adjust to more than one adult, a necessary aspect of social growth. At the same time more children are exposed to a "master" teacher, one who has learned to work most effectively in an open environment; the presence of such a teacher can compensate for that of an occasional less capable or less experienced one. In fact, working in teams may be particularly valuable for beginning teachers, who can be paired with more experienced ones.

With team teaching there is less disruption in a class when one teacher is away for a prolonged period of time, which may make it easier for teachers to exchange classroom visits or to attend conferences during school hours.

Team teaching permits greater use of audio-visual equipment, for the combined budgets of several classes may cover the cost of an overhead, opaque, or film-strip projector; a camera; a tape recorder; a record player; a television set; or the like.

Team teaching also minimizes duplication of effort, for only one center may be established for each interest, and lessons need not be repeated in each individual class .

Finally team teachers have more adult companionship in the course of their working day.

Disadvantages

Some children are said to benefit from close relationships with one classroom teacher, and this type of relationship may be more difficult to achieve in a team.

Furthermore, some children find it difficult to adjust to a larger group, and some may be more easily overlooked. Teachers cannot always come to know all the children in the group as well as they can in a self-contained classroom.

Children may also be confused when different members of the team have different standards, and additional discipline problems may result from putting a larger number of children together.

It is also charged that parent conferences are unwieldy, there is a greater demand for meetings, record keeping may be more time-consuming, and some teachers may find it difficult to work with other teachers because of personality, educational philosophy, or attitudes toward children. Establishing one teacher as a team leader also runs counter to most teachers' preference for equality among all teachers in a school. Yet without such differentiation the team may function less well.

To Team or Not To Team

Having noted both advantages and disadvantages of team teaching, teachers must decide: to team or not to team? The decision in each instance is personal, but certain generalizations may be helpful. Team teaching should be adopted only when it seems a more desirable form of class organization for a particular group of children and teachers—never because it seems "the way" to establish an open classroom or is mandated by a particular administrator. The success of team teaching is much less likely if any member feels that she has been forced to participate. It is true that most people who decide to enter teams do so with some reservations, and a teacher need not wait until she is 100 percent certain.

Teachers who team in open classes do have advantages over those who do so in traditional classes. The "openness" of the classroom is conducive to frank, honest relationships among teachers, as among pupils. Similarly, the noncompetitive atmosphere, so different from that in many traditional classes, also reduces competition among teachers and helps to engender an atmosphere of cooperation. It should be easier in an open classroom for a teacher to admit to shortcomings and to seek help from another teacher. The teacher in an open classroom does not have to know everything. In a successful team a teacher can say honestly to his partner: "Mike is interested in pendulums, but I know nothing about them. Can you help?" or "I'm having no success explaining long division to Dan. Would you work with him?"

Although teams have been known to function adequately even when the members did not work in complete harmony, dissension certainly inhibits the team and often constitutes an emotional drain on the participants. For this reason, the composition of the team is a primary consideration.

Choosing a Team

The first criterion in selecting members of a team is their compatibility. For this reason, before deciding to work together, teachers should explore their own attitudes on several important matters:

1. *Assignment of Responsibilities to Children.* What choices will children be permitted? What degree of freedom to design their own curriculum and to make other decisions about their work?
2. *Mutual Goals.* Is there agreement on goals? Does any teacher believe that certain areas should receive priority?
3. *Initial Organization of the Classroom.* Does any teacher believe that certain activities should be restricted to the morning or afternoon? Should children be permitted free choice of activities throughout the day?
4. *Teachers' Work Habits.* Does one teacher prefer to come in early while others prefer to stay at the end of the school day? If so, they may have difficulty arranging convenient times in which to meet.
5. *Standards for Pupils' Work.* What is considered acceptable from students? What is expected from them within a given period?
6. *Discipline.* What is an acceptable noise level? What is to be considered an infraction? How are infractions to be dealt with?
7. *Working with Children.* Does one teacher prefer group work to individual work? Does one tend to be more successful with low-achieving children? Or high-achieving children?
8. *Division of Labor.* Is there agreement on the philosophy that will govern the division of labor among team members?
9. *Review of Children's Work.* How often and by whom will children's work be reviewed? Will there be daily or less frequent meetings with children? One teacher may feel the need to meet with children daily, even if only for brief periods, to review written work, and she may be irritated if another teacher does not "do her share."
10. *Abilities.* What particular strengths can each teacher bring to the team?

Some teachers are unaccustomed to having other teachers in the classroom. It may cause particular strain when they are also attempting a teaching method new to them. For this reason, it is also important to know something about the personality of each team member, how she deals with frustration and problems, and how adaptable and open to change she is. Fortunately, many of the very traits that lead teachers to embrace open education contribute to their ability to work with other faculty members in teams. But teachers must be certain that other team members agree on the philosophy of open education. A teacher who confuses an open classroom with a free classroom, in the "free school" tradition, can easily destroy the team's effectiveness. Most important, teachers should not join with others whom they do not respect professionally, no matter how close their personal friendships may be. There must be mutual respect for professional ability and confidence in the quality of each teacher's relationship with the children in the team.

Pairs in which one member is a man and the other a woman tend to work well, but only when all the other conditions mentioned have been met. Similarly, teams in which members have different strengths have certain advantages. Nevertheless, in an open classroom it is important that the team not be viewed as a combination of subject specialists. A team may profit from different members' special abilities in creative or academic work, but it is not essential that teachers have complementary skills.

From our stress on compatibility among team members, it should not be concluded that they must hold identical views on all subjects. It is more important to understand where the differences among members lie and to be sure that those differences are ones on which the members are prepared to compromise. Joseph C. Grannis, who was involved in a pioneer team-teaching project, has declared that "idiosyncratic ways are as much to be prized as to be feared in team teaching and we would do well not to ascribe too many of our troubles (in team teaching) to the fact that the teachers are not all dealt out of the same deck."[2] Certainly an open classroom in which individual differences are prized and conformity is rejected as a goal for students should apply the same values to teachers. A combination of unique yet compatible teachers is most desirable in choosing members of the team.

The Size of the Team

There is no single approved size of teams for open education. They generally range from two teachers for about 50 students (the equivalent of two conventional classes) to three or four teachers for 75–100 students (the equivalent of three or four conventional classes); occasionally they are even larger. Several factors determine the size of the team: available space, personnel, and the specific children involved.

Teams of two teachers are a good first step toward team teaching. Before a larger team is organized, the participants must be certain that the advantages of pooling their varied talents will not be offset by the disadvantages of dealing with the larger number of students.

The children involved will have to be carefully reviewed. Inclusion of many children with special problems may exacerbate the difficulties of each. It is also imperative that adequate space be provided. Cramped quarters without provisions for privacy for small groups are bound to inhibit the team's functioning.

[2] Joseph C. Grannis, "Team Teaching and the Curriculum," in Shaplin and Olds, op. cit., p. 138.

Differentiated Staffing

Many teams have adopted forms of differentiated staffing. They may be composed of both professional and nonprofessional personnel; the latter includes paraprofessionals and clerical aides. Teaching interns or students can also be assigned to a team. Some teams are still further differentiated: One of the teachers is designated as team leader or chairperson, with additional authority.

The team leader may be elected by other members of the team or appointed. Some teams rotate this position. The leader's responsibilities usually include coordinating the work of the team, arranging for team meetings, and representing the team in discussions with the administration. The leader may also be expected to delegate tasks among other members.

A team in open education will probably make use of some aides or students. A larger team in particular does seem to require paraprofessional assistance, and the designation of one of its members as team leader. A smaller, two-teacher team is less likely to require either of these measures in order to function effectively.

Planning a Team

Although it may not be advisable to decide in detail beforehand how the team will function, careful initial planning and organization are essential to successful team teaching. British headmasters who had instituted team teaching reported that six months' advance preparation was the minimum time required.[3] Such a planning period enables team members to explore one another's philosophies, to observe the functioning of established teams, and to anticipate many problems that may inhibit their work. They must also decide in advance on their goals, the allocation of responsibilities, record keeping, methods of working together, arrangement of space and resources, and materials to be ordered. Some schools can increase the budget allotment for the first year of team teaching to cover the cost of additional equipment. There must, however, be agreement on how this money is to be allocated.

It may also be necessary to inform parents that team teaching is planned for their children. The extent to which this notification is required varies from community to community, depending upon the relationships between professional staff and parents and the degree of general support for educational innovations among the parents. The roster of students to be included must also be agreed upon. Will the children be grouped vertically or horizontally? By what criteria will children be assigned to the team? Other faculty members may have to be involved in the plans. Although

[3] John Freeman, *Team Teaching in Britain* (London: Ward Lock, 1969), p. 382.

special considerations may be expected in the initial organization of a team, it should demand as little as possible from non-team members.

Organizing the Space

When two or more teachers have decided to work cooperatively, they may request assignment to adjoining classrooms and perhaps even removal of the partition walls. Although a unified space is ultimately desirable, it may not be essential that the walls be removed immediately. Two rooms across a corridor from each other, preferably at the end of the corridor so that it too can be used by the team, will permit free movement between classrooms.

If two separate rooms are used, one can be organized as a reading, language, library, or research center, focusing on quieter activities; the other can be reserved for more noisy activities like music or for messier activities like arts and crafts, mathematics and science projects, and water and sand play. The corridor can hold desks or tables for writing and paper-and-pencil exercises; it can also be used for large constructions and murals. If the entire cluster of rooms on a corridor has been organized for an open approach, the corridor itself can be used for noisy activities.

When a large open space is available, it is still sometimes desirable

Rooms within rooms can be created for quiet work. (Photograph courtesy of Guggenheim School, Port Washington Public Schools, New York.)

to place quieter and more active centers apart. It is important to emphasize once again that large open rooms must contain quiet nooks or corners for either individuals or small groups of children. Some children occasionally need to "escape" from a crowd of fifty or more peers. Quiet corners can be created by partitioning small areas; erecting tents, Indian tepees, "forts," and "houses"; or by leaving "crawl spaces" under a teacher's desk or table; even an upholstered chair turned to face the wall can serve this purpose.

Carrels enclosed on three sides also offer some privacy in large rooms. They can be constructed from commercial components, or a desk or part of a table can be walled in on three sides by heavy corrugated cardboard. Rooms within rooms can be created from plywood or heavy corrugated cardboard. These "rooms" are valuable for small groups.

Organizing the Students

The roster of pupils is often broken down so that each teacher is assigned a "home" group for administrative chores like taking attendance and collecting lunch money. The teacher may also meet with "her" pupils during the day. "Home" groups are established in a variety of ways. Random division of the list into even alphabetical groups is the easiest way. To ensure that each group is representative of the class, teachers can make sure that the age and ability ranges of the class as a whole are reflected in each group. In a vertically grouped class, the "home" groups can be based on age: third-year students assigned to one teacher and fourth-year students to another, for example.

Each of these methods has been used successfully. Proponents of an alphabetical or random distribution argue that grouping children by age emphasizes age differences and undermines the advantages of vertical grouping by making social and instructional intermingling more difficult. They also claim that the children tend to associate one teacher with the younger children and the other with the older children. Others prefer age division because some activities seem more appropriate for one age group than for the other. Grouping the children by age during "home" meetings also facilitates class discussions and assignments. With very young children —kindergartners; and first- and second-graders, the choice of stories for a final story hour each day is easier. Furthermore, when children remain with a team for two years, some of the discussions or activities required of the younger children will already be familiar to older children. Teachers who prefer "home" groups to be representative of the entire class can regroup children for activities when necessary to overcome these difficulties, however.

In some classes teachers who wish to emphasize that all members of the team are responsible for the entire class change "home" groups during the year. Whether or not this change is made depends upon the team. Sometimes one teacher may think that her group is not using the strengths of another teacher sufficiently. Yet, particularly with young children, the presence of one particular teacher may offer an additional bit of security, and it is therefore often best to maintain the same "home" groups.

It should be remembered that, unless there are special reasons, arising from the needs of the children themselves, "home" groups are simply administrative units; their establishment does not imply one teacher's special responsibility for instructing a particular group. Sometimes teachers do decide on greater division of responsibility for individual children, in order to facilitate parent conferences and writing report cards. One teacher may assume responsibility for regular conferences with one group of students and for maintaining their overall records. This group will not necessarily coincide with her "home" group. Teachers may also alternate their work with this "record" group, perhaps after each marking period.

Organizing the Work

Teachers must decide on the division of responsibilities within the team. We have just discussed allocation of overall responsibility for individual children. There may also have to be a division of instructional tasks. Some teams divide some subjects among the members: One teaches reading, for example, and another mathematics. This type of specialization often poses problems in open classrooms, where subjects are not always clearly delineated. If it is used, it is basically so that one member of the team can be familiar with all the children's experiences in a subject, can ensure that all are exposed to certain skills, and can keep track of their progress.

In some teams teachers prefer to assume responsibility for different centers, according to their own interests. For example, one teacher may help children to set up a newspaper workshop and may want to continue working with them on producing newspapers; another may come to be viewed as the "consumer consultant" for the class. Others will be adept at music, art, or craft work. In one open classroom each teacher in a team of three started in one of three areas (arts and crafts, reading and writing, or mathematics) every morning. Children could choose one of these three or could continue with other work, but sometime during the day each child was expected to see each teacher. The teachers rotated their areas weekly.

In organizing the work of the team, nonteaching personnel or teaching interns may be assigned to specific centers for part of the day, again in accordance with their own interests and strengths. For example, in one room a part-time aide may teach a craft or bake with the children; in one school an aide offered weekly guitar lessons. In making these arrangements, teachers are guided by various considerations. First, assignments should be flexible; no one should be so tied to a center that work there becomes isolated from that of the rest of the class. Second, all members of the team should have opportunities to view the total work of the children, so that they will be able to make any one child's experiences more meaningful and to suggest ways in which his growing interests can be extended.

When teachers divide instructional responsibilities, they also tend to change assignments regularly: every week or two or every month. In this way each can be aware of what every child is doing in all aspects of his work and can suggest ways of integrating his studies or recommend instruction as required. Furthermore, no teacher becomes so identified with one field that children do not feel free to ask for other help from him during the course of a day.

Teachers who work in this manner claim that there is another advantage in frequently shifting assignments: The child is exposed to different approaches to curricula. All the teachers are familiar with his work and can cooperate in helping him to solve problems that he may encounter or in suggesting further directions for him. Teachers also insist that they can more

Teachers divide instructional responsibilities in a team. (Photograph courtesy of Merrick Public Schools, New York.)

clearly gauge a child's progress in a specific area when they return to him after a period of time. If he seems to have progressed insufficiently, the teachers can consult about causes.

The basic consideration in organizing the work of the team is how the children react. Are they comfortable with all the teachers in the team? Are they able to profit from the strengths of each? Are they making progress? Is the organization conducive to their growth as self-directed individuals? Whatever arrangements are made, they will have to be reviewed regularly to keep them responsive to the changing needs of the class.

A final note on organizing work: Teachers must make certain that no child is "lost in the shuffle"; that each child knows whom to approach with a problem and that at any one time one of the teachers is clearly responsible for him—"responsible" not in the traditional sense of prescribing his exact course of study but in the sense of awareness of his functioning, his accomplishments, and his interactions with peers.

Planning the Work

Adequate preparation time is essential to the success of a team. A specified period each day (even if only a few minutes in the morning) and a few longer periods each week should be agreed upon in advance for planning sessions. Preferably these periods should occur during the school day. It is difficult for many teachers to plan effectively at the end of the school day, when they are tired. Planning sessions should include, first, a review of the current work of the class. Teachers should examine together what is being accomplished, which centers appear to be used most, which appear to be losing the children's interest, in which topics and projects the children are engaged, the reading and mathematics curriculum, which books are being read.

Second, they should make both short-term and long-term plans for future work. They should project plans for new centers or the launching of new projects that may require ordering of materials or other prior arrangements.

Third, they should review individual pupils' work. Each child should be discussed by all members of the team at least once a month, but those who require more attention can be discussed in these special planning sessions.

Fourth, a brief review of the records is usually helpful, in order to agree that they are sufficiently complete or that some may be unnecessary.

It is clear that planning is not only essential for the efficient functioning of a team but also quite time-consuming. For this reason, it is important that these planning sessions themselves be organized. Too often, without an agreed agenda they may become occasions for social interchange.

Records of the Team

The actual records kept by team teachers need not differ from those kept in other open classrooms. In Chapter 5 we discussed these records in detail. There are a few additional points about records in a team context that bear emphasis, however.

First, records of children's work are even more important in a team situation. When teachers are alternating responsibility for a subject or a center, for example, they will need to know what experiences the children have already had in order to avoid repetition. For this reason team members have a responsibility to keep accurate records of their work with youngsters. Such records make it possible for each team member to plan her work with a child, to hold parent conferences, and to meet with school personnel about a child's particular needs—without always having to call upon other members of the team.

Second, each team member should assume responsibility for checking all the records of particular children regularly. These assignments may be alternated, but clear-cut assignment of responsibility for the total work of each child may be helpful, to ensure that no child will be overlooked.

Finally the cautions offered about records previously are even more applicable in the team situation. Only records that have specific purposes and are of more than fleeting value should be maintained. It is important that teachers not become bogged down in records, that they keep only those that are necessary to the functioning of the team.

Meeting with Parents

There is usually a general meeting of parents and teachers at a "Meet Your Teacher" night, a class tea, or an open house, once a term. It may be burdensome for each team member to attempt to meet each child's parents individually. Individual parent conferences for a large number of students can be quite time-consuming.

Some team teachers have solved this problem by dividing the individual parent conferences among the members but conducting them at the same time. In this way, though a parent meets with only one of the teachers a few minutes can be allotted either at the beginning or end of each conference for brief introductions to the other teachers on the team. If a parent has a particular reason for a meeting with one of the other teachers, it can usually be arranged either during the conference period or at a later time.

There are some pupils for whom teachers will prefer joint conferences, but these conferences should be kept to a minimum. A parent conference may be less relaxed when more than one teacher is present. Some parents find it easier to talk to one teacher at a time. It is important, however, that the teacher who is conducting the conference have accurate records and be adequately briefed by the other teachers so that she is able to discuss the child fully with the parent.

General Comments

In reviewing team teaching, it should be borne in mind that it is basically a method of organizing classes. It does not by itself affect the basic philosophy of the class or even the teaching methods. Openness is independent of team teaching. It can exist in a self-contained classroom yet be completely absent in a team situation. Just as teachers may build invisible walls in classrooms without apparent walls, they may isolate themselves within cooperative or team units.

There is no question that a form of cooperative or team teaching can contribute positively to a teacher's acceptance of open education. Professional support, professional stimulation, and sharing of talents in this situation are valuable assets, which are not easily available otherwise in many American schools. In the final analysis, however, team teaching remains an "optional extra" for open-classroom teachers.

Chapter
EIGHTEEN
Parents,
Volunteers,
and Paraprofessionals

Open education is based on an approach to children and teaching so different from that experienced by most parents in their own education that they are frequently distrustful of it. Even parents who are dissatisfied with the education that they themselves have received and conscious of its limitations may still endorse a similar approach for their children—possibly because the familiar is often preferred to the untried. Or perhaps schools have left the impression that unsuccessful education is the fault of the children and not of the schools. As a result, the adult who is dissatisfied with his own education may assume that the responsibility was his own and that his child can do better within the system.

Gaining the support of parents is a primary objective of open educators, who recognize that the success of an open class may well depend upon it. It is extremely difficult, perhaps impossible, to conduct an open class when parents are hostile. Their fears about a program are easily communicated to their children, which exacerbates the problem. On the other hand, supportive parents are valuable resources for the open class. Similarly, a teacher's understanding of a child's home environment and respect for his background are essential. In their absence, the child may be torn between conflicting pressures and unable to function. It is paramount that the child perceive unity between his teachers and his parents, the significant adults in his life.

For these reasons open educators seek active cooperation between home and school. The Plowden report has stressed this objective: "One of the essentials for educational advance is a closer partnership between the two parties to every child's education. . . . Home and school interact continuously.

An improvement in school may raise the level of parental interest, and that in turn may lead to further improvement in school."[1]

FOSTERING PARENTAL UNDERSTANDING

When an open class is first being established, the extent of parental involvement depends largely upon the existing relations between parents and school. In some schools there is a tradition of leaving educational decisions to professionals and little questioning by parents of educational plans. In others it would be inconceivable to plan open classes without informing parents. Similar considerations determine whether or not certain children should be assigned to established open classes. Some schools that have both traditional and open classrooms may offer parents the choice for their children; others insist on making this judgment themselves.

Whether or not parents are involved before the assignment of their children to the open class, a program of parent education should be undertaken during the school term. There are at least five objectives of such a program:

1. To acquaint parents with the history and philosophy of open education.
2. To relate this philosophy to the educational practices of the specific classroom.
3. To suggest experiences outside of school which supplement the child's work in school.
4. To explain school policies on the work of the class.
5. To secure parental support for and participation in the work of the class.

Concurrent with parent education there must be a process of teacher education. As parents are learning about the school and its objectives for their children, teachers are learning about the children's homes and the parents' objectives for these same children. The significance of this kind of interaction is obvious.

Communicating with Parents

Programs of parent education can take several forms.

Parent-Teacher Meetings Meetings between teachers and parents fall into two categories: those confined to parents of children in the same

[1] Lady Bridget Plowden, *et al*, *Children and Their Primary Schools* (London: H.M. Stationery Office, 1967), p. 37.

class and larger meetings with parents of children in different classes. The smaller meetings focus on a specific class, its organization and its activities. Films or slides of the class in action can be shown, and facets of its work can be discussed: the topics and projects being investigated, the activity centers, and classroom experiences. Together parents and teachers examine how certain aspects of school life can be reinforced at home and how aspects of home life can be expanded at school.

Series of meetings will also be held with larger groups of parents, as part of the regular Parent-Teacher Association meetings or separately. More general topics are on the agendas at such meetings. Speakers may be invited to discuss different features of the philosophy of open education. In some districts teachers or parents lead these discussions themselves. Theories of how children learn as they relate to open education, can be analyzed: For example, the views of Jean Piaget can be discussed. One purpose of these meetings is to explain to parents the sound concepts of child development on which open education is based.

There may also be meetings devoted to aspects of the curriculum in open classes. The importance of play and activity may have to be clarified. Parents may seek reassurance that reading and mathematics will not be neglected, that there is no conflict between the goal of academic achievement and open education. A reading list can be provided, and when possible books and articles can be made available for circulation.[2]

Seminars and Study Groups   Seminars and study groups may focus on any aspect of open education: its philosophy, organization, curriculum, and so on. It may be necessary to schedule meetings at various morning and evening hours to ensure parent participation. Occasionally these groups may meet at the homes of parents. When morning seminars are held at the school, some older children may be asked to baby-sit with younger siblings. Leaders for these groups are usually drawn from among the parents, the school staff or the community.

Study groups can at times be more directly involved in the work of a class. Parents can undertake to develop materials for a project. They may visit (frequently in the company of teachers) other schools or be invited to educational conferences. Seminars may also include sessions devoted to child care, developmental problems, parent-child relations, consumer education, and community problems. These sessions can be led by a school

[2] The following works are recommended for this purpose: John Blackie, *Inside the Primary School* (New York: Schocken, 1971); Charles Silberman, *Crisis in the Classroom* (New York: Random House, 1970); Plowden, *op. cit.*, Joseph Featherstone, "Schools for Children," *The New Republic*, (August 19, 1967); Featherstone, "How Children Learn," *The New Republic* (September 2, 1967); and Featherstone, "Teaching Children To Think," *The New Republic* (September 9, 1967). Reprints of the Featherstone articles are available.

guidance counselor, or a psychologist, or by someone from the community.

Seminars and study groups serve an important function in the school. They are frequently the most effective forum for solving community problems that affect the school. By providing a nonthreatening, often social atmosphere in which different groups of parents can meet, they encourage social contact among parents who may have different cultural backgrounds but common interests. They may provide rare opportunities for many parents to become acquainted with one another. They also offer a forum in which parents can openly express questions, doubts, or endorsements of the program of the open classroom. The reactions of parents can be helpful to teachers who must assess both the positive and the negative aspects of the developing program.

Workshops Workshops for parents should include opportunities to use the materials of the classroom much as children use them. Parents may be invited, for example, to work on some activity cards, and in the process they may learn more about the mathematics program than could be gained from a lecture on the subject. Similarly, parents often enjoy the opportunity

Workshops enable parents to experiment with classroom materials. (Photograph courtesy of Columbus School, New Rochelle Public Schools, New York.)

to bind a book of their favorite poems or use art or craft materials. Workshops can be organized around different curriculum areas: language arts, science, mathematics, arts and crafts.

Arrangement of large-scale workshops often takes a great deal of time, and attendance may not justify the effort. For this reason, some schools have arranged for certain classrooms to be open to parents on specified evenings, usually once a month. Parents come in and use the materials as they choose. A brief discussion precedes or follows the activities.

Newsletters An excellent means of keeping parents informed of the work of the school is a newsletter, usually edited by parents themselves. It communicates items of interest, presents pertinent articles, outlines teachers' plans, reports on future activities, and solicits help and materials from parents as needed. It may also include samples of children's writing.

Presentations Occasionally children prepare presentations for parents. They may mount an exhibition of their art or other work, organize a program of demonstrations, perform a play or a series of skits, or show films or slides of their classroom work.

Coffee Hours and Teas A warm bond between home and school can be established through occasional coffee hours or teas at which parents from one class at a time can drop in to discuss questions or to chat with the principal. Teachers may be excused from their classes briefly in order to attend these occasions. The informal atmosphere and small number of participants create a climate for positive discussion of the objectives of the open classroom.

Visiting Days and Open Houses Many schools have regular visiting days on which parents are invited to come to school, to observe classes, to talk with students, to inspect their work, and to chat with teachers. As so many parents work during the day, it may be advisable to schedule an evening session of school (perhaps in place of part of one day's session), so that more parents can actually observe the schools at work.

The Plowden report offers an interesting suggestion for "open" days: "Invitations can be extended to the community as a whole, and the result, if not the intention, may be to recruit voluntary help for the school."[3] This proposal has many merits. Not only is it, as pointed out, helpful for recruiting volunteers, but it may also lead to other kinds of support for the school. In communities that vote directly on the school budget, it is important for people who do not have children in the school to become acquainted with its work. Close ties with the community also permit greater appreciation of the resources of the community and facilitate arrangements for children to visit places of business and other sites. It may also help the schools to elicit contributions of waste materials, like styrofoam packing, which may have no value to a local firm but is most useful in the classroom.

[3] Plowden, *op. cit.*, p. 41.

Another advantage of visiting days is that they can serve as orientation periods for young children who will soon be entering school. Many schools invite these children in during the semester before their enrollment; the practice appears to facilitate children's later adjustment to school.

Parent-Teacher Conferences   The parent-teacher conference is a primary means of reporting on the work of children to their parents. Many schools arrange for children to be dismissed from school for a few afternoons a year, in order to enable teachers to conduct these conferences. They are frequently the most effective means of explaining the program to parents. The teacher generally keeps a folder of each child's work to show to parents. She uses the conference to gain understanding of the child's home life: his interests, his playmates, his relations with his siblings, the television programs that he prefers, his responsibilities, and the like. The teacher also wants to know whether or not the child continues any of his school interests at home, how he appears to react to school, whether or not he discusses any aspects of it.

At this conference, too, teachers can plan with parents to cooperate on some aspect of a child's emotional or academic growth. They may recognize that the child needs more opportunities for leadership in school or reinforcement of his growing independence. A parent may be encouraged to read with a youngster or to share other experiences. It is essential that an atmosphere of cooperation be engendered.

In planning for a conference teachers must focus on positive aspects of the child's work, not only problems. They must also be certain to report these to the parents. Frequently, because of concern about a problem, a teacher may greet parents with the problem and convey the impression that she has little respect for the child or his capabilities. The result is to alienate the parents, rather than to enlist their support.

Parents as Resources

One of the largest untapped resources for schools is the parents of the students. Parents have a range of occupations and professions and a diversity of interests and abilities. An organized effort to tap these resources for the classroom can enrich the work of the school. There are several ways in which parents can become involved in schools.

Parent Advisory Committees   An advisory board of parents, which may include a few parents from each of the open classes in the school, can frequently be helpful to teachers and parents both. The board members may operate in ways similar to those of the *class mothers* that many classes have established, but their role is oriented more toward parent education. They can help to plan workshops, seminars, and coffee hours in parents' homes or in school; can recruit other parents to work as volunteers; can conduct surveys to determine what skills, hobby experiences, and special abilities parents may be willing to contribute to the school; and can generally act as liaison between the school and the home. They can call the teachers' attention to concerns among parents and can in turn relay to parents information about the school's plans and objectives. They can frequently be used as a sounding board by teachers and administrators seeking to assess probable parental reactions to projected plans. A good functioning parents' committee can make significant contributions to a school.

Parents as Volunteer Aides   Parents can also be enlisted to work in the classroom. Many have professional backgrounds or have interrupted careers to stay at home. They can fill a variety of functions at school. Some may have artistic talent or skill in such crafts as needlework, jewelry making, macramé, costume design, and cooking. They can be invited in regularly to work with interested children. Others can read with children, help type their dictated stories, supervise particular corners, handle clerical details, and help with research. Some may be well versed in poetry, music, or dance. They can act as consultants, enlarging the scope of activities to which children are exposed. Occasionally a school will ask a parent to accompany a small group of children to a museum or to see an exhibition. Field trips in small groups may be more effective than large class trips.

To enlarge the child's conception of the world of work, working parents should be invited to school whenever possible. Children are fascinated when a lawyer, an electrician, a newspaperman, or a nurse explains his work. Many new projects can result from such talks.

Parents in Other Classroom Functions   Parents can be asked to do research for a projected unit of work. They can also help to collect materials for use in the classroom. Community shops are usually generous in contributing to school projects. A local lumberyard may have wood scraps that can be useful. The telephone company will often donate rolls of scrap wire. A fabric store may be asked for remnants, carpet stores for samples (to make "rugs" for activity centers), toy stores for shopworn toys that need repairs or painting, hardware stores for screws and nails, and so on.

Material can be obtained from parents too. In many homes there are bits of carpet, books, cloth remnants, unused furniture, old clocks, plastic bottles, clothes for dress up, idle equipment (for example, woodworking materials or even a typewriter) that parents would be happy to share with the class. The idea is not to turn the classroom into a junkyard but to discover what is available and to plan how it can be used in the classroom.

Parents will often repair, paint, and even make materials for use in a classroom. One parent made a magnetic reading game, another a puppet stage complete with curtains, another a group of geoboards. They may also help to plan a fund-raising fair when a class is trying to raise money for a camera, dark-room equipment, a typewriter, or other equipment. In Oxfordshire, England, children were particularly proud of the minibus used to transport small groups of children on field trips: Parents had collected 1,400 books of green stamps with which to buy it.

The principal of an open school, after praising the contributions of the parents to his building, remarked facetiously: "In the past we used to stage science fairs so that parents could display their talents surreptitiously behind their children; now our parents do not need to hide their work. We invite them to build equipment, displays, and projects for us. The children are proud of their parents' contributions, and it adds a wonderful spark to the school."

WORKING WITH VOLUNTEERS

Aside from parents, there are other sources of volunteer work in the classroom. Although volunteers can be useful, they can also create additional burdens for the teacher. It may be necessary for the teacher to organize volunteers' work in advance and to devote time to training them. Some volunteers are quite reliable in their attendance, but others, because of young children at home or other responsibilities, are unable to maintain a consistent schedule. Teachers must determine the extent to which they are prepared to rely on volunteers' help in class, bearing in mind that properly organized volunteer programs can enrich the classroom experiences of youngsters. In some schools the principals or other staff members undertake to train all the volunteers and then assign them to individual classes. Two frequently untapped sources of volunteers are retired people and older children.

Retired People

Community members who have retired usually have time to work in schools. They have varied abilities and are usually the most devoted volunteers. Their presence in school can help to bridge the gulf that exists between the young and the old in our society and can provide a valuable resource for the classroom. They can be enlisted to serve many of the same functions that we have described for parent volunteers.

In an interesting experiment a school in New York invited retired men to serve as part-time kindergarten instructors. Men with backgrounds in art, mechanics, carpentry, cooking, and police work were included. An evaluation of the program revealed a positive effect on the academic work of children, as well as a greater appreciation by children of the social roles of older people.

Older Students

Teachers of many open classes invite older students, either from the same elementary schools or from nearby junior or senior high schools,

An older child teaches younger ones to use a balance board. (Photograph courtesy of Merrick Public Schools, New York.)

to work in their classrooms. This practice has been beneficial for all involved. The older children's self-concepts are strengthened when they act as "teachers' aides," and the younger children learn through the talents of the older ones. Students can be used to read to young children, to help with activities, to teach foreign languages, to demonstrate crafts, or to share skills and hobbies. An older child who shows his stamp collection, his model planes, or his rock collection can stimulate many new interests.

Students chosen for such a program must be carefully screened in advance and told what is expected of them. They may be asked to list some of the activities on which they would like to work, and members of the class can then sign up for their visits. Sometimes an older student may be assigned to read with a younger one on a continuing basis. Some schools have enlisted for this purpose students who themselves have had some reading difficulties; the results for both parties have been positive.

WORKING WITH PARAPROFESSIONALS

The teacher in an open classroom may be the leader of a team of adults that includes paraprofessionals, teaching interns, and parent volunteers. Some of these adults may be assigned to work full time, others part time, and some only briefly. But all can make significant contributions to open classes.

There is no doubt that regularly assigned paraprofessionals are particularly helpful in open classrooms. In contrast to traditional classrooms, where frequently only one class activity occurs at a time and most revolve around the teachers, in open classrooms, characterized by multiple activities, paraprofessionals can be more readily and consistently absorbed into the work of the classes in a variety of functions.

There are other factors conducive to the use of paraprofessionals in open classrooms. First, another "pair of hands" is most welcome in a highly diversified program, as are additional talents and skills. For example, a paraprofessional, who can bake, sew, or share a craft skill can enrich the program of the class. Second, as paraprofessionals are generally recruited from the community, they have a critical role in fostering the cooperation between home and school that characterizes the open classroom. They can act as a vital pipeline to the community, assisting teachers to understand it, to relate to it, and to be aware of its resources. In addition, from their personal knowledge of the home lives of the students, they can frequently help teachers to structure activities that seem more relevant to the students and suggest directions that will more accurately reflect students' concerns. Paraprofessionals also help to interpret the open classroom to the community.

Paraprofessionals can work either in the classroom or outside it. In school their duties usually include relieving teachers of clerical work; handling audio-visual equipment; preparing materials, displays, and stencils; keeping records of the activities in which children are engaged; tutoring small groups of students or individual children; working with children on specific interests or activities like baking, music, and art; devoting time to children who need attention to their emotional or academical development; assuming routine patrol duties on the playground or in the hall or lunchroom; acting as liaison between home and school.

In some districts, paraprofessionals, work in the community as *family workers* or *family assistants*. It is their job to advise parents on providing preschool experience for youngsters and other matters related to the health education programs and workshops, interpret school policy and the curricuing sessions for parents and youngsters. They may also coordinate adult-education programs and workshops, interpret school policy and the curriculum, work with attendance officers to reach youngsters with special problems, and also act as general liaison between home and school.

There is growing emphasis on providing career ladders for paraprofessionals, as a guarantee that they will not be placed in "dead end" jobs and as an incentive for them to pursue their own education. To encourage the latter, the school may assist by arranging programs, offering released time, and granting free tuition. Educational programs for paraprofessionals may range from a few courses related to the school curriculum to enrollment in college for training as teachers or social workers. Once the paraprofessional has obtained college credits or experience "in the field," he may be eligible for promotion to a higher position. Labor unions like the American Federation of Teachers and the American Federation of State, County and Municipal Workers have demanded career ladders, in some instances providing educational programs and negotiating regular employee benefits like sick leave and vacation pay for paraprofessionals. The result has been increasing acceptance of paraprofessionals as a more stable, better-trained force working in viable careers.

Alan Gartner has studied the impact of paraprofessionals on pupil performance and has concluded that

> . . . paraprofessionals through their direct impact on students positively affect their learning. And, beyond this indication of direct affect on the pupil, there is data as to affect on teachers—changes in the allocation and use of their time and their behavior which allow for greater attention by the teacher to pupils.[4]

GENERAL COMMENTS ON THE USE OF VOLUNTEERS AND PARAPROFESSIONALS

To ensure maximum benefits from the participation of volunteers and paraprofessionals in the open classroom, it is essential that they be aware of educational goals. People who do not understand the philosophy of open education may be uncomfortable with the informality of the classroom, especially with the freedom of children to converse, play, and move about. Although they may not express this discomfort verbally, it may influence their work and their attitudes toward the children, causing them to become impatient when children appear to be *playing* with scales rather than *working* on mathematics or when they talk.

A further consideration in working with volunteers and paraprofessionals is to make sure that they derive satisfaction from their work, watching particular projects reach fruition and using their own individual talents. It would be unfortunate if an adult familiar with a craft or a foreign culture, for example, were never invited to share her knowledge with interested groups of children. It is for these reasons that paraprofessionals in open classrooms are frequently encouraged to participate in workshops and professional meetings, and also contribute to planning the work of the classes.

[4] Alan Gartner, *Paraprofessionals and Their Performance* (New York: Praeger, 1971), p. 24.

Chapter
NINETEEN
Anticipating
Some
Problems

"This has been the most difficult, frustrating, exciting and in a way, satisfying year of my entire teaching career," a veteran of twelve years' teaching recently reported. She was referring to her first year in an open classroom, and her reaction was not unique. Along with the satisfactions, an open classroom undoubtedly brings with it initial problems and frustrations as well. The success of the new approach may depend on how teachers cope with these problems.

"Be patient," was the advice offered by a British teacher who had spent a year in this country as consultant to a school district that was adopting open methods. "Americans are impatient. We have been experimenting with informal methods for over thirty years, and we have not solved all our problems, nor established perfect schools. You are newcomers to informal methods and yet your parents, administrators, and even teachers expect perfection overnight.

"There appears to be a contradiction in your behavior. When I was invited to America, I was told of the problems of your formal schools, yet the minute anything went wrong in an informal class, instead of trying to work it out, there seemed to be a desire to run back to the 'good old days.'"

The attraction of the "good old days" is common in the United States. In many a classroom where problems have been encountered, sometimes because changes have been made too quickly or with insufficient understanding, teachers have suddenly glorified and returned to the traditional approach, moving desks into neat rows where children can be kept quiet, controlled, and apathetic.

There are several common difficulties in the early stage of organization of open classroom. Anticipating these difficulties and some possible solutions may be useful. Some of them have been touched on in previous chapters, but we shall review them here for clarity:

1. Maintaining a healthy working atmosphere.
2. Making sure that each child spends his time constructively.
3. Learning when and when not to intercede in a child's activity.
4. Learning how to sustain a child's interest in an activity.
5. Obtaining sufficient material.
6. Handling negative reactions from others.

MAINTAINING A HEALTHY WORKING ATMOSPHERE

The problem of how to maintain a proper climate for work is most frequently reported by teachers who are adopting the open approach for the first time. They complain that some children seem to "waste time," to complete a minimum of work and in general seem to take advantage of their new freedom. It is necessary that teachers recognize that this behavior is more common in the beginning stages of open education, part of the "growing pains"; otherwise they will be overcritical of their own efforts or, worse, will conclude that "our children are not capable of handling responsibility" and "back go the desks!"

Initially, it should be realized, every child will not be equally prepared to cope with the free environment of the open class; when some restraints are removed it is natural for children to test the new limits. There are many examples of extreme behavior in reaction to removal of restrictions. The child who has always had a strict bedtime hour may remain awake most of the night when visiting a friend, children who have been accustomed to strict discipline may stage a "near riot" when the teacher leaves the room, and even an adult who goes off a rigid diet may indulge in an orgy of overeating.

Children may also be suspicious of their sudden freedom. They may not trust teachers enough to believe that they will really permit children to make meaningful decisions. The open approach is foreign to their expectations of school, and often their doubts are confirmed by the teacher who too quickly reasserts her authority and reimposes restrictions.

Both the teacher and the children must learn to trust each other and to work together. Children gradually become accustomed to responsibility for their own work and behavior. At first, it may be necessary to structure a particular child's work, in order to help him to acquire the confidence to work on his own. But this approach must be carried out with respect for his individual needs and not in a punitive manner.

It is important that children know what is expected of them. Does the teacher say "Choose your own work" and then become angry when they have chosen not to work on mathematics? There is no objection to the teacher's assigning some necessary work. It is also true that even open classrooms must have rules. These rules should be clearly understood. They should be adopted by the teacher and the children in classroom meetings at which open discussion about their necessity is encouraged. In this way all parties have a stake in their enforcement. When rules have been established in this manner, there must be recognized consequences for their violation: "Those who would completely relax rules are so anxious to please . . . that they fail to understand that firm, fair standards of discipline mean that we care; lax standards are interpreted by those who need firm standards as lack of interest."[1]

When teacher and children agree on standards of behavior, the atmosphere of the class is treated as the joint concern of both. Children, as well as the teacher, will want to maintain an environment in which they can function. They will be as aware and as concerned as is the teacher when there is a failure.

The arrangement of the room can also contribute to the problem of a poor climate of work. Have noisy and quiet areas been placed too close together? Are there areas to which children can withdraw when necessary? Some teachers have found that playing soft music in one corner of the room soothes children who may be accustomed to listening to the radio or records while working at home.

A prime consideration in maintaining the working atmosphere is the choice of activities provided for the children. Are they sufficiently challenging to occupy the children? When children are absorbed in a task, they do not pose discipline problems. Is there a broad enough range of activities to suit different children's abilities? Are too many frustrating for some and boring for others? Do they represent the teacher's interests, rather than those of the children? Are there sufficient materials on hand to sustain interest?

Teachers who are concerned about this problem should also clarify their definition of a "healthy, working atmosphere" and should be certain that their expectations are realistic. In a class not characterized by quiet, order, and passivity definition of this term becomes complex. It is possible to become anxious about the noise level, for example, when for many children it may not be bothersome. More indicative of a healthy atmosphere are certain subtle characteristics that are more difficult to measure: the sense of purpose with which children approach their tasks, their growing acceptance of responsibility, evidence of group cohesiveness and mutual concern, and signs that children are finding new interests.

[1] William Glasser, *Schools without Failure* (Harper & Row, 1969), p. 194.

Finally, we must add that the problem of creating a healthy, working atmosphere is one that generally resolves itself as the class acquires more experience in working in the open classrooms. Discipline problems do tend to diminish and children to increasingly concentrate on their work as they accept their responsibilities in the open environment.

MAKING SURE THAT EACH CHILD SPENDS HIS TIME CONSTRUCTIVELY

Making sure that the child spends his time constructively is closely related to maintaining the proper working climate. The word "constructively," however, requires further definition. In the traditional classroom, where each child spends his day on tasks assigned by the teacher, such work is considered constructive. Children who are listening quietly to a teacher's lecture are also considered to be behaving constructively. Yet these children may be only superficially involved in their tasks and entirely absent in spirit from the lecture.

By contrast children in open classes may be talking together or sitting alone examining a rock, yet these may be constructive tasks. In evaluating how children spend their days in open classrooms, teachers must consider that children need some time to socialize, to observe one another's work, to plan, and just to think. Play has also been shown to be a significant component of the program. The fact is that many children in conventional classes are rushed through the day. Questions are posed to them, but a premium is put on quick replies that involve little thought. There is a constant implied scarcity of time. It may be well to recall Jean Jacques Rousseau's admonition: "The most useful rule of education is: Do not save time, but lose it."

Even taking all these considerations into account, however, there will still be children who seem to accomplish little during the day, who tend to ignore certain areas of work, and who do not exhibit the growth that the teacher believes consistent with their abilities. These children may at first require more teacher direction. Several approaches are possible. The teacher may assign some specific tasks and ask that they be completed within a specified period. This approach can be additionally helpful to those children who through lack of confidence hesitate to attempt certain activities for fear of failure. By assigning them in a nonthreatening fashion, the teacher expresses her confidence in the child's ability to execute the task.

Some children need help in scheduling their day. The teacher may ask that they prepare plans at the beginning of each day and review them with her. This also enables the teacher to make sure that children vary their activities. A child who never engages in creative work is as much concern as the child who never schedules mathematics.

Other children may need guidance in more constructive use of time as they work. Suggesting that they check with the teacher before they change activities is often effective. Still others may require immediate feedback as they work. Encouraging them to complete short tasks which can be reviewed at once may help. All the preceding approaches should be viewed as temporary measures, used selectively as children learn to accept more and more responsibility for their own work.

Another facet of this problem is one of standards. It has been noted that high standards are set for children's work in open classrooms. Acceptance of superficial efforts frequently conveys to the child the message that he is not considered capable of better work. However, it is important that children be aware of the standards set for them and accept them as reasonable. Teachers must recognize that children will have more and less productive periods; some will establish their own rhythm for the day, which a sensitive teacher will respect.

Despite all the above measures, children cannot ultimately be expected to spend their days constructively if the range of activities provided for them is too limited or inconsistent with their own abilities, interests and needs. Teachers must make certain that each child has sufficient opportunity to work in a manner satisfying to himself and spends his time in a manner he too perceives as "constructive."

LEARNING WHEN (AND WHEN NOT) TO INTERCEDE IN A CHILD'S ACTIVITY

Two primary kinds of freedom for children in open classrooms are the freedom to make mistakes and the freedom to experience success from their own endeavors. Both are freedoms of which children are often needlessly deprived. For this reason, the teacher in an open classroom hesitates to interfere when a child is actively exploring a problem, even when he is obviously committing an error. For example, one teacher of five-year-olds related: "A boy was busily pacing back and forth across the room, each time measuring its length with his footsteps. As I approached, he turned to me, and said, 'I can't understand how you do it.' 'Do what?' I asked the child. 'Keep changing the size of the room,' was his reply: My first impulse was to explain, but fortunately I remained silent. I was rewarded for not interfering when a few minutes later the child let out a shriek of joy. By careful pacing he had succeeded in getting the 'room to remain fixed in size,' and had solved his problem."

This particular incident posed a relatively easy problem for the teacher. Others will be more difficult, however. Activities frequently take unpredictable turns in open classrooms, some of which may appear less fruitful than the anticipated ones. Yet even so the danger is that in salvaging an activity the teacher may sacrifice the child's confidence in his own ability to solve problems.

Generally it may be said that teachers do not intervene as long as a child is actively engaged in working a problem. They are more likely to intervene when the child is losing interest, is simply repeating an activity without extending his learning; then suggesting a new direction may help him to see the potential of some materials or to revive his flagging interest. This approach will be clearer when we examine another problem that teachers face.

SUSTAINING A CHILD'S INTEREST IN AN ACTIVITY

Children may lose interest in activities before they have investigated them adequately; activities last for brief periods, new ones are constantly demanded, and learning is at a minimum. This problem too is more frequently encountered in newly organized open classes. It may be caused by children's needing to adjust to their unfamiliar responsibilities in the classroom. Whereas in the past the teacher made sure that an activity would continue for a stated period of time along stated lines, when teachers encourage students to find their own paths, they must be prepared for them to stumble or halt in the process.

Teachers can help children to see the potentials of situations without actually becoming completely directive. When an activity seems to have lost interest for children, the teacher may wish to find out whether or not there are sufficient materials on hand so that children of different abilities and interests can explore them. Sometimes the introduction of a new book or a different object can revive interest in an activity. Have the children been made aware of possible directions for investigation? A meeting of the participating students may help. Sometimes new ideas emerge from group interaction.

It may be advisable to schedule a field trip or invite a "resource person" to the classroom to provide further information on an activity. Children can be involved in making the arrangements for these events. "Resource people" may be quite close at hand: an older student from the same school or the high school, a parent, another teacher.

Some teachers have found it inadvisable to introduce too many activities at once. They prefer to start with a few, offering a range of possibilities and expecting children to stay with those that they have chosen to some depth. By emphasizing this expectation, they help students to set more rigorous standards for themselves and to undertake activities in a more inquiring frame of mind.

Some basic questions about the nature of the activities are "Who plans them?" Is it always the teacher? Whose purposes and interests do they express? An activity can be exquisitely planned yet still excite no interest. One teacher gave an example:

"I wanted to get the class interested in art. So I set up an exhibit of prints, and suggested a number of activities related to the prints. I worked hard, going to the museum to collect prints, accumulating information about each, planning a beautiful display, and devising activities.

"The children couldn't care less. Most ignored the display. Those who tried an activity never really became involved with the art. I realized that it had never been the children's activity. It had arisen from my purposes not theirs. I had never involved them in planning the work."

It is unrealistic to attempt to sustain participation in an activity that does not reflect children's interests.

OBTAINING SUFFICIENT MATERIALS

"Children seem to eat up the material. It gets used so quickly," is a common complaint in open classrooms. Two points must be reemphasized. First, housekeeping is extremely important in open classrooms. Unless there is a designated place for each piece of equipment the open classroom will deteriorate in no time into a repository for miscellaneous junk serving no purpose. Children should know where to find the materials that they need. The room must be carefully planned, and children must participate in deciding where to store materials and in the responsibility for their care. Second, teachers should resist putting all available materials on display at once. Introducing a new book, a new game, a different fabric texture can sometimes revive interest in an activity, but too much material at once may be simply confusing.

These cautions aside, it is true that open classes do require an abundance of materials. There are now many commercial kits geared to individual work: science kits, reading kits, mathematics activity cards, art activity cards, and so on. Yet, although these kits are undoubtedly very helpful to teachers, they are expensive, and their use has other disadvantages as well. The most successful activity cards are those that have been constructed by the teacher and children together. Commercial kits may be used as a resource, but they are most effective when they are adapted to the particular interests of the group. Putting out a box with more than 100 activity cards in mathematics is often less valuable than putting out ten or fifteen cards that have been carefully thought out by the class. Similarly, the occasional investment of $25 in paperback books geared to children's current reading interests can sometimes produce a more exciting reading program than can expensive kits.

When buying materials, teachers should carefully consider expenditures in the light of long-range purposes. For example, although paperbacks are cheaper and in some ways preferable to hard-cover books, some-times more expensive equipment may be desirable. If a scale is to be used for mathematics, one good and accurate scale is worth more than three cheap ones. It is better to build up a supply of worthwhile equipment over a few semesters than to give children flimsy materials.

There are many sources of materials. Neighborhood stores, commer-cial firms, and parents generally contribute generously. Parents can fre-quently be enlisted to make objects for the classroom: a playhouse, a store, a puppet stage, bookshelves. Older children can also help. Some enjoy making games for younger children, they collect the materials themselves. The teacher should know just what is needed. When funds are not available, fairs or sales can be organized by the class. One class staged a white-ele-phant sale of used toys that its members had repaired and painted. With the proceeds the class bought a movie camera and film.

Joint concern about obtaining sufficient materials and caring for them properly can contribute much to solving this problem. One teacher encour-aged children to plan the class budget. He told them how much was avail-able for supplies, and they helped to decide what to order. The approach had most gratifying effects.

HANDLING NEGATIVE REACTIONS FROM OTHERS

When open classrooms are established in schools that include con-ventional classes as well, there may be adverse reactions from other mem-bers of the staff. Custodians may resent the additional cleaning required. Other teachers may be unhappy about special consideration given to the open classes in the matter of supplies, visitors, and freedom for the children. Some of these reactions may be unavoidable. Teachers may pay lip service to the goal of educating children capable of exercising initiative and inde-pendent thought, but conforming children are more comfortable to live with. Furthermore, change in itself is threatening to some people.

Open-class teachers must be sensitive to these attitudes, because to some extent they may unwittingly be contributing to negative reactions. Some teachers may seem to denigrate the work of traditional classes, behav-ing as if they alone have "seen the light." The fact is that much superior education is available in traditional classes. As we have shown, open educa-tion itself has deep roots in history; teachers in open classrooms are not alone in recognizing that children learn by doing, can be given responsibil-ity, and require individual consideration. Respect for one's professional colleagues can result in support for the open classroom and in opportunities to test and discuss ideas with other teachers in the school—essential to the open-classroom teacher.

Chapter
TWENTY
Teacher
Centers

Teachers embarking on the path to open education encounter an additional problem: and that is the "loneliness" of the route. They may wish to meet with others interested in open education, to be aware of new materials, to discuss some of their concerns, or to extend their understanding of the philosophy of open education, but they may find few avenues of communication and may be forced to rely primarily on their own resources. One significant response to this problem has been the establishment of teacher centers, to some extent modeled on British centers.

Although the movement toward teacher centers in this country is still very much in the embryonic stage, it is growing in many directions. Basically, centers tend to be found in districts amenable to educational reform. Their major purpose is to stimulate the professional growth of teachers and to enrich the scope of activities that teachers are prepared to offer their students. Some centers provide more direct support to teachers in the classrooms by supplying advisers who visit classes. These advisers always assume a nonsupervisory role, acting mainly as "resources" and consultants for teachers.

Teacher centers may range from one-room clearing houses for materials to separate buildings catering to a large geographical area and housing a multiplicity of services. Their functions may include any or all of those discussed in this chapter.

FUNCTIONS OF TEACHER CENTERS

Clearing Houses for Materials and Equipment

A wide variety of curriculum materials can be displayed in the center. Occasionally there may be special exhibits on specific subjects like

A teacher reviews curriculum materials in a teacher center. (Photograph courtesy of Hannah More Center, Bristol, England.

reading and crafts. Additionally, there may be examples of materials made by teachers, a model interest center, room dividers, equipment for storage, and furniture for use in classrooms.

Resource Center

In addition, files of activities, projects, community resources, and samples of classroom records may be maintained. The staffs of some centers compile extensive materials on topics like African art for loan to schools on a rotating basis.

Workshop

Teachers have opportunities to experiment with materials, to modify them for classroom use, and to construct others. Parents and nonprofessional classroom personnel may also be invited to become acquainted with materials and to work with them in the center.

Preservice and In-Service Education

Students in education courses at local universities may meet at centers for seminars and to explore the materials.

In-service education is a primary function of most centers. It takes many forms. One-session workshops may be offered to acquaint teachers with particular kinds of equipment or skills: Cuisenaire rods, attribute blocks, macramé work. They can be scheduled in the morning, during the lunch hour, after school. Frequently schools release time for teachers to attend such workshops. In-service courses may also be more extensive, lasting for many sessions; in some centers they are conducted by universities for college credits.

In-service education can also be provided for paraprofessionals and other nonprofessional school personnel. Some centers offer special workshops to classroom teams composed of teachers, interns, paraprofessionals, and regular volunteers. These workshops may center around the use of equipment or common classroom problems.

Parental Education

Some centers offer seminars for parents on topics related to the work of the school.

Advisory Service

Centers may provide advisers who will visit teachers' classes. Frequently, this service is provided as follow-up to a workshop or course in order to help the teacher apply what he has learned.

Circulating Equipment

Films, science materials, craft supplies (like weaving looms), videotape cameras, and other audio-visual equipment may be available for loan to individual classrooms.

Display Center

Work completed in different schools can be exhibited in the centers.

Meeting Rooms

The centers may be used for meetings of teachers, parents, and school administrators in the district.

Social Center

Centers provide a place where teachers can meet others in the district, can exchange ideas, and can share concerns. Social events may be scheduled; some centers have catering facilities. (In England some even have bars.)

Library

Professional books, resource books, children's literature, and textbooks are kept in stock. Some centers also collect information about educational conferences, workshops, summer workshops, and university courses.

Miscellaneous

Some centers have the resources to operate darkrooms, "animal banks," woodworking shops, and other special facilities for use by teachers.

ORGANIZATION OF THE CENTERS

Teacher centers are currently being established by individual schools, school districts, and large school systems, frequently in cooperation with teacher organizations. They take different forms. A school may set aside one or a few rooms as a teacher center. A teacher on released time, an outside consultant, or a group of teachers working during the summer may be charged with equipping it. When the center is opened, there will have to be at least one person permanently in charge. Some centers, of course, will have much larger staffs.

The center may be organized as a classroom with different interest areas. Although many possible functions have been noted, at the minimum the center should provide samples of materials and opportunities for teachers to work with them. Supplies for constructing classroom items, lumber, and art materials should be accessible, as should resource books. Most centers provide materials for teachers to make activity cards.

Just as in the classroom, it is important that new materials be introduced frequently to sustain an interest in the center. Even if it is housed in one room, it must be a dynamic area in which teachers are motivated to participate. Experimenting with an activity in the center helps the teacher to envision its possibilities for the class.

It has been noted that in-service training can originate in the center. It may be offered by teachers or by outside consultants. In some centers a group of teachers rotate responsibility for presenting activities and projects, either through demonstrations or exhibitions of some of the work of their classes.

Wherever possible, leadership of the small center should reside with the teachers in that school or district, so that they find it responsive to their needs, rather than to the notions of an outside consultant. If it is not feasible to release one teacher for full-time service in the center, a committee of teachers can be organized to plan and evaluate the development of the center.

This type of small center can serve one school or an entire district. In the latter instance the center must be accessible to teachers from all the schools, and there must be provision for visits during school hours, as well as after school. Some teachers may be excused from their classrooms at regular intervals to participate in work at the center or just to browse and explore.

Some teacher centers in this country are developing with the added cooperation of local universities. The education departments of these universities are indicating interest in off-campus facilities for training teacher candidates. Frequently a local teacher organization, school district, and a university can work together to organize a center. The university provides consultants and courses geared to the needs of teachers. One professor may establish an office at the center and be readily available as an adviser to teachers. In turn, the school offers additional opportunities for education students to participate as interns in the classrooms.

Teacher centers may also be much more ambitious projects. Benjamin Rosner, after a study of British teacher centers, offered a comprehensive proposal for large teacher centers in urban areas. He envisioned them as serving approximately 1,000 teachers each and as employing sizable staffs, including full-time directors and secretaries, part-time deputy directors, media specialists, librarians, and clerical and housekeeping assistants. Consultants would be hired as needed. Physically, the centers would have kitchen and bar facilities, lecture halls and meeting rooms, display areas, audio-visual equipment, libraries, and media-resource collections.

In an area like New York City, Rosner estimated, this kind of center would cost $250,000 annually. Although this figure may seem impossible, Rosner offered several specific suggestions for financing. He pointed out that for 1,000 teachers the cost would be $250 per teacher. "It is interesting to note that even at $250 per teacher, the expenditure is equivalent to the tuition for a three-credit graduate course at most of the universities in the City of New York."[1]

Rosner argued that if they were awarded the equivalent of three credits toward salary increments or advanced certification, teachers might be willing to consider such an investment. This plan could be facilitated by partnership with a university, which might grant graduate credit for in-serv-

[1] Benjamin Rosner, "The British Teacher Center: A Report on Its Development, Current Operations, Effects and Applicability to Teacher Education in the U.S." (New York: Office of Teacher Education, The City University, November 1972), p. 24.

ice courses and for cooperative development of curricula. Teacher funding has the advantage of permitting teachers to assume control of the center, guaranteeing that it is responsive to their needs, although it is unrealistic to expect teachers to accept full responsibility for funding a center.

Other funding possibilities suggested are partnerships among public school districts, teacher organizations, universities, and some private businesses that might use the centers for displays of commercial educational materials. One factor not mentioned in Rosner's report may reduce the cost of centers: Many school districts are experiencing declines in school populations. Space for large centers may therefore be available in school buildings. Kitchen and gymnasium facilities will thus be available too. School districts may be more willing to contribute to the costs of centers if they do not have to pay for leasing additional space.

There is a growing consensus on the need for teacher's centers in this country, on the constructive role they can perform in the continuing professional education of teachers. However, one point must be reemphasized. Whatever the size of the center—whether it be in one room or an entire building—it should be organized not *for* but *by* the teachers in a given area. Just as with open classrooms, teacher centers will vary from community to community; each center must be responsive to the needs of its particular constituency.

Appendix

A

The
British
Scene

British primary schools have been receiving worldwide attention recently. Here in the United States they have aroused particular interest; educators have cited the British approach as a model for educational reform, some schools have imported British headmasters and teachers to help establish open classes, and much of the recent literature on open education published in this country has centered on descriptions of British schools.

Full understanding of open education and its literature therefore compels attention to the British scene: to the historical factors that have contributed to the growth of informal education[1] in Great Britain, to British schools, as they are today, and to some comparisons between British and American cultures.

HISTORY OF INFORMAL EDUCATION IN GREAT BRITAIN

Informal education evolved slowly in Great Britain. D. E. M. Gardner had traced its roots to the early nursery schools, beginning with the one founded by Robert Owen in Scotland in 1816.[2] Owen was a mill owner. At that time many factory owners arranged for supervision of the

---

[1] The term "open education" is rarely used in Great Britain. There are a number of different designations for this approach: "informal," "modern," "progressive," "child-centered," and "integrated." The expression "open school" in Britain generally refers to the physical plan of the school, which includes large open spaces and few partition walls. In discussing British schools we shall use "informal education" and "informal school" as synonyms for our terms "open education" and "open school."

[2] D. E. M. Gardner, *Education Under Eight* (London: Longmans Green, 1949).

311

children of working mothers. Usually they simply provided rooms and older boys and girls who offered minimal care. Owen, however, assumed greater responsibility for the infants. He hired trained personnel and stressed the importance of activities and an environment that would stimulate the children's curiosity. Although his school attracted favorable notice, it was far ahead of its time, and his ideas gradually died out.

It was not until fifty years later that a similar approach was revived in England by disciples of Friedrich Froebel. His ideas were propagated in England through Froebel societies and later in Froebel training colleges for teachers, which to this day remain outstanding centers for training teachers in informal methods.

Other educational theorists influenced British thinking, but according to the Plowden report, "It was rare to find teachers who had given much time to the study of educational theory."[3] It is to other factors, unique in Great Britain, that we can attribute the growth of the informal movement.

One important aspect was the tradition of support for early childhood education. For many years the state had encouraged nursery-school education, particularly for children of working-class parents.[4] As early as 1870 Great Britain became one of the few countries to make education from the age of five compulsory. Infant schools were established to provide a full day's schooling to children between the ages of five and seven. In some infant schools children were admitted to nursery classes at the age of three.

The British infant school is a unique institution with no real counterpart in American education. To this day it is often maintained as a separate school, independent of other primary schools. It was in nursery and infant schools that informal education in Great Britain developed. Although the infant schools were responsible for teaching the children to read and to acquire other basic reading and mathematical skills, they were less constrained by formal curricula and more closely attuned to nursery-school techniques. They stressed play, activities, and learning through interaction with the environment, rather than formal work.

Other events stimulated the development of informal education in Great Britain. John Blackie has stressed the influence of the Hadow Commission. In 1924 a national commission was appointed, under the chairmanship of Sir Henry Hadow, to investigate elementary education. This body issued three rather remarkable reports, which encouraged the informal approach and, according to Blackie were "destined to change the whole face of English education."[5]

[3] Lady Bridget Plowden, et al. *Children and Their Primary Schools*, I (London: H.M. Stationery Office, 1967), p. 189.
[4] In 1972 the British government projected the goal of free nursery-school education by the end of this decade for all children aged three to five years, whose parents request it.
[5] John Blackie, *Inside the Primary School* (London: H.M. Stationery Office, 1967), p. 4.

At that time British elementary schools accommodated students from ages five to fourteen, which was the age for leaving school. One of the Hadow commission's recommendations, which was adopted, was that primary schools be limited to children up to age eleven and that senior, or secondary, schools be established for children aged eleven to fourteen years. In many communities there were separate infant schools for children up to age seven. These remained and junior schools were established for children aged seven to eleven. Thus the primary schools came to include two levels —infant and junior. As a result of this reorganization, primary schools were forced to reevaluate their curricula and more progressive changes resulted.

World War II had a decided impact on the further growth of informal education in Great Britain. During the war teachers were evacuated from the cities with their classes and were forced to live with the children twenty-four hours a day. Education could not be compartmentalized in periods, and classes were necessarily much less formal than in regular schools. When the war ended and schools were reestablished in the cities, teachers were faced with even greater diversity among their students than usual. Some children had been exposed to formal curricula; others had not. Some had learned to read; others had not. The schools were compelled to seek means of individualizing instruction. An additional result of the war was that young men who had been in the armed forces came into the schools. As a result of the shortage of teachers, they were encouraged to take intensive one-year training courses; when they began to teach they tended to be much less constrained by traditional methods.

Even after the war, however, these changes came slowly. An important inhibiting factor was the "eleven-plus" examination, which was administered to all children upon completion of primary school. According to their scores on this examination, children were admitted to either of two kinds of secondary schools: grammar and secondary-modern schools. The first was the route to higher education, originally reserved for the children of the wealthy and for a few bright working-class children. The secondary-modern schools were primarily vocational schools and were intended for the majority of children who were expected to complete their education at the age of fourteen (later raised to fifteen and then in 1972 to sixteen).

The junior schools, particularly in their upper years, were under great pressure from parents to prepare the children to pass the "elevens" examination. This preparation dominated the curriculum of many junior schools. Currently, it is only in those areas where the examination has been eliminated that informal education has been able to penetrate the junior schools.

The open approach continued to spread slowly, confined chiefly to infant schools, but little publicity was given to it. Historically the greatest impetus for the informal movement came from the Plowden report. In 1965, about thirty years after the influential reports of the Hadow Commission, a new commission was appointed, under the chairmanship of Lady Bridget Plowden, to study primary education. For three years the commission conducted an extensive investigation. In 1967 it issued a detailed report in two volumes, which enthusiastically endorsed the informal approach to education. This report sparked an increase in the number of informal schools in Great Britain and, as it has reached the attention of American educators, has contributed to the growth of open education in the United States as well.

Other indigenous factors on the British scene should be noted. One is the unique British system of national inspectors and advisers. Originally appointed to inspect schools for the national government, they now function primarily as advisers who spread new ideas among schools and offer support to teachers who are experimenting with new techniques. They have many duties. They often organize in-service courses, work with new teachers, and help to evaluate teachers who have applied for promotion. A headmaster in London remarked, "For many years, it was said that if you wanted a promotion, you had better not let the inspector find you standing in front of the room lecturing to the whole class." It was clear that in many counties the inspectors used their authority to support the informal approach.

Also decisive in the growth of the informal movement was the autonomy of headmasters, the relative freedom of teachers from fixed curricula, the small size of the schools, teacher centers, and provisions for in-service education of British teachers. These factors will be explored in our discussion of British schools today.

To complete the historical picture, we note that the informal movement in Great Britain, though extremely influential, is still a minority movement concentrated largely in certain geographical areas and in the earlier grade levels (infant classes). The remaining primary schools include some that are still quite traditional and others that are "in between."

BRITISH SCHOOLS TODAY

The British educational system is technically under the national Department of Education and Science, headed by the Secretary of State for Education, who is directly responsible to Parliament. The national government concerns itself with broad policy, including national teachers' salary scales, minimum standards for school buildings, national goals, and a national inspection.

In practice, there is much local autonomy. The school system is divided into education authorities, each of which has primary responsibility for the schools in its area, including the organization of the schools, personnel, and the curriculum. The authorities are governed by local boards; within each authority a few schools are grouped together and placed under the government of a local board of managers. However, their authority rarely extends to professional decisions. It is fairly well established, for example, that curriculum is the responsibility of the headmasters and teachers.

Organization: Primary Years

Most primary schools are divided into two branches: infant schools for children aged four plus to seven plus years and junior schools for children aged seven to eleven plus years. These divisions may be housed in the same building or in completely separate ones. In some authorities schools are currently being reorganized to conform to a recommendation by the Plowden Commission: a first school for children up to the age of eight years and a middle school for those up to age twelve or thirteen, at which point children would attend secondary schools. The primary purpose of such reorganization is to permit children to spend an extra year in the infant school, in order to establish literacy before they leave. The commission was concerned about lack of attention to reading in the junior schools.

British primary schools are generally smaller than their American counterparts. At the time of the Plowden survey the majority of state-maintained primary schools had between 100 and 300 pupils. Classes tend to be larger than those in the United States, however.

Organization: Secondary Schools

For many years there were two kinds of secondary schools: grammar schools (for academically oriented students) and secondary-modern schools (for students who would leave school when they reached the school-leaving age). Admission to these schools was determined by scores on the "elevens" examination. As pressure against relying on this examination mounted from parents and educators who protested that children's futures were being largely determined at the age of eleven, several authorities dropped the examination and switched to "comprehensive" secondary schools that incorporate some features of both the grammar and the secondary-modern schools. In many counties all three kinds of secondary schools still exist, and, though the "elevens" have been eliminated, there is still competition for places in some grammar and comprehensive schools. Except in a few scattered areas, informal education has not been adopted by the secondary schools.

About half the school population still leaves school at the age of sixteen. In Great Britain this phenomenon is widely accepted, and there is no disparagement of these children. They are called "school-leavers," not "drop-outs" as in the United States, and at the end of the school year many job advertisements are addressed specifically to "school-leavers." The remainder of the population generally stays in school for some technical training; only a small minority attends universities. Although patterns are gradually changing, in Great Britain it has been customary for children of working-class parents to leave school early. Higher education has been reserved for the upper classes.

The comparatively early age at which many pupils leave school has its impact on British schools. One primary-school headmaster alluded to it when he compared the educational goals of American and British society. "Unlike the United States, our primary schools do not aim to prepare every child for admission to an academic secondary school or for eventual admission to a university."

Faculties of Schools

The Headmaster The British headmaster is roughly equivalent to our principal, but he may also be described as a combination of our master teacher, guidance counselor, social worker, and principal. It is traditional for parents to consult headmasters about family problems or to drop into school in the morning to explain that "Mary had an upset last night. . . ."

Headmasters exercise more power and have more autonomy than our principals do. They determine the curricula and organization of their schools, the allocation of funds, and the teaching methods. The term "head" implies "head teacher" and most "heads" consider themselves teachers, rather than administrators. They pride themselves on their knowledge of all the children in their schools, and they often continue to teach. In some schools they work with specific classes on a regular basis, in others with small groups or as substitute teachers. "Heads" also frequently assume responsibility for remedial work in reading or mathematics.

There are no regular achievement tests in British schools, but some headmasters personally test all the children in their schools to ascertain their progress. The testing may take the form of listening to each child read a selection once or twice a year or administering individual graded word-recognition tests at specified intervals.

Although headmasters may view themselves as teachers, their status is quite different. They have complete authority in the school and may exercise it autocratically or democratically. There is no special certification or training required for appointment to a headship. Promotion is from the ranks of experienced teachers, who either apply directly to a school that has posted an opening or ask to be included on a promotion list. Selection procedures include observation by a local inspector of the candidate in his classroom; the final choice is the province of the school's board of managers.

Teachers The primary-school teacher in England, as in the United States, is usually a woman, though there are some men on the upper junior-school levels. The majority of "heads" are men (except for the "heads" of separate infant schools). The teacher may be a young woman just out of school or an older woman who has returned to work. Her training, however, is quite different from that received by the American teacher.

A university degree is not required for teaching in Great Britain. There are three routes to qualification: attendance for three years at a college of education, an optional fourth year with a Bachelor of Education degree, or attainment of a university degree which automatically permits her to teach. The overwhelming majority of teachers choose the first alternative.

When she enters the informal classroom the teacher has few written curriculum guides or teachers' manuals to rely on, but she usually has a great deal of direct support from the headmaster, local inspectors to advise her, and a broad choice of in-service training courses. In-service education for teachers is emphasized in informal schools, and courses are offered by local schools, national inspectors, education authorities, the national Department of Science, various colleges of education, and such other groups as the National Teachers Union. When the "new math" was introduced in Great Britain, for example, the Nuffield Foundation scheduled many in-service courses, which were extremely popular.

A network of teachers' centers also contributes support for teachers. Teachers generally receive tenure after one year of probationary teaching.

The Parents

Only a minority of schools have formal parent-teacher organizations. According to the Plowden report: "We do not think that PTAs are necessarily the best means of fostering close relations between home and school. They can be of the greatest value where good leadership is given by the head. They may also do harm if they get into the hands of a small group."[6] It is apparent that even in schools in which parents actively participate, the headmasters and teachers maintain complete control of professional matters.

Evaluation of Informal Schools

There have been few comparative studies of formal and informal education in Britain. The most extensive ones were conducted a number of years ago by Gardner, who was herself a leading theorist and exponent of "progressive" methods. Although her research methods are open to some question, the results are nevertheless of interest. In 1942 she first surveyed

[6] Plowden, *op. cit.*, p. 39.

infant schools that were using "freer methods" and found that in all instances they did as well as or excelled the more traditional schools.

Later Gardner conducted a follow-up study to determine how the children in the freer infant schools had fared in junior schools. She concluded that most children from those infant schools remained superior in such areas as concentration, listening and remembering, friendliness, writing original poems, and ingenuity.[7]

Finally in a long-range study she compared some informal junior schools with traditional ones, reporting that, though the tests did not show an "unequivocal result, [they] nevertheless clearly indicate that on the whole the experimental schools have more instances of surpassing their controls except in the case of arithmetic where the controls are slightly ahead. . . ."[8]

There have been conflicting reports about reading achievement in informal schools, as compared with that in more formal ones. This dimension is difficult to measure, for informal schools do not generally administer standardized reading tests. K. Lovell studied reading achievement in junior schools and found no significant differences between the mean reading scores of children from informal and from formal schools.[9]

Informal education has not been without its critics in Great Britain. Pamphlets containing articles attacking all aspects of "progressive" education in Great Britain, from informal primary schools to comprehensive secondary schools were addressed to members of Parliament. The charges leveled against the progressive primary schools in these papers summarize the most common kinds of criticisms: neglect of the "three Rs," lack of discipline, low standards of work, and poor teaching methods.[10]

While attacks on informal education appear to be confined to a small segment of British society, even its proponents have expressed concern about excesses and have warned that the pendulum may have swung too far toward freer methods in some schools. Sybil Marshall has urged that the "three Rs" not be overlooked in the abundance of activities now included in the primary-school classroom, that pupils not be given freedom to do whatever they like, and that teachers maintain control over the curriculum.[11]

[7] Gardner, *Experiment and Tradition in Primary Schools* (London: Methuen, 1966).
[8] *Ibid.*, p. 199.
[9] K. Lovell, "Informal vs. Formal Education and Reading Attainments in the Junior School" (London: Report of the National Foundation for Educational Research, 1963).
[10] C. B. Cox and A. E. Dyson (eds.), Collections of essays, *A Black Paper: Fight for Education* and *Black Paper Two: The Crisis in Education* (London: Critical Quarterly Society, 1969).
[11] Sybil Marshall, "Back to the Three Rs?" *The Times (London) Education Supplement*, July 2, 1971, p. 37.

ARE BRITISH CHILDREN DIFFERENT?

Many proponents of open education read about British schools—their apparent lack of discipline problems, their responsible and motivated youngsters—and ask "Are British children different?" In a sense, the answer must be in the affirmative. All people are influenced by the society in which they are raised, and our society has undoubtedly left its own mark on our children. It has been said that we live in a materialistic, competitive society in which status is conferred on parents by, among other symbols, the admission of their children to Ivy League universities. British children, on the other hand, are said to be influenced by the class structure of their society, which makes them more respectful of authority. Yet there are many indications that these generalizations are becoming less valid. Today's American youth to some extent rejects the materialism of our society and current concepts of status. In Great Britain youth is rebelling against the inhibitions of class, and discipline problems are increasing in many of the more formal primary schools and in the secondary schools.

There are probably more similarities than differences between British and American children. It is to characteristics of the informal schools that we must look for the explanation of the apparent diminution of discipline problems and of more responsible student behavior. The elimination of competition through an end to grading, minimum regulations, respect for youngsters, and a generally accepting climate all contribute to decreasing problems in British informal schools. If we establish similar classroom environments and eliminate those in which youngsters are made to feel frustrated and inadequate, in which they are constantly regulated and evaluated, we may well find that here, as in Great Britain, discipline problems will abate. This change has already been reported by many teachers who have established open classes in the United States.

The British have also learned that a concomitant of freedom is structure, so that children are not confused about what constitutes acceptable behavior. By setting clear and reasonable standards of behavior, British teachers have also excluded the "testing of limits" that often contributes to discipline problems in our schools.

In conclusion, it should be emphasized that British informal education has been developing for many decades and is still in the process of change. It is unrealistic for Americans to assume that in a short period of time they can create schools in the British image—even if they were considered desirable.

Appendix
B
A Study
of British
Informal Schools

Many early reports on British informal schools tended to be idealized accounts that frequently discussed the accomplishments of many different classes as if they were typical of each. As these reports appeared, there were warnings that they could be misleading. In one article in *The New York Times*, for example, an American educator was quoted as saying of British informal classes: "Children essentially work on their own at whatever they desire."[1] This statement drew letters from two English educators. Allard wrote: "Such statements are so far from the truth that it would be unjust not to draw the attention of your readers to the fact."[2] Moira McKenzie, a headmistress, also warned about misconceptions of British education, explaining, "Good British education has an underlying structure not always immediately apparent to the casual observer."[3]

It was specifically to identify this structure, and to analyze the daily activities of children in British informal classrooms that the author undertook a study of such classrooms: "There has been no systematic observation of a number of British informal classrooms, recording and analyzing all the activities which occur in a search for clarification of the actual work of the classes, their organization and specific opportunities for individuals to make decisions pertaining to their learning."[4]

The study addressed itself to clarifying aspects of British education

[1] William K. Stevens, "Nyquist Backs British Informal Schooling Plan," *New York Times*, December 8, 1970, p. 1.

[2] L. S. Allard, Letter to the Editor, *New York Times*, December 25, 1970, p. 28.

[3] Moira McKenzie, Letter to the Editor, *New York Times*, December 17, 1970, p. 46.

[4] Lillian S. Stephens, "A Study of Aspects of Individualization in Informal British Primary Schools" (Unpublished doctoral dissertation, New York University School of Education, 1972), p. 3.

that are of particular interest to American teachers. Details of the study together with some of the major findings are therefore summarized in this appendix.

DETAILS OF THE STUDY

The sample consisted of sixty-eight different classrooms in twenty-four British informal schools in London, Bristol, Leicestershire, and Oxfordshire. The schools were in different kinds of neighborhoods, and the classes spanned the primary-school years.

Each classroom was observed systematically, and data were recorded on an instrument designed by the author.[5]

MAJOR FINDINGS

The findings can be summarized under three major classifications:

1. The nature of classroom work
2. Organization of classes
3. Division of responsibility

The Nature of Classroom Work

Four hundred activities were observed in the course of the study. They were divided into seven broad categories: reading, mathematics, writing, play and crafts, topics and projects, science, and miscellaneous. Table B.1 shows the number of times that each was observed and the numbers and percentages of children engaged.

The description of informal classrooms as environments in which many activities occur simultaneously was found to be verified. An average of six different activities were observed in each classroom during a forty-five-minute observation period. Furthermore, the "three Rs" were revealed as holding a primary place in the curriculum. Two-thirds of the observed activities were in reading, writing, or mathematics.

Certain subjects that generally form part of the curricula of American elementary schools—for example, spelling and social studies—were absent in England, and only minimal science activities were included. It was pointed out, however, that in the schools visited these subjects are rarely taught separately. Spelling and English are correlated with writing

---

[5] It is entitled *Systematic Observation of Classrooms on a Continuum of Educational Responsibility*, or *SOCCER.*

Table B.1   Activities Observed

Activity	Number of Times Observed	Children Engaged	
		Number	Percentage
Reading	102	511	25
Mathematics	97	524	26
Writing	44	305	15
Play and crafts	89	372	18
Topics and projects	35	163	8
Science	10	58	3
Miscellaneous	23	99	5
Total	400	2,032	100

activities, and social studies and science often form the bases for topics and projects.

Provisions for individual children to pursue interests through topic and project work and frequently freedom to work on topics without adhering to time schedules were also noted. There was special emphasis on writing, play, and crafts. The latter two occupied almost one-fourth of the time of infant-school children, but on the junior levels they had been partly replaced by topic and project work that included craft activities.

Two other major factors affecting the work of these classes were reported: the organization of the school day and the length of assignments given to children:

> The day started between 9:00 and 9:30 and ended between 3:15 and 4:00. . . . Within the school day there was usually an assembly period and two "tea breaks" of 15 to 20 minutes duration, one in the morning and one in the afternoon. Lunch was most frequently a period of an hour-and-a-half. The result was that children were rarely expected to continue to work without interruption for more than an hour or an hour-and-a-half. . . .

> It was evident that assignments were of less length than those encountered in many United States schools. For example, workbook page assignments were generally one or even one-half of a page. Mathematics computations were held to four to six problems. . . .[6] This same philosophy was noted with regard to basal readers: The [short] length of the readers is significant and illustrates a philosophy often encountered in the schools, that the young child should have many opportunities to experience the satisfaction of completing a book. . . . To many of the teachers visited, the prospect of handing a young child a basal reader with 100 or more pages to master is almost incomprehensible.[7]

[6] Stephens, *op. cit.*, pp. 105, 106.
[7] *Ibid.*, p. 70.

Organization of Classes

Classroom organization was investigated at two levels: organization of classes within the school and organization of groups within individual classes.

Organization of Classes within the School A variety of organizational patterns within the school was identified, all based on some form of age grouping. Achievement and ability were not factors in establishing classes. Horizontal, or one-year age grouping, was observed as a total school pattern in one-third of the sample. Vertical grouping, in which children of different ages are grouped in a single class, was the pattern in 29 percent of the schools. A combination of horizontal and vertical grouping characterized the remainder (38 percent).

Organization of Groups within Classes Of the total population of children observed, 2,032 (only 32 percent) were working in organized instructional groups. These groups were usually small, most frequently consisting of two to four members. Of significance too was the finding that of the 400 activities observed during this study, only 6 were lessons directed at whole classes.

Although a majority of the children observed were engaged in individual tasks, they rarely worked in isolation. They were free to gather in informal groups and to seek aid from one another as the need arose. The aid extended by one pupil to another appeared to be a definite factor in enabling the teacher to work informally.

Division of Responsibility

The author identified the locus of responsibility for each of the observed activities by analyzing them to determine whether the teacher, pupil, or both jointly were responsible for each of six kinds of decisions about the initiation and execution of the activity:

> Initiation of the general category of work
> Designation of the specific activity
> Scheduling of the period for its execution
> Continuation or abandonment of the activity
> Determination of materials and procedures to be used
> Choice of participants

The study concluded, "Findings were at variance with those reports of British informal schools which depicted children as being permitted to make the majority of decisions with regard to their work."[8] Of these six

[8] *Ibid.*, p. 155.

kinds of decisions, five were more often made by teachers than by pupils or by teachers and pupils together. The exception was the choice of participants, which was more frequently left to the pupils.

The highest percentage of teacher responsibility was found in initiation of the general category of work. Teachers decided the general areas in which 72 percent of the observed children would work but then delegated a greater degree of responsibility for other aspects of the work.

It was also found that the area of joint responsibility, in which children made choices from limited alternatives presented by the teacher was "pivotal." The teacher could structure the work of the class broadly, yet children could still participate in decision making.

There was a difference in the degrees to which pupils were given responsibility for decisions on the infant and junior levels. The younger children were actually found to exercise more freedom to make decisions. The researcher concluded that "responsibility in the schools studied could not be construed as a function of the maturity of the students, but rather of historical patterns of organization and of differences between the curricula of the two levels."[9]

OTHER FINDINGS

A few peripheral findings are particularly relevant to American teachers.

Team Teaching   Of the twenty-four schools in the sample, one-third had established some degree of team teaching. The organizational patterns varied: "There was an obvious interest in team teaching in Britain. Education officers interviewed stated that they were anxious to encourage its growth and saw it as a necessity for the new 'open-space' schools being built."[10]

Evaluation and Reporting to Parents   The author "never saw a letter or numerical grade assigned to a piece of work. . . . Where answers were available . . . pupils were permitted to make their own corrections."

With respect to report cards, "of the 24 schools in the study, eight issued report cards once a year to parents and 16 did not issue any written reports. . . . There was no provision for a grade defined as 'unsatisfactory' or 'failing.' None of the reports employed numerical grades." When letter grades were used the lowest was "E," defined as "poor" or in one school as "well below average." "Heads reported no anxiety on the part of children with respect to report cards or grades."[11]

[9] *Ibid.*, p. 156.
[10] *Ibid.*, p. 140.
[11] *Ibid.*, p. 141, 142.

Parent-School Relations There were parent organizations in only ten of the schools in the sample. The organizations were described by the headmasters as ranging from those that "hardly function at all" to those that were "active." "In the schools with PTAs heads made it clear that parents did not 'run' the schools. The heads and teachers maintained complete control of professional matters. . . . All the schools had regularly established parent days. . . ."[12] In many schools parents were active and made important contributions in time, raising of funds for equipment, or donations of materials to the schools.

Homework There was no regularly assigned homework in any of the schools studied. "Children are encouraged to work at home to pursue an interest, or if a child is behind in his work and wants homework, a teacher may assign some."[13]

Size of the School The size of the school is a decisive factor in British informal education. The average size of the schools in the study was 330 pupils in ten classes. "In this size school . . . a closeness is engendered which is conducive to informal education."[14]

Role of the Headmaster The British headmaster "is an important component of informal education. . . . There is an implication that it may be difficult or even impossible to create the environment for open education in the United States if there is only tacit approval or even some opposition from the principals."[15]

Some findings from this study have been reported because they should help to dispel misconceptions about British informal classes and thus explicate the practice of open education. They confirm the existence of structure in British schools, which has undoubtedly contributed to the growth of the informal movement in Great Britain. There is much evidence that here in the United States it is coming to be recognized that open schools will also have to establish structures, frameworks within which children will be free to function as independent and capable human beings while remaining cognizant of their responsibilities not only to themselves but also to the other members of the school community.

---

[12] *Ibid.*, p. 143.
[13] *Ibid.*, p. 144, 145.
[14] *Ibid.*, p. 160.
[15] *Ibid.*, p. 161.

Annotated Bibliography

There are increasing numbers of books available in the field of open education. The following is a select list for the reader who wishes to pursue the subject or is interested in further resources for its implementation in the classroom.

Books of General Interest

Barth, Roland S., *Open Education and the American School* (New York: Agathon Press, 1972).

Analyzes some of the assumptions about learning and knowledge held by open educators. Also contains frank description of author's early unsuccessful attempts to establish open classes in two urban schools.

Blackie, John, *Inside the Primary School*, American ed. (New York: Schocken Books, 1971).

Short paperback originally written for British parents by a retired British school inspector. Valuable introduction to open education and its rationale.

Bremer, Anne and John, *Open Education: A Beginning* (New York: Holt, Rinehart and Winston, 1972).

Illustrates how a theme can be used to integrate different subjects and gradually lead teachers to an open approach.

Brown, Mary and Norman Precious, *The Integrated Day in the Primary School*, American ed. (New York: Agathon Press, 1970).

Two British heads describe a Leicestershire open school.

Featherstone, Joseph, *Schools Where Children Learn* (New York: Liveright, 1971).

Includes author's excellent articles that first appeared in the *New Republic* in 1967 and which stimulated American interest in British schools.

Gartner, Alan, Mary Kohler, and Frank Reisman, *Children Teach Children* (New York: Harper & Row, 1971).

Good description of how children can serve as teaching aides. A number of programs utilizing this approach are described.

Informal Schools in Britain Today (New York: Citation Press, 1971).

This collection of 23 pamphlets is produced jointly by Anglo-American Primary Education Project, Schools Council, and Ford Foundation with an introduction by Joseph Featherstone. Recommended for American readers are the pamphlets: "The Pupil's Day"; "The Teacher's Role"; "An Infant School"; and those on subjects: Mathematics; Science; Art; and so on.

Marsh, Leonard, *Alongside the Child* (New York: Praeger, 1970).

A British educator describes the theories behind informal schools, and the work of the children and role of the teachers.

Marshall, Sybil, *Adventures in Creative Education* (London: Pergamon Press, 1968).

Report of a twelve-week workshop designed to orient primary teachers to informal ways.

Murrow, Casey and Liza, *Children Come First* (New York: American Heritage Publishing Company, 1971).

Sensitive description of British schools by two American teachers. Details many classroom activities observed.

National Froebel Foundation, 2 Manchester Square, London, W1.

Publishes a journal, extensive bibliography, and pamphlets on open education. Particularly helpful are: *Activity and Experience in the Infant School* and *Activity and Experience in the Junior School* by E. H. Walters; *The Junior School Today*, by Beryl Ash and Barbara Rapaport; *Learning through Creative Work* by Beatrice Mann; *The Place of Play in an Infant and Junior School* by Gertrude Cooper; and *Some Aspects of Piaget's Work* by Evelyn Lawrence, T. R. Theakston, and Nathan Isaacs.

Ewald B. Nyquist and Gene R. Hawes (eds.), *Open Education*. (New York: Bantam, 1972).

Anthology of significant pieces on open education.

Perrone, Vito, *Open Education: Promise and Problems*. (Bloomington, Ind.: Phi Delta Kappa Educational Foundation, 1972).

Excellent short pamphlet describing open education and its implementation in some North Dakota classrooms.

Plowden, Lady Bridget et al., *Children and Their Primary Schools: Report of the Central Advisory Council in Education*, Volumes I & II (London: H.M. Stationery Office, 1967).

Volume I is a comprehensive explanation of philosophy and practices of British informal schools. Particularly significant is Part Five on curriculum. Volume II summarizes research and is of less interest to Americans. Available at British Information Services, Sales Section, 845 Third Ave., New York City 10022.

Rathbone, Charles (ed.), *Open Education: The Informal Classroom* (New York: Citation Press, 1971).

A collection of pieces written between 1966 and 1970 with an introduction by John Holt. Offers good exposition of the philosophy of open education.

Ridgway, Lorna and Irene Lawton, *Family Grouping in the Primary School*, American ed. (New York: Agathon Press, 1971).

Rationale for family grouping in British informal schools with examples of classroom practices.

Rogers, Vincent (ed.), *Teaching in the British Primary Schools* (New York: Macmillan, 1970).

Compilation of articles primarily by British teachers and heads describing various aspects of informal schools and their curriculum.

Sargent, Betsye, *The Integrated Day in an American School* (Boston: National Association of Independent Schools, 1970).

Account of author's experiences in 1968–1969 school year with open class of five-, six-, and seven-year-olds. Includes useful suggestions for activities and materials.

Silberman, Charles, *Crisis in the Classroom* (New York: Random House, 1970).

One of the most influential of the early books that called attention to open education as an alternative to the "joylessness" of American classrooms.

Weber, Lillian, *The English Infant School and Informal Education*
Englewood Cliffs, N.J.: Prentice-Hall, 1971.

Careful exploration of theories upon which British informal education are based with description of British nursery and infant schools.

Yardley, Alice, *Reaching Out*; *Exploration and Language*; *Discovering the Physical World*; *Senses and Sensitivity*; *The Teacher of Young Children*; *Young Children Thinking*, American eds. (New York: Citation Press, 1973).

Series of six short books originally written to reorient older British women who were returning to teaching to the progressive philosophy. Good explanation of basic elements of open education.

Resources for the Classroom

Ascheim, Skip (ed.), *Materials for the Open Classroom* (New York: Dell, 1973).

Large soft-covered book. Catalog of materials, activities, resources, and suppliers.

Early Childhood Education Study, *Building with Cardboard* (Cambridge, Mass.: 90 Sherman Street, 02140).

Booklet describing how to make classroom furniture from cardboard.

———, *Building with Tubes*.

Booklet describing how to make classroom furniture, toys, and instruments from discarded cardboard tubes.

———, *Materials: A Useful List of Classroom Items That Can Be Scrounged or Purchased*.

Mimeographed list of materials for open classrooms.

———, *Single Sheets*.

Individual cards with suggestions for activities for young children.

Education Development Center, *Instructional Aids, Materials and Supplies*. (Newton, Mass.: 55 Chapel St., 02160).

Mimeographed lists of materials for general classroom use and in specific curriculum areas.

Kaplan, Sandra and JoAnn, Sheila Madsen, Bette Taylor. *Change for Children*. Pacific Palisades, Cal.: Goodyear Publishing, 1973.

Collection of ideas, activities, games for use in open classrooms. Includes suggestions for learning centers.

Nelson, Leslie W. and George C. Lorbeer, *Science Activities for Elementary Children* (Dubuque, Iowa: William C. Brown, 1972).

Numerous suggestions for activities which can be used in open classrooms although the book is not specifically directed to open schools.

Pluckrose, Henry, *Creative Themes* (London: Evans Bros., 1969).

An English headmaster suggests ways of developing themes into classroom projects. Although addressed to a British audience, ideas are applicable. Themes include magic and fantasy, ice and snow, the sea, ships, sailors and pirates, animals.

Rance, Peter, *Teaching by Topics* (London: Ward Lock, 1968).

A British headmaster discusses the use of projects in the classroom with specific reference to their organization, development, and culmination. Examples at various age levels are included.

Rowen, Betty, *Learning through Movement* (New York: Teacher's College, 1963).

A short booklet with excellent suggestions for incorporating movement activities into the curriculum.

Schmidt, Victor F. and Verne N. Rockcastle, *Teaching Science with Everyday Things*. New York: McGraw-Hill, 1968.

Good suggestions for classroom science activities using readily available materials.

Wiseman, Ann, *Making Things* (Boston: Little, Brown, 1973).

Set of pamphlets with directions for making paper, toys, books, candles, belts, bags, and basics of Batik.

Workshop for Learning Things, Inc., *Our Catalog* (Watertown, Mass.: 5 Bridge St., 02171).

Lists interesting and unusual materials and techniques that can be used in open classrooms. Also publishes series of pamphlets on *cardboard carpentry* with instructions on items teachers can make.

Wurman, Richard S. (ed.), *Yellow Pages of Learning Resources* (Cambridge, Mass.: MIT Press, 1972).

Crammed with suggestions for using cities as learning resources. Many ideas are geared to school field trips and are also excellent for inspiring classroom projects.

Yanes, Samuel and Cia Holdorf (eds.), *Big Rock Candy Mountain* (New York: Dell, 1971).

Catalog of articles and ideas adaptable for use in open classrooms.

Index

Ability grouping, 52, 160, 243, 248–249, 258–259, 268
Activities, description of, 11, 42, 58–59, 68–70, 73, 80, 90, 96–97
    See also Arts and crafts; Cooking and Baking; Drama; Language; Living things; Mathematics; Movement; Music; Projects; Reading; Science; Social Studies; Writing
    sustaining interest in, 70, 302–303
    teachers interceding in, 301–302
Activity box, 65, 98, 153, 185, 188, 231
    See also Science, resource box
Activity cards, 96–99, 112, 113, 115, 185–187, 198, 213–215, 231, 303
Activity corners (or centers), arrangement of, 62, 299
    art, 226–227, 229
    cooking and baking, 220–221
    mathematics, 66, 112, 199, 212–213
    museum, 229
    reading, 62, 63–64, 172
    science, 67, 153
    suggestions for additional, 67–68
    writing, 65–66, 184, 186, 187
Activity methods, 2, 3, 4, 24, 25, 59, 124, 130
Activity period, 58–59
    starting the day with, 77–78
Allard, L. S., 320

Ames, Louise Bates, 258
Animals, 67, 155–157
Aquariums, 157
Aristotle, 1
Arts and crafts, 226–232
    activities, 58, 227–231
    in Britain, 228, 231–232, 321, 322
    corner (*see* Activity corners)
    materials for, 225–227
    with waste materials, 230–231
Assessment, of achievement, 254–256
    of intelligence, 252–254
    See also Tests and Testing
Assigning work, 41, 44–47, 85–99, 177, 197, 300, 322
Authority, 26, 30, 38, 39

Baking (*see* Cooking and Baking)
Becker, Carl, 144
Behavioral objectives, 242, 243
Bigge, Morris L., 254
Blackie, John, 288*n.*, 312
Bookbinding, 58, 68, 139, 192, 290
    directions for, 192–193
Brainstorming, 135
Breakthrough to Literacy, 167
Brealey, M., 236
Bristol Education Authority, 127, 128
British children, 5, 319
British education general), faculties in, 316–317, 325

British Education (*cont.*)
  organization of, 315, 316
  role of parents in, 317, 325
  size of schools in, 262
British informal education, 5, 12, 27, 31–32, 88
  art in, 228, 231–232
  beginning reading in, 166
  creativity in, 226
  curriculum of, 123–124
  evaluation of, 317–318
  family grouping in, 261–262
  history of, 311–314
  special children in, 250
  study of (*see* Study of British schools)
  writing in, 181
Bruner, Jerome, 4, 158
Bulletin board, 59, 66, 70, 75, 79, 85, 88, 92, 133, 139, 269

Camera, pinhole, 69
Carrels, 70, 280
Changing from a traditional classroom, 51–75
Check lists, 112–113, 116
  samples of, 113, 114
Chickens, incubating in the classroom, 157
Child development, 16–19
Children and childhood, 13–14
Children and learning, 19–25
Choices, 3, 4, 12, 31, 39, 40, 56, 70, 80, 81, 101, 131, 245
  See also Decisions; Freedom; Responsibility
Cinquains, 188
Class, book of facts, 216
  lessons, 26, 27, 82
  meeting, 77, 82–83, 137, 299
Classroom management, 76–99
Clegg, A. B., 190
Comenius, John, 2
Competitiveness, 36, 46
Conferences, 88, 115, 116, 281
  reading, 175–178
  parent-teacher, 281, 284–285, 291–292
Content approach, 14–15
Contracts, history of, 88
  for general work, 92–95
  in open classrooms, 88–96

problems in the use of, 96
  in specific areas of work, 89–92
  samples of, 78, 91, 93, 94, 95
Control, 35, 36, 37
Cooking and Baking, 182, 205, 218–221
  corner (*see* Activity corners)
  recipes, 221–223
Cooper, Gertrude E., 127
Cooperative teaching 263, 271–273
  See also Team teaching
Cox, C. B., 318
Creative arts, 87, 128–129
  See also Arts and Crafts; Dance and Movement; Drama; Music
Creativity and creative activities, 26, 72, 80, 224–226
Curriculum, 4, 14–15, 19, 22, 23, 26, 37, 45, 123–129, 245
  integrated, 12, 29, 124–125, 141
  See also Arts and Crafts; Cooking and Baking; Dance and Movement; Drama; Mathematics; Music; Reading; Science; Social Studies; Topics and Projects; Writing
Curve stitching, 212

Daily plans, samples of, 78
Daily programs, samples of, 80–81
Dance, 226, 233–236
Dearden, Robert, 25–26, 126
Decisions, 27, 37, 38, 39, 41–47, 323–324
  about routines, 41–42
  about work, 26, 31, 42–47
  See also Choices; Freedom; Responsibility
Decroly, Ovide, 130
Dennison, George, 5, 30
Desks in open classrooms, 60
Dewey, John, on freedom, 40–41
  on learning, 20
  philosophy of, 3
  and progressive education, 28
  on stimulating interests, 247
  on Three Rs, 29
Diagnosis, 34, 46–47, 101–102, 116–117, 173, 175–176, 177
Diaries, 182
Dictionaries, 65, 191–192
Differentiated staffing, 278
Discipline, 13, 35–36, 299, 300, 319

Drama, 226, 236
Dyson, A. E., 318

Ellis, Michael, 127
English schools (*see* British informal education)
Environment of open classes, 4, 16, 24, 26, 27, 29, 38, 40, 72–75, 87, 123, 232, 299–300
Environmental studies, 130, 137, 183, 184, 187, 229
Errors, 24, 38, 101, 249, 301
Evaluation, 26, 36, 43–44, 46–47, 100–102, 116, 175, 244, 252, 324

Family grouping, 261–262
Featherstone, Joseph, 5, 288*n*
Film, 58, 68, 69, 163, 175
Flitting, from activity to activity, 15, 46, 84
Flow charts, 131, 135, 138
    sample of, 136
Folders of work, 62, 79, 108, 115, 116–117
Folk songs, use of in social studies, 146
Foshay, Arthur, 224
Free schools, 5, 27, 30–31, 241
Freedom, 24, 26, 29, 38, 39, 40–47, 80, 107, 163, 245, 250, 251, 256, 298, 301
    See also Choices; Decisions; Responsibility
Froebel, Friedrich, 2, 3, 126, 312

Games, in mathematics, 216
    in reading, 178
Gardner, Dorothy, 127*n*, 247, 311, 317–318
Gartner, Alan, 296
Geoboards, 211
Gestalt field theory, 244
Gifted children, 250
Goodman, Kenneth S., 169, 174
Grammar, 125, 141, 181
Grannis, Joseph C., 277
Graphs, as record of work, 107
    in mathematics, 196, 203–204
Groos, Karl, 126
Grouping, 257–270
    ability (*see* Ability Grouping)
    family, 261–262

heterogeneous vs. homogeneous, 258–259
    horizontal, 258, 323
    in open education classes, 26, 131, 250, 267
    kinds of groups, 268
    leadership of, 250, 269, 270
    organization of, 46, 56, 268–270
    for project work, 134, 139
    for reading, 172–173, 174, 176
    in open education schools, 259–267
    vertical, 259–262, 323
Guilford, J. P., 253

Haddon, F. A., 226
Hadow commission, 312–313
Haiku, 188
Hall, Stanley, 126
Handwriting, 182
Herbart, Johann Friedrich, 2
Holt, John, 5, 30
Home and school, 20, 286–287, 317
    See also Parents
Homework, in British informal schools, 325
Housekeeping, 74–75, 77, 227, 303
Hunt, J. M., 22
Hunt, Maurice P., 254

Illich, Ivan, 5, 36
Individual children, 2, 4, 19–25, 26, 241–256, 267
    assessment of, 251–256
Individualization of instruction, 22, 45, 241–242
    in open classes, 244–247, 267
    in traditional classes, 242–244
Individualized reading, 162, 173–178
Informal education (*See* British informal education)
Integrated curriculum, 2, 12, 26, 29, 124–125, 141
Integrated day, 47, 124–125
Intelligence tests, 252–254
Interage grouping, 27
    See also grouping, vertical
Interest areas (*See* Activity corners)
Interests, 2, 27, 29, 39, 131, 133, 134, 141, 146, 245–247, 322
Isaacs, Nathan, 4, 21
Issacs, Susan, 4, 127

Jackson, Philip W., 244
James, Albert, 152
Jenkinson, Marion, 101–102
Junk art, 137, 230–231

Key decisions, 42–47, 323–324
Kilpatrick, William H., 3
Koch, Kenneth, 189
Kozol, Jonathan, 5, 30
Krauss, Ruth, 189

Ladybird Key Words Reading Scheme, 171
Language, activities, 87, 163, 178–180
   development, 18, 24, 163
   and movement 234
Learning, corners (see Activity corners)
   open educators' views of, 19–25
Limericks, 188
Lipton, Aaron, 176–177
Locke, John, 2
Logs, 92, 110–111, 115
   sample of, 111
Lovell, K., 318
Lytton, H., 226

McKenzie, Moira, 320
Mailboxes, 77, 79, 88, 108, 109
Mann, Beatrice, 127
Marshall, Sybil, 47, 318
Materials, 12, 26, 29, 40, 62, 72, 73–74,
      84, 87, 99, 225, 226–227, 292,
      302, 303–304
   care of (see Housekeeping)
   See also Activity Corners for mate-
      rials listed in each corner
Mathematics, 22, 30, 36, 58, 59, 79, 86,
      87, 113, 114, 194–197, 245
   activities, 198, 199, 200–215
   activity cards, 198, 213, 214, 215
   in British Schools, 321, 322
   computations, 73, 96, 196, 197, 200,
      204, 216–217
   in cooking and baking, 205, 218, 219
   corner (see Activity corners)
   curriculum in open classes, 124, 195,
      196–199
   in integrated curriculum, 125
   and movement, 234
   and music, 232
   Piaget's theories related to, 19, 195–
      196

   in project work, 141
   recording findings in, 196, 203, 215–
      216
   records, 117, 119
      samples of, 113, 114
   scope of, 199–200
   textbooks, workbooks, kits, 197–198
   See also Three Rs
Mercer, James R., 253
Meredith, Robert, 169
Merriam, Junius, 3
Minischools, 263
   See also Schools within schools
Montaigne, Michele de, 1, 2
Montessori, Maria, 4
Mosaics, 136, 229
Motivation, 3, 21–22
Movement, 82, 226, 233–236
   activities, 234
Moyle, Donald, 167
Music, 141, 163, 226, 182, 232–233
   and poetry, 189
Musical instruments, 163
   directions for making, 233

Nasca, Donald, 246
Nash, Doris, 166
Notebook, 78, 88, 106, 109–110, 112
Nuffield Mathematics Project, 214n

Olds, Henry F., Jr., 272
Open classrooms, activity cards in, 96–
      99
   characteristics of, 25–27
   contracts in, 88–96
   establishment of, 52–75, 297–304
   organization and assignment of work
      in, 41, 44–47, 76, 83–88, 177,
      197, 300–301, 322
      See also Team Teaching, organiza-
      tion
   organization of school day in, 46, 76,
      77–83, 300, 322
Open corridor schools, 12, 32
Open education, definition of, 12–13, 27
   history of, 1–6
   philosophy of, 11–32
Open-plan schools, 12, 27, 264–267
Open schools, other terms for, 12
Open-space schools (see Open-plan
      schools)

Original sin, doctrine of, 13
Owen, Robert, 311–312

Pantomime, 236
Paperbacks, 63, 171, 303–304
Paraprofessionals, 110, 167, 189, 219, 251, 263, 272, 278, 281, 294–296
Parents, 115, 286–293
    in British schools, 31, 317, 324–325
    communicating with, 287–291
    orientation of, in establishment of open classes, 53–54, 287
        in planning for team teaching, 278
    as resources, 135, 231, 233, 251, 263, 291–293, 304
    teacher conferences with, 281, 284–285, 291–292
Parker, Francis, 3
Pegboards, 107
Pendulums, 213
Pestalozzi, J. H., 2
Philosophy of open education, 11–32
Phonics, 96, 174, 178
Photography, 68, 69, 227
Piaget, Jean, 4, 288
    on child development, 17–18, 20, 22
    implications of theories for teachers, 19
    on language and thought, 18
    on mathematics, 19, 195–196
    on play, 126
Pictures on light-sensitive paper, 58, 69–70
Planning, by children, 78, 79, 125
    for project work, 138–139
    in team teaching, 278, 283
    See also Decisions; Responsibility
Planning period, 79
Plans, sample forms for, 78
Plants in classroom, 158
Plato, 1
Play, in British schools, 321, 322
    definitions of, 126–127
    early theories of, 14, 126
    Froebel on, 3
    Plato on, 1
    Montaigne on, 2
    and work, 3, 125, 126–127
    values of, 127–128

Plowden Report, 288n, 313–314
    on British teachers, 312
    on curriculum, 124
    on gifted children, 250–251
    on home and school, 286–287
    on integrated day, 125
    on learning, 22
    on open house, 290
    on parents, 317
    on play, 126
    on school size, 262
    on writing in informal schools, 181
Poetry, 64, 186–189, 227
Postman, Neil, 5, 30, 159
Printing, 229
Problems, in organization of open classes, 297–304
Process approach, 14–15
Progressive education, 3, 27, 28–30, 88
    project method in, 3, 29
Projects, 29, 59, 80, 81, 134–135
    activities related to, 11, 134–139
    advantages of, 141
    choice of, 135–137
    culmination of, 139
    definition of, 130, 131
    examples of, 142
    groups for, 139
    multiple-class or school-wide, 138
    planning of, 138–139
    in science, 155
    in social studies, 146–148
    See also Topics; Topics and Projects
Puppets, 229–230
Purkey, William W., 16

Rabelais, François, 1
Rance, Peter, 131–132
Reading, 30, 59, 85, 86, 113, 159–180, 245
    basal readers, 63, 160, 161, 167, 169, 170–171, 173, 175, 243, 322
    beginning readers, 166
    beginning reading, 165–168
    in British schools, 159, 321, 322
    conference, 175–178
    corners (see Activity corners)
    developmental, 168–178
    experience charts, 167–168
    grouping for, 172–173, 174, 176
    individualized, 173–178

Reading (*cont.*)
  instruction in open classrooms, 124, 160, 161–180
  language activities related to, 163, 178–180
  materials for, 169–172
  oral, 172, 176–177
  readiness for, 162–165
  records, 116–117, 177
    sample of, 118
  in traditional classes, 160–161
  and writing, 166–168
  See also Three Rs
Reasoner, Charles F., 161
Recordkeeping, 100–119
Records, anecdotal, 114–115
  for attendance, 103–104
  baskets, 108
  check lists, 112–113, 116
    samples of, 113, 114
  cumulative, 105
  folders of work, 62, 79, 108, 115, 116–117
  guidelines for, 102
  grade books, 100, 113–114
  graphs, 107
  index cards, 110, 119
  logs, 92, 110–111, 115
    sample of, 111
  lunch and milk, 304
  mailboxes, 108–109
  mathematics, 117, 119
  notebook, child's, 79, 88, 109–110, 112
    teacher's, 106
  pegboards, 107
  photographs, 106
  reading, 116–117, 177
    sample of, 118
  scope and purpose of, 101–102
  sign-in sheets, 108
  in team teaching, 104, 109, 110, 284
Reich, Charles, 5
Responsibility, in British schools, 47, 323–324
  child, 4, 24, 26, 29, 42, 56, 80, 89, 104, 298
  for decisions about work, 43–47
  notion of, 39–40
  teacher, 37–38, 41
Retired people in the classroom, 293

Rogers, Carl, 4
Room arrangements, 60–73, 299
  diagrams of, 71
Rosner, Benjamin, 309–310
Rousseau, Jacques, 2, 300
Rowen, Betty, 234

Scheduling, 26, 27, 37, 41, 43, 44, 45, 46, 59, 76, 79–82, 83–84, 86, 87, 125, 300, 301
Schiller, F. S. C., 126
Schmuck, Richard and Patricia, 262–263
School day, integrated (*see* Integrated day)
  organization of, 46, 77–83, 322
  schedule of (*see* Scheduling)
    sample schedules, 80–81
  starting, 77–79
School organization, 257–267, 323
Schools within schools, 32, 262, 263
Science, 55–58, 59, 87, 130, 149–158
  activities, short-term, 153–154
    with living things, 155–158
    long-term, 154–155
  activity cards, 153–154
  in baking, 218–219
  in British schools, 321–322
  corners (*see* Activity corners)
  5/13 Project, 154*n*
  in open classes, 134, 141, 152–158
  questioning in, 151–152
  resource box, 57–58, 90
Shaplin, Judson T., 272
Signing-up for activities, 84–85
Silberman, Charles, 5, 288*n*
Skinner, B. F., 242
Smith, E. Brooks, 169
Smith, Peter, 37
Social Studies, 55, 59, 90, 130, 143–148
  activities, 146–148
  in British schools, 321–322
  through folk songs or postage stamps, 146
  in open classrooms, 134, 141, 145–148
Socrates, 1
Somerset Authority, 264–265
Special children, 247–251
  child who needs structure, 251
  in England, 250

gifted, 250–251
notion of, 247–248
in open classes, 249–251
in traditional classes, 248–249
Spelling, 125, 141, 181, 321
Spencer, Herbert, 126
Standards, 38, 66, 191, 231–232, 276, 299, 301
Stephens, Lillian, 47, 128, 262, 320–325
Stimulus-response theory, 242–243
Stretch, Bonnie B., 41
Structure, 76, 251, 298, 300
in British schools, 47, 319, 325
See also Freedom
Study of British schools, comparison of formal and informal schools, 317–318
creativity, 226
by Plowden commission, 313–314
reading, 318
by Stephens, 47, 128, 262, 320–325
Task cards (*see* Activity cards)
Teacher centers, 32, 305–310
Teachers, aides (*see* Paraprofessionals)
and child responsibility, 38–47,
See also responsibility
relations with children, 26, 37–38, 145, 298
role of, 12, 29, 30, 31, 33–47
in developing interests, 246–247
in topic work, 132–133
Team teaching, 27, 267, 271–285
advantages of, 273–274
in British schools, 324
choice of members for, 276–277
and cooperative teaching, 271–272
decision to participate in, 275
definition of, 272
disadvantages of, 274–275
history of, 271
in open classes, 273–285
organization, 279–283
planning for, 278–279
records, 104, 109, 110, 284
reporting to parents in, 281, 284–285
in schools within schools, 263
size of team in, 277
staffing, 278
starting day in, 77
Television sets, mock, 230
Terrariums, 158

Tests and testing, 31, 32, 36, 99, 159, 161, 251–256
See also Evaluation
Themes (*see* Topics and Projects)
Three Rs, 29, 47, 54, 80, 81, 96, 141, 128–129, 321
See also Mathematics; Reading; Writing
Tolstoy, Leo, 3
Topics, 130–134
choosing, 131
definition of, 130
examples of, 134
in Science, 154–155
in Social Studies, 146
See also Projects; Topics and Projects
Topics and Projects, 43n, 58, 89, 130–142, 146, 245
in British schools, 321, 322
See also Topics; Projects
Trust, 14, 26, 36, 298

Van Til, William, 28
Venn diagram, 136, 204
illustration of, 204
Vertical grouping, 259–262, 323
Volunteers, 167, 219, 272, 293–294, 296
retired people as, 293
students as, 293–294
See also Parents, as resources

Walton, Jack, 125, 137
Watson, Peter, 253
Weber, Lillian, 5, 32
White elephant sale, 220, 304
Writing, 79, 86, 181–193
activities, 182–191, 192–193
activity cards, 185, 186
in British schools, 181, 321, 322
corner (*see* Activity corners)
corrections of, 191
functional, 189–191
notebooks, 182–183
poetry, 186–189
prose, 182–186
and reading, 166–168
resource box, 65, 185, 188
See also Three Rs

Yardley, Alice, 74